The Art of
PREACHING

The Art of PREACHING

FIVE MEDIEVAL TEXTS & TRANSLATIONS

SIEGFRIED WENZEL

THE CATHOLIC UNIVERSITY OF AMERICA PRESS
WASHINGTON, D.C.

The paper used in this publication meets the minimum
requirements of American National Standards for Information Science—
Permanence of Paper for Printed Library Materials,
ANSI Z39.48-1984.
∞

Library of Congress Cataloging-in-Publication Data
Wenzel, Siegfried, 1928–
The Art of Preaching : Five Medieval Texts and Translations /
Siegfried Wenzel.
pages cm
Includes bibliographical references and index.
ISBN 978-0-8132-2137-3 (cloth : alk. paper) 1. Preaching.
2. Rhetoric, Medieval. I. Title.
BV4222.W46 2013
251—dc23 2012045868

CONTENTS

PREFACE

In presenting five medieval works dealing with the art of preaching I have wanted to make available several treatises of a genre that has attracted far too little attention. Of the roughly two hundred forty *artes praedicandi* known to exist, only two dozen, or 10 percent, have been edited, and many of them without a translation. To increase this small corpus, I here present five such treatises, of which four have never been edited, while the fifth is available in a modern text but has been found to require a new edition. All five are presented with translations. Both texts and translations aim primarily at students of medieval preaching, rhetoric, and culture in general, as well as non-specialists interested in the subject. It is my hope that these texts, in their Latin form as well as their translation, will help students of medieval preaching to become familiar with the technical language as well as the grammatical, logical, and stylistic concerns that pervade treatises on how to structure a (scholastic) sermon. This technical language is often highly difficult to grasp, quite apart from the handwritten form in which these works have been preserved, and it has been my aim to understand and elucidate the finer and sometimes recondite points of medieval teachers who instructed their readers and perhaps listeners in how to structure a scholastic sermon in a way that is pleasing, logical, and fruitful for their audiences. Part of my aim in editing and translating these texts is, therefore, pedagogical. I hope that the fruit of these labors will help others to find their way into and through a literary genre whose technical advice lies behind—or perhaps rather was based on—countless medieval Latin sermons.

My thanks are due to the libraries, and their staffs, that hold the manuscripts on which the edited texts are based. Permission to use their manuscripts as base for the editions has been graciously granted by the Warden and Fellows of Merton College Oxford; the Biblioteca Nacional de Portugal; and the Dean and Chapter of Lincoln Cathedral. In particular, I am indebted for various pieces of information to Dr. Bart Jaski, Grace Swart, and Sr. Gimbrère at the Utrecht University Library; to Dr. Bertram Lesser at the Herzog August Bibliothek, Wolfenbüttel; and to Prof. Richard W. Pfaff, Prof. Ralph Hanna, and Fr. Simon Tugwell, OP. To all of these as well as to the director of the Catholic University of America Press, Trevor Lipscombe, and his editorial staff, my warmest thanks.

ABBREVIATIONS

PUBLISHED WORKS

Bloomfield	Morton W. Bloomfield et al., eds., *Incipits of Latin Works on the Virtues and Vices, 1100–1500 A.D.* (Cambridge, Mass.: The Mediaeval Academy of America, 1979). Quoted by item number.
Caplan	Harry Caplan, *Mediaeval "Artes Praedicandi": A Hand List,* Cornell Studies in Classical Philology 24 (Ithaca, N.Y.: Cornell University Press, 1934). Quoted by item number.
Caplan Suppl	Harry Caplan, *Mediaeval "Artes Praedicandi": A Supplementary Hand List,* Cornell Studies in Classical Philology 25 (Ithaca, N.Y.: Cornell University Press, 1936). Quoted by item number.
CCSL	Corpus Christianorum, Series Latina (Turnhout: Brepols, 1954–). Quoted by volume and page.
Charland	Th.M. Charland, *Artes praedicandi: Contribution à l'histoire de la rhétorique au moyen âge* (Paris: De Vrin, 1936). Quoted by page.
Kaeppeli	Thomas Kaeppeli, OP, *Scriptores ordinis praedicatorum medii aevi,* 4 vols. (Rome: Ad S. Sabinae, 1970–93). Quoted by volume and page.
PL	J. P. Migne, ed., Patrologiae cursus completus, Series Latina, 217 vols. (Paris: J. P. Migne, 1844–64). Quoted by volume and page.
Sharpe	Richard Sharpe, *A Handlist of the Latin Writers of Great Britain and Ireland Before* 1540, Publications of the Journal of Medieval Latin 1 (Turnhout: Brepols, 1997). Quoted by page.
Walther *Initia*	Hans Walther, *Initia carminum ac versuum medii aevi posterioris latinorum,* 2nd ed. (Göttingen: Vandenhoeck u. Ruprecht, 1969). Quoted by item number.
Walther *Proverbia*	Hans Walther, *Proverbia sententiaeque latinitatis medii aevi,* 6 vols. (Göttingen: Vandenhoeck u. Ruprecht, 1963–67). Quoted by item number.

MANUSCRIPTS

A	London, BL Additional 24361	*Quamvis, Hic docet, Vade*
B	Basel, Universitätsbibliothek B.ix.4	Fusignano
C	Cambridge, Corpus Christi College 423	*Quamvis*
E	Incunable	Fusignano
G	Cambridge, University Library Gg.6.20	*Quamvis*
L	Lincoln, Cathedral Library 234	*Quamvis, Hic docet, Vade*
M	Oxford, Merton College 102	Fusignano
O	Oxford, University College 36	Fusignano, *Quamvis*
P	Lisbon, BN Alcobaça 130	Rochelle
R	London, BL Arundel 275	Rochelle
U	Utrecht, University Library 317	*Quamvis*
V	Vatican, Ottoboni 396	Rochelle
W	Wolfenbüttel 4047	*Vade*

INTRODUCTION

All human activities that require skill and a certain know-how sooner or later beget technical manuals that, at whatever level, provide instruction on how to do things, from the *Sabiston Textbook of Surgery* to *The Joy of Cooking* and *Seven Weeks to Better Sex.* So it is also with preaching in the Middle Ages. Proclaiming the Good News had already been the work of Jesus and his apostles, and it continued as a central feature in Christian society through the succeeding centuries. But it was not until the High Middle Ages, the early thirteenth century, that separate technical treatises on this activity began to be written.[1] Some of them would comprehensively discuss everything belonging to this office, from the moral qualification of the preacher to his voice modulation and gestures and further to the sources and the structure of his sermon. Others would more narrowly furnish complete instruction on how to build a good sermon. And yet others would limit their scope even further and deal with a single aspect of sermon building, such as the ways in which a preacher could develop or expand his chosen text. All such treatises, generically called *artes praedicandi,* as their authors clearly indicated followed actual practices used by preachers who learned and practiced their craft in university milieus—Paris, Oxford, and others.[2] Though the earliest works of this kind were written

1. For the history and typology of *artes praedicandi* see Marianne Briscoe, *Artes Praedicandi,* together with Barbara H. Jaye, *Artes Orandi,* Typologie des sources du moyen âge occidental 61 (Turnhout: Brepols, 1992); and James J. Murphy, *Rhetoric in the Middle Ages: A History of Rhetorical Theory from Saint Augustine to the Renaissance* (Berkeley, Los Angeles, London: University of California Press, 1974), 269–355. Besides Murphy's work for medieval rhetoric in general, the basic studies of medieval *artes praedicandi* are Caplan, Caplan Suppl, and Charland (see the abbreviations list above). The relevance of such *artes* to medieval literary criticism is discussed in Siegfried Wenzel, "The Arts of Preaching," in *The Cambridge History of Literary Criticism. Vol. 2: The Middle Ages,* ed. Alastair Minnis and Ian Johnson (Cambridge: Cambridge University Press, 2005), 84–96.

2. The interrelation between the teaching of *artes* and actual sermons, especially at the

by theologians of various affiliations (friars, monks, secular masters, etc.), *artes praedicandi* benefitted greatly from the great impulse that preaching itself received from and within the new religious orders, the Dominicans and the Franciscans.

It is not entirely manifest to what extent this new rhetorical art depended and continued to depend on classical rhetoric, such as was known to medieval students from Cicero's *De inventione* and the *Ad Herennium*.[3] But however close the connection may have been originally, medieval preachers very quickly developed and described a sermon structure very much their own. This new form has been labeled the modern, or university, or thematic, or scholastic sermon, and throughout the later Middle Ages, from the thirteenth to at least the end of the fifteenth century, it remained the dominant sermon form, attested by the *artes* as well as by countless extant sermons. It is typically based on a relatively short string of words from Scripture, the thema (hence its being called "thematic sermon"), which is then divided into parts that could be further developed in a variety of ways.[4] It is important to realize that the (biblical) thema and its division are the main constituent features of a scholastic sermon. In other words, a preacher might well speak about temptation, but his discourse would not be like a Baconian essay "On Temptation" but rather a rhetorical exegesis of *Beatus vir qui suffert temptationem* (James 1:11) with the purpose of leading his audience to practice virtue and avoid sin.

University of Paris, has been studied with much detail from unedited sermon collections by Nicole Bériou, *L'avènement des maîtres de la parole: La prédication à Paris au XIIIe siécle*, Collection des Études Augustiniennes—Série Moyen Age et Temps Modernes 31 (Paris: Institut d'Etudes Augustiniennes, 1998). Robert of Basevorn frequently distinguishes sermon usages at Oxford from those at Paris.

3. The case has been made by Margaret Jennings, "*Rhetor Redivivus?* Cicero in the *Artes Praedicandi*," *AHDLMA* (1989): 91–122. See also Kimberley Rivers, "Memory and Medieval Preaching: Mnemonic Advice in the *Ars Praedicandi* of Francesc Eiximenes (ca. 1327–1409)," *Viator* 30 (1999): 252–84, with special attention to memory; the article has now been incorporated in Rivers, *Preaching the Memory of Virtue and Vice: Memory, Images, and Preaching in the Late Middle Ages* (Turnhout: Brepols, 2010), 161–79. Franco Morenzoni, in his edition of Thomas de Chobham, *Summa de Arte Praedicandi*, Corpus Christianorum Continuatio Mediaevalis 82 (Turnhout: Brepols, 1987), xlviii–lxiv, gives a nuanced view of the development of the scholastic art of preaching in relation to classical rhetoric.

4. The term "thema" is not to be confused with the "theme" or main topic of a sermon. It is in order to avoid this confusion (which runs through a good deal of modern literary criticism) that I have, in earlier writings and here, preferred the term "scholastic sermon."

While the *artes praedicandi* that have been studied may acknowledge the existence and use of different structures, such as the older homily or preaching without division, they are remarkably consistent in teaching the "modern" form, the pattern just outlined.[5] Yet besides consistently embracing thema, division, and development as the basic constituent parts, they may differ in regard to other features of the sermon. For example, the thema may be introduced in a variety of ways, including a "protheme" based on a different scriptural passage, or it may be connected with the division in different fashions, and the development can take a multitude of different forms. One even finds terminological innovations, such as *pedis positio* or *radix sermonis,* which label parts of the sermon structure as they were being used by sermon makers. In other words, while medieval *artes praedicandi,* on the whole, are remarkably uniform in teaching the basics, they also show signs of innovation, of an ongoing development.

Treatises that describe and teach such a verbal structure, the *artes praedicandi,* were surveyed and listed in the 1920s and 1930s by Harry Caplan.[6] His *Hand-List* and its *Supplement* identify about two hundred forty works extant in manuscripts and early printed books. Of these, only two dozen are available in modern editions, listed below in appendix D, and very few additional treatises of the kind have been noted since[7]—a rather small sample for studying the genre let alone the connections between individual works.[8] Furthermore, even readers with a good knowledge of Latin will find many of these texts very hard going,

5. Preaching without dividing the thema is recognized as a possibility used in former ages, for example, by John of Wales (ed. Ulm 1480, f. 418) and Waleys (Charland 356).

6. Caplan and Caplan Suppl. In collaboration with Henry H. King, Caplan also published a series of lists of post-medieval treatises on preaching, in Latin (*Harvard Theological Review* 42 [1949]:185–206), Italian (*Speech Monographs* 16 [1949]: 243–52), French (*Quarterly Journal of Speech* 36 [1959]: 296–325), Spanish (*Speech Monographs* 17 [1950]: 161–70), Scandinavian (ibid., 21 [1954]: 1–9, and Dutch (ibid., 235–47).

7. For example Nicholas d'Oresme and the anonymous "Dic ut vides," listed in appendix D.

8. One of the foremost contemporary students of medieval *artes praedicandi* declared, not too long ago, that for lack of edited texts and understanding their interrelations any synthesis of the genre is premature: Franco Morenzoni, "La littérature des *artes praedicandi* de la fin du XIIe au début du XVe siècle," in *Sprachtheorien in Spätantike und Mittelalter,* ed. Sten Ebbesen, *Geschichte der Sprachtheorie* vol. 3 (Tübingen: Gunter Narr Verlag, 1995), 339–59, at 339.

and of the Latin texts available in print only nine have been translated into modern English. In fact, only five of these give a full account of scholastic sermon structure, and one of them—Robert of Basevorn—in its complexity and peculiarities is hardly representative of the genre.[9] As a result, modern students have only a very limited access to a genre that holds some importance for the study, not only of medieval preaching, but also of medieval rhetoric and literary criticism in general. It is the aim of the present work to broaden this access by presenting five medieval *artes praedicandi* in their original Latin together with a modern translation, in the hope to stimulate further explorations.

For the first work I have chosen a treatise by Jacobus de Fusignano (henceforth referred to as Fusignano), an Italian Dominican writing around the year 1300 or a little later. His *Libellus artis predicatorie* has survived in a fairly large number of manuscripts and in several early prints, but has so far not found a modern editor. I have placed it first because its instruction on how to build a scholastic sermon is complete and detailed, and it uses a clear and leisurely exposition that is easier to follow than many other treatises, especially Basevorn's, one of the few *artes praedicandi* available in an English translation. In particular, Fusignano's constant practice of illustrating the points he is making with one or more examples is of great help, not only for novice readers but also for seasoned medievalists, in understanding matters that elsewhere can get rather complicated, even muddled. Next I offer three shorter *artes* that present what is essentially the same subject matter in different approaches. The first, *Quamvis,* is in one of its manuscripts ascribed to an English Dominican (though nothing seems to be known about him) and was used by another English writer, the Benedictine Ranulph Higden (about 1340). In two manuscripts it is immediately followed by two other *artes,* where they have escaped previous scholars (*Hic docet* and *Vade*).[10] I have edited all three because, although they basically agree in their teaching of the scholastic sermon structure,

9. Those by Henry of Hesse, Pseudo-Aquinas, Ranulph Higden, Robert Basevorn, and Thomas Waleys, the last an unpublished MA thesis. For publication details see appendix D.

10. They are not listed in Caplan or Caplan Suppl, and Charland knew only of *Vade* in one Continental manuscript (106); nor did the modern cataloguer of the Lincoln Cathedral manuscripts notice them: R. M. Thomson, *Catalogue of the Manuscripts of Lincoln Cathedral Chapter Library* (Woodbridge, Suffolk; Wolfeboro, N.H.: D. S. Brewer, 1989), 194.

they do so with peculiar emphases of their own, such as the house image in the third *(Vade)* or the distinction between *sermo* and *collatio* and the analytical attention to such refined processes and their names as *claves, sufficientia,* and *pedis posicio,* in the second *(Hic docet)* and third *(Vade),* or the closer attention to modes of speech (exhortation, question, command, etc.) in the second *(Hic docet).* That these three are distinct works is shown by their separate preservation. In addition, the varying forms and manuscript contexts of the first, *Quamvis,* open a window on the work of usually unknown late-medieval writers in composing a treatise—especially an *ars praedicandi*—by conflating material from different sources and by copying it together with other works of the same kind into one and the same manuscript, which is explored in appendix B. Finally, I offer the *Processus negociandi themata sermonum* by Jean de la Rochelle (henceforth referred to as Rochelle), an early Franciscan master at Paris. As the title of his work indicates, this is a partial or limited *ars praedicandi,* dealing only with ways of developing the sermon thema and thus not commenting on what a sermon's main parts are or how to choose a fitting thema. It therefore shows a university master dealing with the grammatical and logical analysis involved in building a scholastic sermon. More than the preceding four treatises, its Latin text demonstrates how difficult the exposition can be, and I hope my translation, which accompanies the newly edited text, will clear a way through what may well seem to be an impenetrable jungle.

To the texts and their translations I add several reflections on this material. Appendix A will highlight three main features of medieval preaching as constantly set forth and emphasized in the *artes praedicandi.* Appendix B summarizes insights into their preservation and "life" during the later Middle Ages, continued in appendix C with a comparison between *Quamvis* and the art of preaching by Ranulph Higden, a work that has received more careful and extensive scholarly investigation than other *artes* in recent years. Finally, appendix D lists modern editions and translations of medieval *artes praedicandi.*

In editing these works I have aimed at presenting texts that make sense. This has been relatively easy in the case of Fusignano but rather more difficult in the other four treatises, whose extant witnesses are full of scribal errors including misunderstandings of "hard words," eyeskips (that is, omission of text between two identical or similar words, where the copyist's eye has "skipped" from the first to the second), and other omissions—errors for whose correction comparison with other witnesses of the same work has very often been impossible or of no help. Given the paucity of witnesses and their general corruption, I had to rely a good deal on my understanding of the techniques of sermon building that are there described and exemplified (including, for example, parallelism and end rhyme)—a procedure that may raise the eyebrows of scholars trained in the principles of classical text criticism, such as creating a stemma, which unfortunately in these cases will simply not help. Further explanations of my procedures will be found in the introductions to the individual treatises. As a general rule, I have followed the spellings of the base manuscripts. I have silently expanded abbreviations and contractions and have introduced punctuation and sentence and paragraph divisions as seemed to be required by the logical and grammatical sense of the text. Interlinear words are presented between \slashes/, marginal material between <angle brackets>, words not found in the manuscripts, such as folio numbers, in [square brackets]. I have written out numerals except for chapter numbers and in biblical references, which are reproduced as they appear in the manuscript.

The translations that accompany these texts are my own. They aim at providing an English text that is clear and readable yet remains reasonably close to the Latin original. To achieve this, I have allowed myself some freedom, especially in rendering Latin passive constructions with various active ones (by using "one" or "we," etc.). In rendering biblical quotations I have been guided by the Douay-Rheims version but have occasionally updated its language, using for instance "you" instead of "thou." Both edited texts and translations preserve the scriptural *loci* as given by the base manuscripts, even where they are wrong or disagree with modern book divisions (such as the four Books of Kings, which are now divided into 1–2 Samuel and 1–2 Kings). The source notes to all quotations, however, as found at the foot of the translations, follow modern usage, except that for the Psalms I have kept the numbering and verse divisions of the medieval Vulgate followed in parentheses by the respective modern numbering. In both texts and translations I have occasionally added numerals and letters in square brackets to guide the reader's understanding of the treatises' structure; and in the translations I have further added an occasional word or phrase in square brackets, for the same purpose.

TEXTS AND TRANSLATIONS

I
JACOBUS DE FUSIGNANO

FUSIGNANO WAS A DOMINICAN FRIAR of the Roman province, who held various offices in his order during the 1280s and 1290s and ended his life as bishop of Mothon in 1333.[1] His *Libellus artis predicatorie* (or similar titles; Caplan 115 and 220; Caplan Suppl 115) enjoyed much popularity: it survives in more than twenty manuscripts, including one of English provenance (O), and was included in several incunable editions of the equally very popular *Manipulus curatorum,* a pastoral manual written in 1333 by Guido de Monte Rocherii (or Rochen).[2] Like some other *artes* it begins with a scriptural verse that is then applied to the preacher's art, and from it Fusignano develops a fairly leisurely exposition of the parts which a (scholastic) sermon should have, from the chosen thema to ways of developing or expanding the sermon to its

1. Kaeppeli, vol. 2, 321–22.

2. Leonard E. Boyle, O.P., "The Fourth Lateran Council and Manuals of Popular Theology," *Tennessee Studies in Literature* 28 (1985): 30–43, at 39, note 8.

final prayer. In each case he points out what is essential for a preacher to observe and frequently warns against going in wrong directions. Of the greatest value are the examples with which he illustrates each point as he proceeds. His treatise, therefore, holds a place of great importance in the genre of *artes praedicandi* because it is complete (in that it covers all aspects of sermon making) and is easier to follow than many other works of this kind.

The work contains nineteen chapters. It opens with the scriptural words *Oro ut caritas vestra magis ac magis abundet* (Philippians 1:9–10), which are applied to the classical four causes as they relate to preaching (I).[3] Then Fusignano treats the major parts and features of a scholastic sermon: the initial prayer, the thema, its qualities and choice (II–III), the protheme (IV), the division of the thema (V), the subdivision of the parts (VI), twelve ways of developing the sermon (VII), namely: by further biblical quotations that agree with the thema (VIII), discussing individual words (IX), interpreting a name and defining or describing a noun (X), using the fourfold sense of Scripture (XI), using degrees of comparison and compound words (XII), using synonyms (XIII), discussing the properties of things (XIV), exemplification with exempla, miracle stories, fables, and the like (XV), exploring the opposite of a word in the thema (XVI), dividing a whole into its parts (XVII), discussing the causes and effects of a vice or virtue (XVIII), and employing various processes of reasoning (XIX).

SOURCES

For editing the text I have relied on three fourteenth-century manuscripts and one early print. These are:

Oxford, Merton College, MS 102 (M).[4] Parchment, fourteenth century, 295 folios, written throughout in two columns in good Gothic bookhands. It contains:

3. The four causes, established by Aristotle, are used in a number of *artes praedicandi* besides the present one, for example those by Eiximenes, Martin of Cordoba, Thomas of Todi, John of Wales, Basevorn, Higden, and "Dic nobis."

4. R. M. Thomson, *A Descriptive Catalogue of the Medieval Manuscripts of Merton College, Oxford* (Cambridge: D. S. Brewer, 2009), 88–89. I follow Thomson's foliation (old 278–[283]).

(1) Mauritius, *Distinctiones,* by the Franciscan Maurice de Provins, ff. 1ra–276vb, preceded by a partial table of articles, *Abiectio–Auxiliator* (f. 1v).
(2) Jacobus de Fusignano, *Libellus artis predicatorie,* ff. 277ra–284va.
(3) A short commentary without title on *Liber sextus* I.1, in the preceding hand (ff. 284va–286ra), followed by short excerpts or notes in a cursive hand (f. 287).

The manuscript, "M," was produced in Italy, and its hands and orthography are Italian (see below). According to various inscriptions, it belonged to Mag. Alan of Corbrigge, who sold it to Mag. Thomas of Farnelow of Merton College, probably in the 1340s or 1350s.[5]

Basel, Universitätsbibliothek, MS.B.ix.4 (B).[6] Parchment, ca. 1400, eighty-eight folios. A composite volume, from the Dominican convent at Basel.

(1) Aldobrandinus, *Scala fidei,* "Cum intrasset," ff. 1–50va.
(2) *De peccatis,* "Notandum quod peccatum significatur per somnum," fragmentary, ff. 51ra–54va.
(3) Twenty sermons *de sanctis,* ff. 55ra–76ra.
(4) Iacobus de Fusignano, *De arte praedicandi,* "Oro ut caritas vestra magis ac magis abundet," ff. 77–88.
(5) Charter, fragmentary, i and ii.

Oxford, University College, MS 36 (O).[7] Parchment, end of the fourteenth century, 154 folios. Written in two columns; articles 1–6 in an Anglicana bookhand, 7–8 in Secretary hands.

(1) *Speculum laicorum,* "Quoniam ut docet Apostolus," ff. 1–114rb. Elsewhere attributed to John of Howden (died 1275) and edited by J. T. Welter (Paris, 1914).[8]

5. For details see Thomson, *Catalogue,* 89.

6. A detailed description in Gustav Meyer and Max Burckhardt, *Die mittelalterlichen Handschriften der Universitätsbibliothek Basel. Beschreibendes Verzeichnis.* Abteilung B: Theologische Pergamenthandschriften. Zweiter Band: Signaturen B VIII 11–B XI 26 (Basel: Verlag der Universitätsbibliothek, 1966), 128–31.

7. Henricus O. Coxe, *Catalogus Codicum Manuscriptorum qui in collegiis aulisque Oxoniensibus hodie adservantur. Catalogue of the Manuscripts in the Oxford Colleges,* 2 vols. (Oxford: Oxford University Press, 1852; repr. 1972), vol. 1, 10–11.

8. Cf. Sharpe 267.

(2) Commentary on the Decalogue, "Si vis ad vitam ingredi," ff. 114va–116ra, imperfect. Bloomfield 5612.

(3) *De modo et forma componendi* (corrected to *concionandi* in a modern hand), "Predicacio est thematis assumptio," a short *ars praedicandi* sometimes attributed to John of Wales, ff. 119ra–120ra. Caplan 121. Edited by Woodburn O. Ross, "A Brief Forma Praedicandi," *Modern Philology* 34 (1937): 337–44, from London, British Library, MS Royal 5.C.iii, with variants.

(4) *Alius modus tractandi seu compilandi sermones,* "Quamvis de sermonibus faciendis," anonymous (see below, the section on *Quamvis,* etc.), ff. 120ra–124va.

(5) Jacobus de Fusignano, *Libellus artis predicatorie,* without title or author's name, ff. 124vb–130vb, incomplete.

(6) *Tractatus de venenis,* here as elsewhere ascribed to Lincolniensis, i.e., Grosseteste, ff. 131ra–150vb.

(7) *Sermo sancti Athanasii* (thus colophon), "Eleuate oculos sensus vestri," ff. 151ra–152va. The story about an image of Christ in Beyrut, pierced by a group of Jews and shedding blood, which heals and leads to conversion.[9]

(8) A series of short theological notes: the seven deadly sins with exemplary biblical figures (ff. 152vb–153rb); rhyming lists of the Ten Plagues of Egypt (153rb) and of the five books of Moses (153va); why the Blessed Virgin is worshiped on Saturdays (153va); *casus reservati episcopo* (153vb); the seven gifts of the Holy Spirit (153vb); "Caput meum doleo, caput meum turpis [*sic*] est" (f. 154ra); the gifts of the Holy Spirit, ascribed to "Thomas," from Hugh of Strasburg, *Compendium theologicae veritatis* 5.1 (f. 155ra); "O sponsa, inquit, mea, oportet te habere quinque exterius et quinque interius. . . . Hec doctor optimus, scilicet Dominus Iesus, ad sanctam Bigittam" (f. 155va).[10]

9. For the story and its connection with the feast of *Iconia Domini Salvatoris,* see Richard W. Pfaff, *New Liturgical Feasts in Later Medieval England* (Oxford: Clarendon Press, 1970), 116–28, and more briefly in Pfaff, *The Liturgy in Medieval England. A History* (Cambridge: Cambridge University Press, 2009), 541–42. I am grateful to Prof. Pfaff for referring me to his work.

10. For the last item, see Sancta Birgitta, *Revelaciones,* Book V, ed. Birger Bergh (Up-

Guido de Monte Rocherii, *Manipulus curatorum* (E). Printed book, Cologne: Bartholomaeus de Unkel, 1476. I have used a film of the copy in the Berkeley Law Library: BX 2200 .G 948 1476 Incun. Fusignano's treatise appears without title or author's name on ff. 101ra–115v and is immediately followed by another *ars praedicandi,* "Ad, quare, per, propter, notat, in, similat, que, gerundi," elsewhere attributed to Simon Alcok (died 1459; Caplan 8 and 9).

THE TEXT

As already stated in the Introduction, in editing this as well as the other four works it has been my aim to present a text that is readable as well as semi-critical: made readable by dividing the text into sentences and paragraphs and correcting evident scribal errors in the manuscript on which the edition will be based, and semi-critical as a result of collating and inspecting all witnesses used for this edition.

For the choice of a base manuscript for this treatise, U can be at once eliminated because its texts breaks off in chapter X. B can be similarly eliminated because against the other witnesses it contains only eighteen instead of nineteen chapters (cf. textual note 38). Of the remaining two—and indeed of all four witnesses—M is the best text. Of the four it contains the smallest number of omissions by eyeskip: one (at textual note 115) in contrast to at least six in B and at least seven in E (and three in the imperfect U). But M contains its own peculiar readings, which often go against the sense of the sentence or paragraph, or are evidently scribal errors, and hence have to be emended.

Fusignano's style is very deliberate. He announces the parts of a topic and then treats them in order, marking them numerically ("one," "two," "three"). He defines terms that he evidently considers to be unfamiliar to his readers, such as *totum potestativum* (chapter XVIII). He illustrates every point he makes with one and often more examples, always introduced with *verbi gratia* or *puta.* And when he has given an example, he makes sure his readers get what he has illustrated by saying

psala: Kuningliga Vitterhets Historie och Antikvitets Akademien, 1971), where the same text (with slightly different wording) is spoken by Mary to her *filia,* not by Christ to his *sponsa,* as here.

ecce quomodo or *qualiter.* These features tend to make his style pedestrian, but they offer his editor the advantage of discerning irregularities that must have come from the scribe's pen. For instance, it is unlikely that Jacobus wrote *(auctoritas) conducta* when in the next sentence and throughout the treatise he used *inducta* (see textual note 42). Similarly, the reading *uirtutum* at note 27 must be a scribal error for *in truncum,* which is not only demanded by the sentence sense but is in fact used in the immediately following sentence and later on. (One might call this the "the dropping penny phenomenon"—the scribe first writes an erroneous form but a little later, perhaps even in the next sentence, gets it right.) I have, therefore, examined M in terms of the logical flow as well as the grammar and syntax of its exposition, have compared it with the other witnesses, and have corrected readings that strike me as scribal errors. Usually the emended reading is attested in at least one witness. My corrections, however, are not the result of following a *stemma codicum.* For that, a complete recension of all extant witnesses would be necessary, which is not my purpose here. Critical readers may quibble with this procedure, and admittedly a number of cases remain open to disagreement. However, the *apparatus criticus* to the Latin text records the readings of all four witnesses (or three, in the later parts) wherever I have rejected the reading of M. It also includes a few instances where I cannot decide what the original reading may have been (e.g., notes 62 and 73) or where readings from outside M may be of some interest for the textual history of the work (e.g., 24, 26, 122).

That this *ars praedicandi* is the work of an Italian author is neatly shown by his use of *moteti* (in chapter XV; see note 121 to the translation). M itself was produced in Italy and shows such Italianisms as writing *qui* as *q* with a horizontal stroke through its descender,[11] apparently on occasion misread as *que* by the exemplar on which the 1476 edition was based.[12] Also, the exemplar of our witnesses seems to have written -ct- for -tt-[13] and is in this fairly consistently followed not only

11. See for example S. Harrison Thomson, *Latin Bookhands of the Later Middle Ages 1100–1500* (Cambridge: Cambridge University Press, 1969), plate 67 (Italy 1289), right column, lines 13, 31, 33, etc.; and plate 69 (Italy 1308), line 29 *(require).*

12. *actus nostros que* (see below 00); *ab aliis libris que* (00).

13. See also Thomson, *Latin Bookhands,* plate 69 (Italy 1308), line 25: *obmictas.*

by M (with a ligature) but also by B. I have reproduced it as -tt-. Otherwise, I have preserved the spellings of M, including an occasional oddity like *theuma* for *thema,* and its use of *-ti-* and *-ci-* (not always clearly distinguishable) as well as the *u/v* distinction. But *j* has been consistently transcribed as *i.*

FUSIGNANO

TEXT

Oxford, Merton College MS 102.
[f. 277ra]

INCIPIT LIBELLUS ARTIS PREDICATORIE compositus a fratre Iacobo Fusignani ordinis fratrum predicatorum.[1]

[I]
Primum capitulum: De quatuor causis diuine exhortationis.

Oro ut caritas uestra magis ac magis habundet in scientia et in omni sensu, ut probetis pociora et sitis sinceres et sine offensa in diem[2] *Christi.* Philippensium i.

Omni operi omnique actioni non solum debetur efficiens quod opus agit, verum etiam exigitur finis quem agens intendit, materia quam agens assumit, forma quoque quam suo operi agens imponit. Vnde et ad doctrinam sancte eruditionis quatuor ista concurrunt, que in assumptis uerbis conuenienter possunt notari. Causa namque efficiens diuine exhortationis duplex est, scilicet principalis et instrumentalis. Principalis causa Deus est, cui nostras orationes offerre debemus, iuxta illud Psalmi *Ad te orabo, Domine.* Vnde causa agens principalis insinuatur cum dicitur *oro,* scilicet Deum, principalem actorem[3] predicationis. Causa uero instrumentalis predicator est, cuius lingua debet a

1. Incipit...predicatorum] M.E (*with* predicacionis); incipit libellus seu tractatus de arte predicandi B; *om.* O.

2. diem] B *and source;* die M.E.O.

3. actorem] M *and* E *here and later write* actor(em); B *and* O alternate *between* actor(em) *and* auctor(em).

FUSIGNANO

TRANSLATION

HERE BEGINS THE BOOK ON THE ART OF PREACHING composed by Friar James of Fusignano, of the Order of Preachers.

[I]
Chapter One: The four causes of divine exhortation.

I pray that your charity may more and more abound in knowledge and in every sense, that you may test the better things and be sincere and without reproach unto the day of Christ, Philippians 1.[1]

Every deed and every action must not only have something efficient that carries it out, but also an end which its agent intends, a subject matter that its agent works with, and a form which he imposes on his work. These four things also apply to the teaching of holy knowledge, and they can be conveniently found in the [biblical] words that have been quoted. The efficient cause in divine exhortation is twofold, one principal, the other instrumental. The principal cause is God, to whom we should offer our prayers, after the words of the Psalm *To you will I pray, O Lord.*[2] Here the principal efficient cause is expressed in the words *I pray,* namely to God, the principal agent of preaching. But the instrumental cause is the preacher, whose tongue must be moved by God to preach, after the words of the Psalm *My tongue is the pen of a*

1. Phil 1:9–10.
2. Ps 5:4 (5:4).

Deo moueri ad predicandum, iuxta illud Psalmi *Lingua mea calamus scribe.* Christus enim loquitur per predicatorem ueritatis, prout testatur Apostolus secundo Corinthiorum xiii, dicens: *An experimentum queritis eius qui in me loquitur Christus?* Causa igitur agens instrumentalis datur intelligi per hoc quod dicitur *caritas uestra.* Causa uero formalis insinuatur cum dicitur *magis ac magis habundet.* Debet enim predicator habundare auctoritatibus, rationibus, similitudinibus, et exemplis uariis modis, sicut infra patebit. Et hoc est quod Apostolus dicit prima Corinthiorum xiiii: *Quoniam emulatores estis spirituum, ad edificationem Ecclesie querite ut habundetis. Scientia enim sapientis tanquam inundatio habundabit,* ut dicitur Ecclesiastici xxi. Causa quoque materialis insinuatur per hoc quod in auctoritate concluditur *in scientia et in omni sensu.* Dicit autem *in scientia* ad insinuandum diuine ueritatis notitiam, que sola ueraciter scientia et sapientia dici debet, iuxta illud Ecclesiastici xv: *Dedit scientiam sanctorum.* In sola enim sacra scriptura traditur notitia illorum omnium que sunt necessaria ad salutem, secundum illud Sapientie ix, *Scit illa omnia et intelligit.* Quinimo qui sine scriptura sacra se putat scientem, inanis est, quia *uani sunt omnes homines in quibus non subest sapientia Dei,* ut habetur Sapientie xiii. Causa igitur materialis, que est sacra scriptura, insinuatur in nomine *scientie.* Sed addit *in omni sensu,* quia scriptura sacra habundat multiplici sensu, quorum quilibet potest esse utilis predicatori, ut infra patebit. Finis autem predicationis est inducere ad uirtutes et reuocari a uitiis et peccatis. Vnde causa finalis insinuatur [f. 277rb] cum dicitur *ut probetis potiora,* quantum ad uirtutum exercicium, *et sitis sinceres,* idest sine carne corruptionis, quantum ad detestationem uitiorum. Subdit autem *in diem*[4] *Christi,*

4. diem] B *and source;* die M.E.O.

scribe.[3] For it is Christ who speaks through the preacher of the truth, as the Apostle witnesses in 2 Corinthians 13, where he says: *Do you seek proof of him who speaks in me, Christ?*[4] Hence the instrumental efficient cause is indicated [in the initial quotation] by the words *your charity.*[5] But the formal cause appears in the words *that it may more and more abound.* For the preacher must abound variously in authorities,[6] reasons, similitudes, and examples, as will be shown below. This is what the Apostle says in 1 Corinthians 14: *Since you are zealous of spirits, seek to abound to the edification of the Church.*[7] *Because the knowledge of a wise man shall abound like a flood,* as is said in Ecclesiasticus 21.[8] And the material cause is indicated when our [initial] authority concludes with *in knowledge and all understanding.* By saying *in knowledge* it indicates the cognizance of divine truth, which alone can be said to be truly knowledge and wisdom, according to Ecclesiasticus 15: *She* [i.e., Wisdom] *gave him the knowledge of holy things.*[9] For only in Holy Scripture is the cognizance of all things handed on that are necessary for salvation, after the words of Wisdom 9, *She knows and understands all things.*[10] Therefore, whoever deems himself to be knowledgeable without Holy Scripture is hollow, for *vain are all men in whom there is not the wisdom of God,* as is said in Wisdom 13.[11] Thus the material cause, namely Holy Scripture, is indicated in the noun *knowledge.* But the authority then adds *in every sense,* for Holy Scripture is full of multiple senses,[12] each of which can be useful to the preacher, as will be shown below. And lastly, the end of preaching is to lead to virtues and to call back from vices and sins. Thus its final cause is indicated [in our authority] when it says *that you may test the better things,* with respect to practicing virtues, *and be sincere,* that is, without the corruption of the flesh,[13] with respect to detesting vices. And the authority then adds

3. Ps 44:2 (45:1).
4. 2 Cor 13:3
5. Evidently here understood as an address of the recipient of the letter, "Your Charity."
6. "Authorities," in the technical language of preachers, are quotations or proof texts from Scripture and other authoritative sources.
7. 1 Cor 14:12.
8. Sir 21:16.
9. Rather Ws 10:10.
10. Ws 9:11.
11. Ws 13:1.
12. Referring to the fourfold sense of Scripture; see below, chapter XI.
13. The "etymology" of *sincerus* was thought to be *sine corruptione*; cf. Isidore, *Etymologies* 10.242.

idest perseueranter usque ad finem uite, ad ostendendum quod tam exercicium uirtutum quam detestatio uitiorum requirit finalem perseueranciam.

[II]
Secundum capitulum: Quod predicator debet thema assumere et orationem premittere.

Qvia igitur predicator est causa agens instrumentalis sacre eruditionis, ut ex dictis patet, ideo secundum tria que circa causam instrumentalem considerantur tria incumbunt predicatori. [1] Primum autem quod cause instrumentali conuenit est quod preter illam actionem quam habet instrumentum prout est motum ab agente principali, habet aliquam aliam actionem ex propria natura. Sicut securis preter actionem que instrumentaliter pertingit ad formam suam, habet ex natura sui acuminis quod diuidat. Vnde non solum prout mouetur a carpentario sed etiam cadens habet quod diuidat. [2] Secundum est quod sicut agens principale dicitur quod est primum mouens, ita agens instrumentale est mouens motum. [3] Tercium est quod agens instrumentale aliquando quidem pertingit ad ultimum effectum principalis agentis, aliquando uero non, sicut qualitates elementorum in rebus inanimatis pertingunt usque ad educendas formas materiales de materia, sed in homine non pertingunt usque ad producendam[5] animam rationalem, que est forma substancialis in homine. Considerandum ergo quod effectus Dei, qui est principalis actor predicationis, est conferre fidelibus gratiam et gloriam, iuxta illud Psalmi *Gratiam et gloriam dabit Dominus.* Ad quos effec-

5. producendam] B.E.O; perducendam M.

unto the day of Christ, that is, by persevering until the end of life, showing thereby that practicing virtues as well as rejecting vices demands perseverance to the end.

[II]
Chapter Two: The preacher must choose a thema and begin with a prayer.

Since, then, the preacher is the instrumental efficient cause of holy learning, as was shown above, three things are incumbent on him, according to three things that can be discerned in an instrumental cause. [1] The first thing that belongs to an instrumental cause is that, apart from the act an instrument carries out in accordance with the way it is moved by the principal agent, it has some other action that derives from its own nature. Thus, a knife, apart from the act that belongs to it insofar as it is [used as] an instrument, possesses of its own nature sharpness that cuts away. Therefore it cuts not only as it is moved by the carpenter but it also has the power to cut when it falls.[14] [2] The second thing is that, just as the principal agent is said to be the first mover, so the instrumental agent as a mover is himself moved. [3] And the third thing is that the instrumental agent sometimes attains the ultimate effect of the principal agent, and sometimes not, just as the qualities of the elements in inanimate beings attain the material forms that are to be brought out in their subject matter, though in man they do not attain the production of a rational soul, which is the substantive form in a human being.[15] Therefore we must consider that the effect produced by God—who is the principal agent of preaching—is to give the faithful grace and glory, after the words of the Psalm *The Lord will give grace*

14. On this distinction see, for example, Thomas Aquinas, *Summa theologiae* III, a. 1, ad 2.

15. Cf. Thomas Aquinas, *In IV Sententiarum,* distinctio 1, quaestio1, art. 4, quaestiuncula 1: "Sed sciendum, quod actio instrumenti quandoque pertingit ad ultimam perfectionem, quam principale agens inducit, aliquando autem non; semper tamen pertingit ad aliquid ultra id quod competit sibi secundum suam naturam, sive illud sit ultima forma, sive dispositio, alias non ageret ut instrumentum: sic qualitates activae et passivae elementorum pertingunt instrumentaliter ad formas materiales educendas de materia, non autem ad productionem animae humanae, quae est ab extrinseco."

tus nulla rationalis creatura potet pertingere saltem immediate. Quod dico propter sacramenta noue legis, que dicuntur a quibusdam gratiam causare.

Propter primum itaque horum (quia uidelicet instrumentum habet aliquam actionem ex propria natura seu uirtute) conuenit predicatori quod seipsum applicet ad materiam sue predicationis. Quod facit assumendo thema[6] scripture. Cum enim predicator sit instrumentum animatum, seipsum potest ad materiam applicare. Propter secundum (scilicet quia est mouens motum) debet premittere orationem ut eius lingua dirigatur a Deo sicut ab agente principali. Sicut enim non sufficit bonitas seminis ac seminatoris ad fructificandum sine adiutorio pluuie et uirtutis corporum celestium, sic nec sermo predicatoris sine beneficio diuine gratie. Vnde Moyses scripturus canticum nomen Domini inuocauit, Deuteronomii xxxii, dicens: *Concrescat ut pluuia doctrina mea, fluat ut ros eloquium meum, quia nomen Domini* [f. 277va] *inuocabo.* Propter tertium (quia uidelicet non potest pertingere ad causandum gratiam uel gloriam) debet suum sermonem concludere per orationem qua petat gratiam in presenti et gloriam in futuro a Deo, cuius solius est gratiam et gloriam conferre, ut dictum est. Sic ergo debet quidem predicator premittere auctoritatem quasi tocius sermonis fundamentum siue materiam.

Sed attendendum quod sicut scientie humanitus inuente quandoque quidem utuntur propriis[7] et necessariis argumentis, quandoque uero propriis et probabilibus, quandoque autem probabilibus extraneis tantum,[8] ita etiam doctor seu predicator diuine ueritatis diuersorum auctoritatibus potest diuersimode uti. Cum enim principia sacre doctrine habeantur per reuelationem, oportet predicatorem uti auctoritatibus sacre scripture, per quam nobis huiusmodi principia innotuerunt, tanquam auctoritatibus propriis et de necessitate ueritatem concludentibus. Vnde patet quod sicut in omni artificio debet artifex pro-

6. theuma] M *with* u *expuncted.*

7. propriis] B.E; *om.* M.O.

8. tantum] E.O; tam B; tamen M.

and glory.[16] These effects no rational creature can attain immediately. I say this because of the sacraments of the New Law, which are said by some to cause grace.[17]

Now, because the first of these (namely, that an instrument exercises some action from its own nature or virtue), it is necessary that the preacher apply himself to the subject matter of his preaching. This he does by choosing a thema from Scripture. For since the preacher is an animate instrument, he is able to apply himself to the subject matter. Because of the second (namely, that as a mover he himself is moved), he must begin with a prayer, so that his tongue may be led by God as the principal agent. Just as the good quality of a seed and of the sower is not enough for producing fruit without the help of rain and the power of the heavenly bodies, so does the preacher's sermon not produce fruit without the benefit of divine grace. Thus Moses, when he was about to write his song, invoked the name of the Lord, saying in Deuteronomy 32: *Let my doctrine gather as the rain, let my speech distil as the dew, because I will invoke the name of the Lord.*[18] With respect to the third thing (namely, that he is not sufficient to cause grace and glory), the preacher must close his sermon with a prayer in which he asks for grace in the present and for glory in the future from God, whose alone is the power to confer grace and glory, as has been said. In this way, then, the preacher must begin with an authority that is, so to speak, the foundation or material of his entire sermon.

But we must be aware that just as sciences that are of human origin sometimes use arguments that are proper and necessary, sometimes those that are proper and probable, and sometimes those that are probable and only external, so the teacher or preacher of divine truth can also use authorities from different sources in different ways. Since the principles of sacred doctrine rest on revelation, the preacher must use authorities from Holy Scripture, through which these principles have become known to us, as proper authorities that prove the truth by necessity. Thus it is clear that, just as in any craft the craftsman has to

16. Ps 83:12 (83:12).

17. Cf. Thomas Aquinas, *In IV Sententiarum,* d. 1, qu. 1, art. 4, quaestiuncula 1, arg. 5: "Ergo sacramenta novae legis gratiam causant." Also *Summa theologiae* III, d. 62, a. 1.

18. Dt 32:2–3.

priam materiam assumere, ita predicator debet sumere[9] thema et materiam sue predicationis de textu scripture sacre.

Quia uero sancti doctores Spiritu Sancto reuelante plurima de canonicis scripturis exposuerunt, potest predicator uti auctoritatibus sanctorum ad suum propositum probandum, tanquam propriis quidem probabilibus tamen. Sed quia fides nostra non innititur reuelationibus factis sacris doctoribus set solis apostolis et prophetis qui libros canonicos conscripserunt, ideo non est utendum auctoritatibus sanctorum pro themate principali. Vnde beatus Augustinus dicit in *Epistola ad Ieronimum:* "Solis eis scripturarum libris qui canonici appellantur didici hunc honorem deferre, ut nullum actorem eorum scribendo errasse aliquid firmissime credam. Alios autem ita lego ut quantalibet scripturarum auctoritate prepolleant, non ideo uerum putem, quia ipsi ita senserunt." Auctoritatibus uero philosophorum, maxime de libris ad mores pertinentibus, potest quidem predicator uti, parce tamen et tanquam extraneis et probabilibus, et hoc dumtaxat in hiis in quibus per naturalem rationem ueritatem cognoscere potuerunt. Vnde et Paulus Actuum xvii usus est auctoritate Arati poete dicens: *In ipso uiuimus, mouemur, et sumus,* sicut et quidam nostrorum poetarum dixerunt. Et beatus Augustinus dicit in libro *De doctrina christiana:* "Si qua ueritati consona a philosophis dicta sunt, non solum non sunt pertimescenda sed ab ipsis tanquam ab iniustis possessoribus in nostrum usum uendicanda." Cum autem sancti doctores titulo sanctitatis habeant auctoritatem, decens est quod predicator alleget dicta sanctorum cum titulo sanctitatis dicendo "beatus Augustinus" uel "beatus Ieronimus" et huiusmodi. Et eodem modo quia dicta philosophorum gentilium extranea sunt [f. 277vb] a doctrina sacra, ut dictum est, decens est quod predicator qui uult adducere uerbum alicuius philosophi ostendat uerbum illud extraneum esse a doctrina sacra. Quod facit dicendo "sicut habetur in alia doctrina" uel "in alia scientia" aut "in aliis litteris" et huiusmodi, tacendo tamen nomen philosophi et etiam libri, licet in

9. sumere] M.O; assumere B.E.

choose the proper material, so the preacher must take the thema and material of his sermon from the text of Holy Scripture.

But insofar as our holy teachers have explained much of the canonical Scriptures by revelation from the Holy Spirit, the preacher may well use authorities from the saints to prove his point, but as properly probable ones. Yet since our faith rests on revelations, not given to holy teachers but only to the apostles and prophets, who wrote the canonical books, one must not use authorities from the saints as one's main thema. Thus Augustine says in his *Epistle to Jerome:* "I have learned to give this honor only to those books of Scripture that are called canonical, that I may firmly believe that none of their authors has in any way erred in his writing. Others, however, I read in such a way that I do not consider them of equal authority with [Holy] Scripture, however much they may be endowed with scriptural authority—their authors themselves felt this to be so."[19] Authorities from philosophers, however, especially from books dealing with morals, the preacher may indeed use, but sparingly and only for external and probable proof, and this particularly in those matters in which the philosophers could find the truth by their natural reason. Paul, too, in Acts 17, used the authority of the poet Aratus when he said: *In him we live and move and have our being,*[20] as also some of our poets have said. And blessed Augustine says in his book *On Christian Doctrine:* "If anything that is in agreement with the truth has been said by philosophers, not only should it not be feared but it should be taken over from them as if from unrightful owners, for our own use."[21] Now, since our holy teachers, on account of their holiness, possess authority, it is fitting that the preacher should quote the sayings of the saints with their title of holiness and say "blessed Augustine" or "blessed Jerome" and the like. And in the same way, since the sayings of pagan philosophers are outside holy doctrine, as has been said, it is fitting that a preacher who wants to quote the saying of some philosopher should indicate that that saying is from outside holy doctrine. This he can do by saying "as is said in some other teaching" or "in another science" or "in other books" and the like. He should however pass over the name of the philosopher and the book as

19. Augustine, *Ep.* 82.

20. Acts 17:28.

21. Cf. Augustine, *De doctrina christiana* 2.40.

scribendo sermonem possit ponere nomen libri pro maiori certitudine lectoris.

[III]
Tercium capitulum: De qualitate thematis assumendi. Rubrica.

Circa thema uero quod predicator assumit de scriptura sacra debet tria attendere. [1] Primum est quod uerbum assumptum habeat perfectum sensum, ita quod si nichil aliud precederet aut sequeretur in scriptura de qua sumitur thema, nichilominus uerbum sui thematis haberet perfectum sensum. Nec tamen oportet quod totum uersum assumat qui in scriptura scribitur, set tantum quantum sufficit ad suum propositum prosequendum. Uerbi gratia, Iacobi primo scribitur: *Beatus uir qui suffert temptationem, quoniam cum probatus fuerit, accipiet coronam uite quam repromisit Deus diligentibus se.* Licet autem omnia uerba hec sub uno sensu scribantur in textu, tamen si predicator intendat loqui de sufferencia temptationum tantum, non oportet omnia uerba hec proponere, sed sufficit quod proponat sic: *Beatus uir qui suffert temptationem.* Nam hec sola uerba perfectum sensum habent, etiam si nichil aliud sequeretur. Si autem intendit loqui de sufferencia simul et probatione, potest sic proponere: *Beatus uir qui suffert temptationem, quoniam cum probatus fuerit, accipiet coronam uite.* Ista enim sola uerba sine sequentibus habent perfectum sensum. Potest nichilominus et totum uersum proponere secundum materiam de qua proponit loqui, ita dumtaxat quod nimis prolixum thema non proponat. Fecunda[10] sunt namque uerba scripture, et ex breui themate longus potest sermo dilatari.

[2] Secundum est quod coniunctiones et aduerbia quibus thema continuatur uel respicit ad precedencia obmittat in themate assumpto, et specialiter ubi non mutatur sensus scripture. Uerbi gratia, in Psalmo scribitur: *Dixit Dominus domino meo, Sede a dextris meis donec ponam inimicos tuos,* etc. Si ergo predicator uelit

10. Fecunda] *corrected from* sequenda *or the reverse* M; fecunda B; fructuosa E; secunda O.

well, except that when he writes out his sermon he may put down the name of the book, for greater assurance to his reader.

[III]
Chapter Three: The quality of the chosen thema.

Regarding the thema which the preacher takes from Holy Scripture he must attend to three things. [1] The first is that the quotation he chooses must make perfect sense, so that, if nothing else were to precede or follow in the scriptural passage from which he chooses his thema, the words of his thema would nevertheless give a complete meaning. It is, however, not necessary that he quote the entire verse written in Scripture, but only as much as is sufficient to pursue his purpose. For example: In James 1 it is written: *Blessed is the man who endures temptation, for when he has been proved, he shall receive the crown of life that God has promised those who love him.*[22] In the text, all these words appear with a single meaning. However, if the preacher wants to speak only about suffering temptation, he need not quote all these words, but it is sufficient if he says: *Blessed is the man who suffers temptation.* For these words by themselves make perfect sense, even if nothing else were to follow. But if the preacher wants to speak about suffering together with being tested, then he can say: *Blessed is the man who endures temptation, for when he has been proved, he shall receive the crown of life.* These words alone have a complete meaning without anything to follow. Nonetheless, he may also quote the entire verse according to the matter about which he intends to speak, as long as he does not quote an exceedingly long thema. For the words of Scripture are pregnant, and from a short thema one can develop a long sermon.

[2] Second, in the thema he chooses he must omit conjunctions and adverbs by which the thema continues or which link it to what has preceded, and especially so when the sense of Scripture does not change. For example: In the Psalm it is written: *The Lord said to my lord, "Sit at my right hand until I make your enemies,"* etc.[23] Now, if the preacher

22. Jas 1:12.
23. Ps 109:1 (110:1).

suum thema sumere sic: *Donec ponam inimicos,* etc., patebit derisioni, quia hoc aduerbium temporis *donec* respicit precedencia de quibus in[11] suo themate non est facta mentio. Item Luce i scribitur: *Posuerunt omnes qui audierant in corde suo dicentes, Quis putas puer iste erit? Etenim manus Domini erat cum illo.* Si ergo predicator sumat thema sic: *Etenim manus Domini erat cum illo,* male assumet, quia hec causalis[12] coniunctio *etenim* respicit precedencia, de quibus nichil ipse dixit. Et simile [f. 278ra] obseruandum est in aliis. Sciendum est autem quod si in textu sit aliquod pronomen relatiuum uel demonstratiuum, potest predicator proponere thema sicut iacet in textu et tamen prosequi acsi in textu esset ipsum primitiuum, uel ipsum antecedens. Uerbi gratia: Luce xix scribitur de Zacheo quod *precurrens ascendit in arborem siccomorum ut uideret \eum/.* Potest ergo predicator proponere uerba sicut hic posita sunt, et deinde prosequi sermonem suum acsi in textu[13] ubi est *eum* esset *Iesum.* Vnde dicere potest "uisio Iesu, de qua[14] hic agitur, ualet ad hoc et ad illud," ita tamen quod si intendit uocaliter concordare, non concordet de uocabulo quod non est in textu sed de aliqua alia dictione que sit in suo themate.

[3] Tercium quod predicator debet specialiter attendere est ne assumat thema in contrarium sensum scripture quam assumit, ita quod suam expositionem nullus uerus sensus patiatur. Uerbi gratia: Luce xvi scribitur: *Mortuus est diues et sepultus est in inferno.*[15] Si ergo predicator uelit hoc uerbum assumere de Christo, ut dicat "*Mortuus est diues,* idest Christus, *et sepultus est in inferno,*[16] idest descendit ad inferos," male assumeret, quia huic expositioni contrariantur sequencia uerba, nam sequitur quod ille diues dixit *Crucior in hac flamma* et quedam alia que maxime ostendunt quod talis expositio nulli uero sensui consonat. Et ideo in omni expositione scripture quam predicator fa-

11. in] B.E.O; *om.* M.
12. causalis] B.E.O; casualis M.
13. textu] M *followed by* esset *erased.*
14. uisio Iesu de qua] B; uiso (*corr from* uisio) Iesu de qua M; viso Iesu de quo E; visio Iesu de quo O.
15. inferno] B.E.O *and source;* infernum M.
16. inferno] B.E; infernum M.O.

wants to take as his thema *Until I put your enemies,* etc., he opens himself to ridicule, because the temporal conjunction *until* refers back to the preceding words, of which no mention is made in his thema. Likewise, in Luke 1 it is written: *All who had heard them laid them up in their hearts saying, "What, do you think, will this child be?" For the hand of the Lord was with him.*[24] Now, if the preacher takes as his thema *For the hand of the Lord was with him,* this is a bad choice, because the causal conjunction *for* relates back to what has preceded, of which the preacher has said nothing. And the like must be observed elsewhere. But if there is a relative or demonstrative pronoun in the text, one should know that the preacher may quote the thema as it stands in the biblical text and yet proceed as if the text had the original word or the relative's antecedent. For example: In Luke 19 it is written about Zacheus that *running ahead he climbed up into a sycamore tree that he might see him.*[25] The preacher may say the words as here quoted and then develop his sermon as if instead of *him* the text had the word *Jesus.* Thus he may say: "Seeing Jesus, which is here dealt with, is good for this and that." He must do so, however, that if he wants to use verbal agreement [in his further development], it must not agree with a word that is not in his text but with some other word that does appear in his thema.

[3] The third matter the preacher must take special care about is not to choose his thema in a sense that is contrary to the meaning it has in Scripture, so that his exposition would make no true sense. For example, in Luke 16 it is written: *The rich man died and was buried in hell.*[26] Now, if the preacher wanted to take this thema with reference to Christ and say, "*The rich man died,* that is, Christ, *and was buried in hell,* that is, he descended into hell," he would take his thema wrongly, because the next words contradict his exposition, for in what follows the rich man says, *I am tormented in this flame* and other things that show quite clearly that the preacher's exposition does not agree with the true sense [of the biblical text]. Therefore, in any exposition of Scripture that the preacher intends to offer he must pay attention to what precedes and

24. Lk 1:66.
25. Lk 19:4.
26. Lk 16:22.

cere intendit debet attendere ad precedencia et sequencia, ne forte sua expositio precedentibus uel sequentibus contrarietur. Et hoc specialiter in expositione litterali. In expositione autem morali uel allegorica aut anagogica[17] non oportet quod omnia precedencia et sequencia possint exponi secundum eandem expositionem, dummodo litteralis sensus non contradicat expositioni litterali.

Non conuenit autem predicatorem latere quod in omnibus diebus dominicis, quando de tempore agitur, assumendum est thema de euuangelio dominicali uel de epistola, aut etiam de introitu misse quando dominica habet sollempnem et famosum introitum, sicut prima et quarta dominica Aduentus, uel dominica de *Letare* et dominica *Quasimodo geniti,* et si qua alia dominica habet sollempnem introitum. Potest quoque aliquando sed raro sumi thema de ipsa ystoria que cantatur. Excipiuntur autem ab ista regula euangeliorum et epistularum dominicalium prima dominica Aduentus, dominica in Ramis Palmarum, dominica Resurrectionis Domini, dominica in Penthecostem, et dominica de Trinitate.

In sermonibus autem festiuis potest sumi thema de omni loco scrip- [f. 278rb] ture, sed[18] quod melius competit sollempnitati. Sunt tamen quedam sollempnitates que principaliter dependent ex suis euuangeliis, sicut festum Circumcisionis, festum Epyphanie, festum Purificationis, festum Anunciationis, festum Natiuitatis Iohannis Baptiste.[19] In talibus festiuitatibus conueniens est quod de ipso euangelio thema sumatur, licet non sit necessarium. In sermonibus etiam defunctorum potest sumi thema ubi predicatori uisum fuerit diuersimode secundum diuersas conditiones personarum defunctarum.

17. anagogica] B.E.O; anegogica M.
18. sed] B.M.O; secundum E.
19. Baptiste] E *adds* Marie Magdalene.

what follows, lest his exposition contradict the preceding or following words. This applies especially to the literal exposition, whereas in the moral or allegorical or anagogical exposition it is not necessary that all that precedes and follows can be explained according to the same exposition, as long as the literal sense does not contradict his literal exposition.

I should not conceal from the preacher that on all Sundays that are *de tempore*[27] the thema must be selected from the Sunday gospel or epistle, or also from the introit of the Mass[28] when the Sunday has a solemn and well-known introit, such as the first and fourth Sunday in Advent, or the Sunday *Laetare*[29] or *Quasimodo geniti*,[30] and whatever other Sunday has a solemn introit. The thema may sometimes, but rarely, be taken from the narrative that is sung.[31] But from this rule regarding the Sunday gospels and epistles should be excepted the first Sunday in Advent, Palm Sunday, Easter Sunday, Pentecost, and Trinity Sunday.

In sermons on feast days the thema may be taken from any place in Scripture, but one that best suits the feast. Some feasts depend essentially on their gospels, such as Circumcision, Epiphany, Purification, Annunciation, and the Nativity of John the Baptist.[32] On these feast days it is fitting that the thema be taken from the gospel itself, though this is not necessary. And in sermons for the dead, the thema may be taken from wherever the preacher thinks it fitting for the character of the deceased.

27. Sundays throughout the year.

28. Introit: the opening verse of the medieval and Tridentine mass, such as *Laetare, Jerusalem, et conventum facite omnes qui diligitis Dominum* ("Rejoice, Jerusalem, and come together all you who love the Lord," fourth Sunday of Lent).

29. Fourth Sunday of Lent.

30. First Sunday after Easter.

31. Probably referring to gospels that are essentially a narrative.

32. That is, the feast derives from the account given in the gospel; for instance, the feast of the Circumcision celebrates Jesus' circumcision as told in Luke 2:21.

[IV]
Capitulum quartum: De protheumate et modo orationis.

Circa[20] \o/rationem uero premittendam duplex solet modus seruari: aut enim post thema propositum subiungitur oratio absque alio prothemate scripture, puta cum predicator dicit in principio sermonis "Rogemus Dominum," etc.; aut post thema propositum subiungitur prothema de textu scripture sacre. Primus quidem modus facilis est et breuis. Circa secundum uero modum est obseruandum quod \pro/thema sit consonum themati. Quod fit duobus modis. Vno quidem modo, quando prothema consonat themati in ea dictione in qua predicator intendit concordare uocaliter. Uerbi gratia: Si predicator proponat hoc thema *Verbum caro factum est,* deinde loco prothematis subdatur *In uerbo tuo laxabo rethe,* et concordat in suo sermone de *uerbo,* erit modus conueniens et pulcer. Alio uero modo, quando predicator non intendit concordare de una dictione sed predicare de toto themate assumpto uel de toto euangelio; et tunc pulcher et conueniens modus est quod in ea dictione sumat prothema inicium in qua thema terminatur. Uerbi gratia: Si predicator proponat hoc thema *Beatus uir qui suffert temptationem, quoniam cum probatus fuerit, accipiet coronam uite,* deinde loco prothematis subdat *Vita erat lux hominum,* erit modus pulcher, licet non usitatus. Et eodem modo si proponat hoc thema *Ecce rex tuus uenit tibi mansuetus,* et loco prothematis subdat *In mansuetudine suscipite inscitum uerbum,* pulcer modus erit, etiam si in sermone non concordet de ea dictione in qua consonat prothema themati assumpto. Quod si fortassis neutro modo prothema themati consonet, saltem attendat quod prothema non discrepet a materia orationis, aut sapientie, aut scientie seu eruditionis, aut uerbi, uel ceterorum similium. Debet autem in prosecutione prothematis semper uitare pro-

20. Circa] Ciirca M.

[IV]

Chapter Four: The protheme and the form of the prayer.

Concerning the prayer that should be said at the beginning, two types are in use: either a prayer is added after the thema has been stated, without another protheme from Scripture, as when the preacher says in the beginning of his sermon: "Let us pray the Lord," etc.; or else, after the stated thema a protheme is added from the text of Holy Scripture. The first type is easy and short. About the second type, however, we should observe that the protheme must agree with the thema. This is done in two ways. In the first, the protheme echoes the word with which the preachers intends to have a verbal agreement.[33] For example: if the preacher proposes the thema *The Word was made flesh,*[34] and then for his protheme adds *At your word I will let down the net,*[35] and his sermon deals with *the word,* it will make a fitting and beautiful discourse. In the second way, when the preacher does not intend to focus on a single word but wants to preach about the entire thema he has chosen or the entire gospel, it would be fitting and beautiful if his protheme begins with the same word that ends his thema. For example, if the preacher announces as his thema *Blessed is the man who endures temptation, for when he has been proved, he shall receive the crown of life,*[36] and then for his protheme adds, *The life was the light of men,*[37] it will be a beautiful way, though not often used. In the same fashion, if he proposes as his thema, *Behold, your king comes to you meek*[38] and then adds for his protheme, *With meekness receive the ingrafted word,*[39] it will be a beautiful way even if in his sermon he does not focus on the word that links his protheme to the announced thema [i.e., *meek*]. However, if in either case his protheme does not agree with this thema, he must diligently see to it that his protheme does not disagree with the matter of the prayer or of wisdom, or knowledge and learning, or the word, or other similar things. In developing his protheme he must

33. I.e., the word that will be developed after the protheme.

34. Jn 1:14.

35. Lk 5:5.

36. Jas 1:12.

37. Jn 1:4.

38. Mt 21:5.

39. Jas 1:21.

lixitatem, quia sicut dicitur II Machabeorum ii: *Stultum est ante ystoriam effluere, in ipsa autem ystoria subcingi.*

Consueuit autem hec oratio dirigi ad Deum sub patrocinio Beate Uirginis tanquam ducis diuini uerbi, ut que nobis protulit Uerbum increatum procuret sua intercessione uerbum creatum. Petitur autem in huiusmodi oratione loqui et audire quod sit ad honorem [f. 278va] Dei et sancti de quo predicatur in sermonibus festiuis et ad salutem et consolationem audiencium. In sermonibus uero defunctorum talis oratio non consueuit premitti, forte quia olim in huiusmodi predicationibus insistebatur testimonio defuncti et consolationi amicorum plus quam expositioni sacrarum scripturarum.

[V]
Capitulum quintum: De diuisione thematis. Rubrica.

Predicto itaque modo sumpto themate et oratione premissa, procedere debet predicator ad prosecutionem sui sermonis. Quod quidem consueuit fieri tribus modis.

[1] Vno quidem modo quando proposito loco thematis principio euuangelii alicuius predicator prosequitur tocius euangelii explanationem. Et hic quidem modus antiquitus satis fuit communis, sicut maxime ostendunt omelie beati Gregorii et aliorum sanctorum doctorum. Vnde usque hodie quidam predicatores obseruant ut totum euangelium exponant populo, etiam si de una tantum particula predicare intendunt. Est autem hoc satis rudi populo utile. Ceterum litteratis et intelligentibus auditoribus huiusmodi popularis expositio non est necessaria.

[2] Secundo modo solet fieri sermonis prosecutio quando proposito themate omissa thematis diuisione procedunt ad aliquam distinctionem. Et hoc quidem aliqui faciunt specialiter in sermonibus defunctorum. Puta si predicator proponat hoc thema *O mors, quam amara est memoria tua,* deinde absque horum uerborum diuisione subiungatur sic:

always avoid prolixity, for as it is said in 2 Maccabees 2, *It is a foolish thing to make a long prologue and to be short in the story itself.*[40]

The prayer itself is usually directed to God under the tutelage of the Blessed Virgin, as guiding the divine word, so that she who has brought us the uncreated Word may through her intercession obtain for us the created word. In this prayer we ask to speak and to hear what is to the honor of God and of the saint about whom we preach in festival sermons and for the salvation and consolation of our audience. In sermons for the dead, however, such a prayer is usually not said, perhaps because formerly in sermons of this kind the preacher was more concerned with praising the deceased and consoling his friends than with explaining Sacred Scripture.

[V]
Chapter Five: The division of the thema.

After he has chosen his thema and begun with a prayer in the way I have shown, the preacher must then proceed to develop his sermon. This has customarily been done in three ways.

[1] One way is when the preacher in place of his thema selects the beginning of the gospel lection and then goes on to explain the entire gospel. This mode was very common in former times, as the homilies of Blessed Gregory and of other holy doctors show best. Thus some preachers follow this even in our days, so that they explain the entire gospel lection to the people, even if they intend to preach only on part of it.[41] This is very helpful for simple people. Otherwise, for educated and intelligent people such popular exposition is not necessary.

[2] The second way to expand the sermon is used when, after announcing their thema, preachers omit the division of the thema and go on to some distinction. Some preachers do this especially in sermons for the dead. For instance, a preacher may propose the thema *O death, how bitter is your memory.*[42] Then he continues without dividing the quoted words as follows:

40. 2 Mc 2:33.

41. Good examples are the sermons of collection L in Siegfried Wenzel, *Latin Sermon Collections from Later Medieval England: Orthodox Preaching in the Age of Wyclif* (Cambridge: Cambridge University Press, 2005), 91–94.

42. Sir 41:1.

Amatoribus huius mundi amara est mortis memoria propter tria:
Primo quidem propter mundum quem deserunt,
secundo propter futurum supplicium quod metuunt;
tercio[21] propter carnis delicias quas amittunt.

Ecce quomodo proposito themate absque eius diuisione processum est ad eius distinctionem.

[3] Tercio quoque modo solet hoc fieri quando proposito themate proceditur ad eius diuisionem. Et hic quidem modus modernis predicatoribus communior est. Circa istum autem predicandi modum duo sunt attendenda, [i] quorum primum est quod priusquam predicator procedat ad diuisionem thematis, premittat aliquid cui thematis diuisio coaptari possit. Quod utique multis modis fieri potest. Aliquando enim potest premitti aliquod prouerbium notum. Uerbi gratia: Si proponat hoc thema *Nisi habundauerit iusticia uestra plus quam Scribarum et Phariseorum, non intrabitis in regnum celorum,* deinde priusquam ad diuisionem huius thematis procedat, premittat sic:

Prouerbium est "Nouus rex, noua lex," et ideo Christus tanquam rex nouus per carnis resurrectionem nouam legem proponit de iusticie perfectione, dicens: *Nisi habundauerit iusticia uestra,* etc. In quo quidem uerbo tria possumus attendere, etc.

Aliquando uero potest premitti aliquod simile naturale, puta si proposito eodem [f. 278vb] themate procedatur sic:

Sicut in generatione naturali proceditur de imperfecto ad perfectum, ita et in manifestatione legis gratie. Et ideo Christus, per quem gratia et ueritas facta sunt, legem proponit de perfectiori iusticia dicens: *Nisi habundauerit iusticia uestra,* etc. In quo uerbo tria possumus considerare, etc.

Aliquando autem potest sumi aliquod[22] simile morale, puta si eodem themate sumpto dicatur sic:

Mos solet esse illorum qui discipulos cupiunt ad magna prouehere, ut a minoribus incipiant et[23] ad maiora gradatim perducant. Et ideo Dominus

21. tercio] B.E.O; tercium M.
22. aliquod] B.E; ad O; aliquid M.
23. incipiant et] B; incipiendo E; incipitur O; *om.* M.

For those who love this world the memory of death is bitter for three reasons:

First, because of the world they leave,
second, because of the coming punishment they fear,
and third, because of the fleshly delights they lose.

Lo, how after announcing the thema the preacher has without dividing it gone on to a distinction based on it.

[3] In the third way the preacher expands his sermon when after announcing his thema he proceeds to its division. And this mode is more common among modern preachers. Concerning this way of preaching, two things must be attended to. [i] The first is this: before the preacher goes on to divide his thema, he may say something that can fit the division of his thema.[43] This can be done in many ways. Sometimes a well-known proverb may be quoted. For example, if the preacher proposes the thema *Unless your righteousness is greater than that of the scribes and Pharisees, you will not enter the kingdom of heaven,*[44] he then, before coming to the division of his thema, may first say:

There is a proverb "A new king, a new law."[45] Thus, Christ, like a new king in the resurrection of his flesh sets forth a new law about perfect righteousness when he says, *Unless your righteousness is greater,* and so on. In this quotation we can find three things, etc.

Sometimes however a simile from nature may be used. Thus, if after proposing the same thema one proceeds as follows:

Just as in a natural development things progress from the imperfect to the perfect, thus also in the manifestation of the law of grace. Therefore Christ, through whom grace and truth have come, teaches the law of a more perfect righteousness when he says, *Unless your righteousness is greater,* and so on. In which we may consider three things, etc.

Sometimes a moral simile may be taken, as when after proposing the same thema one says:

It is a custom among those who want to advance their disciples to greater things to begin with smaller things and lead them by degrees to larger ones.

43. In the following, Fusignano calls this part of the sermon *prelocutio,* "preamble."

44. Mt 5:20.

45. Listed in Walther *Proverbia* 18,860c.

noster, qui est humani generis creator, quasi a minoribus incipiens sub tempore legis scripture de minori iusticia dedit mandatum, sed in tempore gratie quasi gradatim ad maiora perducens de habundantiori iusticia ponit edictum dicens: *Nisi habundauerit iusticia uestra,* etc. In quo quidem uerbo, etc.

Aliquando uero potest sumi aliquod uerbum scripture sacre ante thematis diuisionem. Puta si assumpto predicto themate subdat sic:

> Habetur Prouerbiorum x *Iusticia preseruat a morte.* Et ideo Dominus noster, qui uenit uitam suis fidelibus dare, mandatum dat de iusticia dicens: *Nisi habundauerit iusticia uestra,* etc. In quo uerbo, etc.

Et eodem modo post thema propositum potest subiungi uerbum alicuius sancti consonum diuisioni quam intendit. Aliquando quoque potest predicator ex se ipso distinctionem aliquam inuenire, ad quam consequatur et coaptetur diuisio thematis. Uerbi gratia: Si proposito hoc themate *Induamur arma lucis* ante diuisionem premittat sic:

> Ignominiosum est esse nudum in spectaculo, periculosum est esse inermem in prelio, turpe est non lucere in exemplo. Ideo, ne inueniamur in spectaculo nudi, monet nos Apostolus ut uestiamur, dicens *Induamur.* Secundo, ne deprehendamur in prelio inermes, monet nos Apostolus ut muniamur, dicens *arma.* Tercio, ne in exemplo appareamus obscuri, monet nos Apostolus ut luceamus, subdens *lucis.*

Ecce quomodo ex prelocutione premissa subsecuta est diuisio thematis. Hic autem modus, etsi non sit facilis in quibusdam thematibus, pulcher tamen est et acceptus. Multis etiam aliis modis potest huiusmodi prelibacio fieri, quos hic exprimere breuitatis gratia non oportet.

[ii] Aliud autem quod ante diuisionem thematis debet predicator attendere est ne in nimias partes diuidat thema suum. Quod quidem contingit quando diuisio quaternarium numerum excedit. Cum enim auditores gaudeant breuitate, in ipso sermonis principio deterrentur quando de quinque uel eo numero amplius predicator promittat[24] seu pretendat se locuturum. Est enim modus compe-

24. promittat] M; premittat B; premittit E.O.

Thus also our Lord, who is the creator of the human race, began as it were with smaller things when, in the time of the [Mosaic] Law, he gave a commandment about a smaller degree of righteousness. But in the time of grace, leading us so to speak by degrees to larger things, he gives a law of a greater righteousness when he says, *Unless your righteousness is greater,* and so on. In this saying, etc.

Sometimes a word from Holy Scripture may be used before the division of the thema, as when after the chosen thema one adds:

In Proverbs 10 it is said, *Righteousness preserves from death.*[46] Thus our Lord, who came to give life to his faithful, gives a commandment about righteousness when he says, *Unless your righteousness is greater,* and so on. In this saying, etc.

In the same way, one can, after the proposed thema, add the pronouncement of some saint which fits the division that one intends to make. And at other times the preacher may invent for himself some distinction which the division of the thema follows upon and is fitted to. For example, if the announced thema is *Let us put on the armor of light,*[47] he may say before the division:

It is shameful to be naked in the theater, dangerous to be unarmed in battle, and vile not to shine as an example. Therefore, that we may not be found naked in the theater the Apostle admonishes us to be clothed, saying *Let us put on.* Second, that we may not be caught without arms in battle, he admonishes us to be shielded, saying *the armor.* And third, that we may not appear dark in being an example, he admonishes us to shine, saying *of light.*

In this way, from the preamble that was stated before has followed the division of the thema. Even if this way may not be easy with some themata, it is nevertheless beautiful and in use. Such a foretaste can be created in many other ways, which for the sake of brevity it is not necessary to list here.

[ii] The other thing the preacher needs to pay attention to before dividing his thema is that he should not divide it into too many parts. This happens when the division goes beyond four parts. Since his audience likes shortness, they would be put off at the very beginning of his sermon if the preacher promises or pretends that he will speak of five or even more things. A fitting way is to divide his thema into three parts,

46. Prv 10:2. The Vulgate reads *liberabit,* "will deliver from."
47. Rom 13:12.

tens ut suum thema diuidat in tria, si talis diuisio themati competit, uel ad plus in quatuor. Diuisio autem que in [f. 279ra] duo tantum est tolerabilis est, licet non sit pulcra, sicut et diuisio que est in quatuor, licet sit habundans. Sciendum est autem quod si predicator habeat loqui de duobus, puta de consecratione ecclesie et de aliquo sancto, uel de natiuitate Domini et de aliquo sancto occurrente, et de similibus, tunc modus decens est ut tale thema assumat quod utrique conueniat, et ipsum thema principali diuisione diuidat in duo, secundum illa duo de quibus proponit loqui; ac deinde utrumque membrum subdiuidat in tria, uel saltem in duo, sicut uiderit thema pati. Uerbi gratia: Si oporteat predicare de Natiuitate Christi uel Domini et de sancto Stephano, potest hoc thema assumere *Sol egressus est super terram, et Loth ingressus est Segor,* Genesis xx. Deinde prius premissa locutione sicut in hoc eodem capitulo dictum est, ipsum thema diuidat in duo, dicens:

In hoc uerbo notatur temporalis natiuitas regis cum dicitur: *Sol egressus est super terram,* et natiuitas militis cum subiungitur: *et Loth ingressus est Segor.* Circa primam particulam thematis, que pertinet ad Christi Natiuitatem, tria possunt considerari, etc. Circa secundam autem particulam, que pertinet ad laudem beati Stephani, tria notantur, etc.

Debet autem predicator in tali casu circa principalem[25] diucius immorari et de secundario seu accessorio breuiter pertransire. Verbi gratia: quia in festo beati Stephani est officium de ipso festo[26] et de Natiuitate Domini fit memoria tantum, debet plus insistere circa ea que pertinent ad beatum Stephanum quam circa ea que pertinent ad Natiuitatem Domini. Quod si fortassis nesciat inuenire thema complectens utraque, querat thema pertinens ad principalem et de illo tantum procedat, diuidendo secundum modum in hoc capitulo positum.

Illud quoque latere non oportet quod apud modernos solet huiusmodi diuisio fieri per quasdam uerborum consonancias, de quibus prioribus predicatoribus nulla aut modica cura fuit. Ob-

25. principalem] M.O. *Here and later in this paragraph* B *and* E *write* principale.
26. festo] M, *perhaps read* sancto, *as in* E.O; *om.* B.

if such a division agrees with the thema, or at most into four. A division into only two parts is tolerable, even if it is not elegant, as is a division into four, even if it provides a lot of material. But if the preacher has to speak of two [different] topics, say, about the consecration of a church and a saint, or about the Lord's birth and a saint whose feast day comes at the same time, and the like, we must know that in such cases it is fitting to select a thema that suits both topics, and this thema he must, in the major division, divide into two sections according to the two topics he proposes to speak about. And after that he must subdivide each section into three or even into two parts, as he finds his thema to allow it. For example, if he needs to preach about Christ's Nativity and about St. Stephen, he can take as his thema *The sun rose upon the earth, and Lot entered into Segor,*[48] Genesis 20. Then, after saying something before the division, as was stated earlier in this chapter,[49] he may divide his thema into two sections and say:

> In this verse is indicated the birth of a temporal king, when it says *The sun rose upon the earth,* as well as the birth of a knight, when it states *and Lot entered into Segor.* With respect to the first section of the thema, which refers to the birth of Christ, we can reflect on three things, etc. With respect to the second section, which concerns the praise of blessed Stephen, three things are shown, etc.

In this case, the preacher must dwell longer on the main section and deal with the second or additional one more briefly. For example, since at the feast of St. Stephen the Office is about that feast while the Nativity of Our Lord receives only a *memoria,*[50] the preacher must dwell more on what concerns St. Stephen than on what concerns the Nativity of Our Lord. If by chance he cannot find a thema that contains both, he should look for one that deals with the principal topic and preach only on that, dividing it in the way that has been shown in this chapter.

We must not overlook that among modern preachers such a division is customarily made with verbal rhymes, which earlier preachers did not

48. Gn 19:23.

49. The "preamble," mentioned above in the paragraph beginning "In the third way."

50. *Memoria:* commemoration of a saint or feast on a day devoted to another feast or occasion.

seruant autem circa hoc moderni quod fines membrorum diuisionis in consimiles sillabas desinant, puta si dicatur sic: "Iste sanctus est admirabilis, est uenerabilis, est imitabilis," et similia.

[VI]

Capitulum vi: De subdiuisione thematis uel membrorum.

Sciendum quoque est quod predicatio uidetur arbori simulari. Arbor enim cum ex radice in truncum[27] conscenderit et truncus in principales ramos pululauerit, adhuc ipsi principales rami in alios secundarios multiplicantur, sic et predicatio, postquam ex themate in prelocutionem[28] processerit, tanquam ex radice in truncum, ac deinde ex prelocutione in principalem diuisionem thematis tanquam in ramos principales, [f. 279rb] debet ulterius per secundarias distinctiones multiplicari. Quod quidem consueuit fieri duobus modis.

[1] Vno quidem modo subdiuidendo principalia membra thematis, et hic modus est communis modernis predicatoribus. Verbi gratia: Si predicator assumat hoc thema *Sol egressus*[29] *est super terram, et Loth ingressus est Segor* et diuidat in duo sic:

> In hoc uerbo insinuatur nobis natiuitas Christi cum dicitur *Sol egressus*[30] *est super terram,* et natiuitas beati Stephani cum subditur *et Loth ingressus est Segor,*

ac deinde subdiuidat sic:

> Circa Christum autem natum insinuantur hic tria, scilicet—
> splendor diuinitatis, cum dicitur *sol;*
> secundo manifestatio humanitatis, cum subiungitur *egressus*[31] *est;*
> tercio status humilitatis, cum subinfertur *super terram.*

Et simili modo potest subdiuidi secundum membrum thematis. Ecce qualiter[32] post principalem diuisionem subsecuta est subdiuisio.

In isto autem modo subdiuisionis duo debet predicator obseruare. Quorum primum est quod non subdiuidat aliquod principalium membrorum in nimias partes, sed seruet regulam que de principali diuisione

27. in truncum] B, *and see the following main clause;* uirtutum M.E.O.
28. prelocutionem] B.E; prelocutione M.O.
29. egressus] B.E.O; ingressus M.
30. egressus] B.E.O; ingressus M.
31. egressus] B.E.O; ingressus M.
32. qualiter] M; quomodo B.E.O.

care about at all or only moderately. Modern preachers, however, see to it that the parts of their division end in similar syllables, as when one says, "This saint was admirable, venerable, and imitable," and the like.

[VI]
Chapter 6: The subdivision of the thema or its parts.

We must also know that a sermon can be likened to a tree. For as a tree rises from the root to its trunk, and its trunk divides into the main branches, and these main branches further multiply into secondary ones, thus the sermon, after it has proceeded from the thema to the preamble, as if from its root into the trunk, and then from the preamble into the main division of the thema, as if to the main branches, it must be further multiplied with the help of secondary distinctions. This is usually done in two ways.

[1] One is by subdividing the main parts of the thema, and this way is common among modern preachers. For example, if the preacher takes the thema *The sun rose upon the earth, and Lot entered into Segor,* and divides it into two parts, such as:

> This verse indicates to us the birth of Christ when it says *The sun rose upon the earth;* and the birth of blessed Stephen when it adds, *and Lot entered into Segor,*

he then subdivides in this way:

> With respect to Christ in his birth, three things are here indicated, namely—
> the brightness of his divinity, when it says *The sun;*
> second, the manifestation of his humanity, when it adds *rose;*
> and third, the condition of his humility, when it ends with *upon the earth.*

The second part of the thema can be subdivided similarly. Notice then how the main division is followed by a subdivision.

But in this way of subdividing the preacher must observe two things. First, he must not subdivide any of the main parts into too many subparts but observe the rule that was given about the main division of the thema in the preceding chapter. Second, he must subdivide all parts into the same number of subparts. It would be unseemly if one member were to be subdivided into three parts, another into four or two.

thematis data est in capitulo precedenti. Alterum[33] uero est quod omnia membra subdiuidantur in partes equales. Nam indecens esset quod unum membrum subdiuideretur[34] in tria et aliud in quatuor uel in duo.

[2] Alio uero modo per secundarias distinctiones predicatio dilatatur quando absque subdiuisione[35] membrorum principalium proceditur ad aliquam distinctionem. Uerbi gratia: Si proposito et diuiso themate predicto non procedatur ad subdiuisionem alicuius membri sed immediate subdatur sic: "Assimilatur Christus soli propter tria"; uel sic: "Dicitur autem Christus egredi in sua temporali natiuitate propter tria."

Multis quoque aliis modis potest predicatio dilatari absque principalium membrorum subdiuisione; de quibus in sequentibus dicetur. Sciendum tamen est quod quando thema diuiditur in duo tantum, pulcrior modus est quod membra subdiuidantur quam quod absque diuisione procedatur ad distinctionem aliquam, quia diuisio que est in duo tantum est diminuta, ut superioribus dictum est. Et ideo per subdiuisionem membrorum suppletur diuisio thematis.

[VII]

Capitulum vii: De modis dilatandi sermonem.[36]

Ut autem similitudinem sermonis ad arborem prosequamur, considerandum est quod sicut arbor postquam in secundarios ramos germinauerit, adhuc per ramusculos dilatatur, sic et predicatio non debet sistere in sola diuisione thematis et subdiuisione membrorum, sed oportet ipsam ulterius dilatari, ut decenti modo texatur.[37]

Modi uero quibus sermo dilatari potest sunt duo- [f. 279va] decim:[38]

Primus modus est per concordancias auctoritatum;
secundus modus est per uerborum discussionem;
tercius modus est per multiplicationem sensuum seu expositionum;

33. Alterum] E.O; secundum B; altera M.

34. subdiuideretur] E.O; diuideretur B; diuidatur M.

35. subdiuisione] B; diuisione M.E.O.

36. E *reads:* Incipit ars dilatandi sermonem. *A separate treatise beginning with the following words ("Ut autem," etc.) is listed as Caplan* 175.

37. texatur] B.E.O; texeatur M.

38. duodecim] M.E.O; B *reads* undecim *and indeed gives only eleven chapters on* dilatatio, *in a changed order; see the notes at the beginnings of the respective chapters.*

[2] The other way of amplifying the sermon through secondary distinctions is when one proceeds to some distinction without subdividing the main parts. For example, if after announcing and dividing the aforementioned thema one does not continue with subdividing any of its parts but at once adds: "Christ is like the sun in three things," or thus: "Christ is said to come in his birth in time for three reasons."

The sermon can also be amplified in many other ways without a subdivision of its main parts, which will be dealt with in what follows. But one must know that when the thema is divided into only two parts, it is more elegant if the parts are subdivided than if one continues without subdivision to a distinction, because a division into only two parts is limited,[51] as has been said earlier. Therefore, the [main] division of the thema is enriched by subdividing its parts.

[VII]

Chapter 7: Ways of amplifying the sermon.

Continuing our comparison of a sermon to a tree, we must consider that, just as a tree, after it has sprouted secondary branches, still expands through twigs, so a sermon must not rest with the division of the thema and the subdivision of its parts alone, but must have it expanded further, so that it is built up in a proper way.

There are twelve ways in which a sermon can be expanded:

1. with the help of concordant authorities;
2. by discussing words;
3. by multiplying the meanings or explanations [of words];

51. Limited in not furnishing much material for the development.

quartus modus est per nominis interpretationem et descriptionem;
quintus modus est per comparationes et diuersas expositiones;
sextus modus est per synonimorum multiplicationem;[39]
septimus modus est per rerum proprietates;
octauus modus est per similitudines;
nonus modus est per oppositi[40] assignationem;
decimus modus est per diuisionem tocius in partes;
vndecimus modus est per considerationem seu assignationem causarum et effectuum;
duodecimus modus est per ratiocinationem.[41]
De quibus omnibus per ordinem est dicendum.

[VIII]

Capitulum viii: De dilatatione sermonis per concordancias auctoritatum.

Per concordancias quidem auctoritatum potest sermo dilatari tribus modis: [1] aut enim auctoritas inducta concordat cum theumate in sententia et non in uoce; [2] aut in uoce et non in sententia secundem sensum litteralem (set potest coaptari secundum aliquem sensum spiritualem); [3] aut in uoce et sententia. Si autem nec in uoce nec in aliquo sensu auctoritas inducta[42] cum themate concordet, pocius erit derisio quam concordantia.

[1] Primus quidem modus, scilicet quod auctoritas inducta concordet cum theumate in sententia et non in uoce, apud quosdam modernos multum uiluit.[43] Potest autem conuenienter fieri quando post unam auctoritatem concordantem in uoce cum themate ad sermonis dilatationem[44] inducitur alia concordans expresse[45] in sententia, licet non in uoce. Verbi gratia: Assumatur hoc thema *Ecce rex tuus uenit tibi mansuetus,* et premissa diuisione dicatur sic:

39. sextus...multiplicationem] *this mode omitted in* B.

40. oppositi] B.E.O; appositi M.

41. ratiocinationem] M *usually writes* rationatio *and related forms, usually abbreviated;* B.E.O *use* ratiocinatio, *etc. I have silently corrected to ratiocinatio, etc. throughout.*

42. inducta] B, *and see the following sentence;* conducta M.E.O.

43. uiluit] M.E; inualuit B; valuit O.

44. dilatationem] B.E.O; dilationem M.

45. expresse] B.E.O; expressa M.

4. by interpreting or describing a name;
5. by comparisons and different expositions;
6. by multiplying synonyms;
7. with the help of the properties of things;
8. by similitudes;
9. by indicating the opposite;
10. by dividing a whole into its parts;
11. by considering or indicating causes and effects;
and 12. by reasoning.
All of these will now be dealt with in order.

[VIII]

Chapter 8: Expanding the sermon with the help of concordant authorities.

With concordant authorities a sermon can be expanded in three ways: [1] either a quoted authority agrees with the thema in its meaning but not its verbal form; [2] or in its verbal form but not in its meaning in the literal sense (though it can be made to fit according to some spiritual sense); [3] or in both its verbal form and its meaning. But when the quoted authority does not agree with the thema in either its verbal form or in any meaning, the result will be contempt rather than concordance.

[1] The first way, that is, when the quoted authority agrees with the thema in its meaning but not in its verbal form, has a bad reputation with some modern preachers. Yet it can be conveniently used when after one authority that agrees with the thema in its verbal form, another authority is quoted for the expansion of the sermon which clearly agrees in its meaning, even if not in its verbal form. For instance, let the thema be: *Behold, your king comes to you in meekness,*[52] and after the division one says:

52. Mt 21:5.

Mansuetudo Christi maxime apparuit in eius passione, iuxta illud Ieremie xi, *Ego quasi agnus mansuetus qui portatur ad uictimam.*

Deinde subdatur:

De sua autem mansuetudine loquitur ipse Dominus Mathei xi, *Discite a me quia mitis sum et humilis corde.*

Ecce quomodo[46] secunda auctoritas concordat cum themate in sententia et non in uoce satis decenter. In hoc tamen casu debet plus predicator insistere ad exponendum[47] primam auctoritatem (que consonat in uoce) quam secundam (que in uoce dissonat et in sententia consonat). Et eodem modo fieri potest quando auctoritas inducta post auctoritatem uocalem est figuratiua respectu thematis. Uerbi gratia: Assumatur hoc thema quod scribitur Romanorum primo, *Dicentes se esse sapientes stulti facti sunt,* et post diuisionem thematis adducatur auctoritas uocalis sic:

Stulti sunt sapientes mundi, quia sapientia mundana deducit ad mortem eternam, iuxta illud Romanorum viii, *Sapientia carnis mors est.* Vnde et Genesis iii legitur quod collocauit Dominus *che-* [f. 279vb] *rubin ad custodiendam uiam ligni uite. Cherubin* interpretatur plenitudo sciencie. Cherubin *uiam ligni uite* claudit quia sciencia seu sapiencia mundana claudit multis uiam intrandi ad ueram uitam.

Ecce qualiter post auctoritatem uocalem dilatari potest sermo per aliam auctoritatem figuratiuam que nec in uoce nec in sensu litterali concordat cum themate.

[2] Secundus autem modus, scilicet quod auctoritas consonet themati in uoce et non in sensu litterali, difficilis est, eo quod oportet auctoritates inductas exponere secundum aliquem sensum spiritualem, quod non est facile nouo predicatori. Valet autem ad hoc multum noticia librorum beati Gregorii, qui in suis *Moralibus* isto modo precipue usus est. Non debet uero predicator timere quod exponendo

46. quomodo] B.E.O; quod M.
47. exponendum] M; exponendam B.E; exponend' O.

Christ's meekness appeared most in his passion, according to Jeremiah 11, *I am like a meek lamb that is carried to be a victim.*[53]

Then one adds:

Of his meekness the Lord himself says, in Matthew 11, *Learn from me, for I am gentle and humble of heart.*[54]

Here the second authority agrees with the thema quite fittingly in its meaning though not in its verbal form.[55] In such a case, however, the preacher must put greater stress on explaining the first authority (which agrees in its verbal form) than the second (which is different in its verbal form but agrees in its meaning). And the same can be done when the [second] authority quoted after a verbally agreeing authority is figurative with respect to the thema. For example, take as thema what is written in Romans 1: *Professing themselves wise they became fools,*[56] and after dividing the thema quote a verbally agreeing authority thus:

The wise of the world are fools, because worldly wisdom leads to eternal death, after the words of Romans 8, *The wisdom of the flesh is death.*[57] Thus in Genesis 3 we read that the Lord placed Cherubim *to guard the way of the tree of life.*[58] *Cherubim* means "fullness of knowledge." The *Cherubim* closes *the way of the tree of life* because worldly knowledge or wisdom closes for many people the way of entering true life.

Thus, after a verbally agreeing authority, the sermon can be expanded through another figurative authority which does not agree with the thema in either its verbal form or its literal meaning.

[2] The second way—that is, when an authority agrees with the thema in its verbal form but not in its literal meaning—is difficult, because in that case the quoted authorities must be interpreted in some spiritual sense, which is not easy for a beginning preacher. But for this purpose a knowledge of the books of blessed Gregory helps a lot, who used this way predominantly in his *Moral Commentary on Job.* The preacher must not be afraid if in interpreting his authorities he digresses from

53. Jer 11:19.

54. Mt 11:29.

55. "But not in its verbal form" because the *mansuetus* of the thema and the first authority is now expressed by the synonym *mitis.*

56. Rom 1:22.

57. Cf. Rom 8:6–7.

58. Gn 3:24.

auctoritates deuiet a principali proposito dummodo que ad instructionem audientium occurrunt rimetur, sed ut dicit beatus Gregorius hunc rectum loquendi ordinem putet, ut ubi opportunitas edificationis occurrit ab eo quod loqui ceperat utiliter deriuet ac deinde propositi sermonis cursum resumat. Caueat tamen ne assumat auctoritatem in sensu penitus contrariam sensui litterali, sicut supra in tercio huius operis capitulo dictum est. Exemplum huius secundi modi est si sumatur hoc thema quod scribitur Actuum ix: *Vas electionis est michi iste ut portet nomen meum,* etc. Deinde premissa diuisione dicatur sic:

De isto uase potest exponi quod habetur Exodi xvii, *Sume uas unum et mitte in illud man. Vas unum* Paulus fuit, *assumptus* ad unitatem fidei et colligationem caritatis. In quo uase missum est *man,* idest nomen Christi, quod propter dulcedinem *man* dicitur.

Ecce quod auctoritas inducta consonat themati in uoce et non in sensu litterali, sed in morali.

[3] Tercius uero modus—scilicet quod auctoritas consonet themati in uoce et sententia—pulcer est et non indigens magna expositione. Uerbi gratia: Sumatur hoc thema quod scribitur Actuum xi: *Erat uir bonus plenus Spiritu Sancto et fide,* et post diuisionem dicatur sic:

Fuit sanctus iste *vir bonus* propter toleranciam tribulationum, iuxta Iacobi i, *Beatus uir qui suffert temptationem,* etc.

Ecce quod auctoritas ista et est consona in uoce et non indiget expositione in sententia.

Sciendum autem est quod isti duo modi sepe commiscentur ad inuicem, ita quod post auctoritatem que consonat in uoce tantum adducatur alia[48] que consonat in uoce et sententia, uel e conuerso. Illi uero qui delectantur predicare per distinctiones morales conari debent quod membra suarum distinctionum probent per auctoritates uocales, quia iste modus conenienci-

48. alia] B; illa M.E.O.

his main purpose while he explores things that occur to him for his audience's instruction. Rather, as blessed Gregory says, he should consider this the right way of speaking if, where there is an opportunity to edify his audience, he digresses from what he had set out to say and later resumes the course of his intended sermon.[59] But he must be careful not to use an authority in a sense that is totally contrary to its literal meaning, as was shown above in the third chapter of this work. An example of this second way is this: if he takes as his thema the words of Acts 9, *This man is to me a vessel of election, to carry my name,* etc.[60] Then, after the division, let him say:

> Of this vessel can be said what is written in Exodus 17, *Take a vessel and put manna into it.*[61] A *vessel* was Paul, *taken* up for the unity of faith and the bond of charity. In that vessel was *put manna,* that is, the name of Christ, which is called manna because of its sweetness.[62]

Thus the quoted authority agrees with the thema in its verbal form and not in its literal meaning, but in its moral sense.

[3] The third way—that is, when an authority agrees with the thema in both verbal form and meaning—is elegant and does not need much explanation. For example, let the thema be what is written in Acts 11: *He was a good man, full of the Holy Spirit and of faith.*[63] After the division may be said:

> This saint *was a good man* for enduring tribulations, according to James 1, *Blessed is the man who suffers temptation,* etc.[64]

Thus, this authority both agrees in its verbal form[65] and does not require an explanation of its meaning.

But we should know that often these two ways are mixed with each other, so that after an authority that agrees only in its verbal form another is added that agrees in both verbal form and meaning, or vice versa. But those who like to preach with the help of moral distinctions[66] should try to prove the parts of their distinctions with authorities that

59. Cf. Gregory, *Moralia in Job,* Epistula ad Leandrum 2 (PL 75:513).

60. Acts 9:14.

61. Ex 16:33.

62. Cf. the hymn *Jesu, dulcis memoria.*

63. Acts 11:24.

64. Jas 1:12.

65. It actually does not, because *bonus* and *beatus* are different words.

66. For examples see chapters V and VI.

[f. 280ra] or est. Sciendum quoque quod si aliquid continetur indeterminate in themate, potest sermo dilatari per auctoritates determinantes ipsum thema. Uerbi gratia: Proponatur hoc thema quod scribitur Ecclesiastici xxxvii, *Qui abstinens fuerit adiciet uitam.* Deinde subdatur sic:

> A quibus autem homo debet esse abstinens ostendit apostolus Petrus prima Petri ii dicens: *Obsecro uos tanquam aduenas et peregrinos, abstinere uos a carnalibus desideriis.* Quod etiam Paulus demonstrat prima Ad Thessalonicenses iiii dicens: *Hec est uoluntas Dei, sanctificatio uestra, ut abstineatis uos a fornicatione,* etc.

Ecce quod illud quod indistincte continetur in themate determinatur per auctoritates introductas quibus sermo dilatatur.

Non oportet enim latere quod circa concordancias auctoritatum est quedam diuersitas apud modernos. Quidam enim concordant de tot dictionibus in themate positis in quot partes ipsum thema diuiserunt. Quidam uero in toto sermone concordant de una tantum dictione. Licet autem secundus modus uideatur pulcrior, potest tamen uterque fieri prout predicatori uidetur vtilius ad fructum animarum, qui principaliter in predicatione debet intendi.

[IX]

Capitulum ix: De dilatatione sermonis per uerborum discussionem.

Circa uerborum autem discussionem multum debet predicator attendere, quia hic modus plurimum utilis est in sermone. Sciendum est ergo quod non solum uerba thematis sed etiam uerba auctoritatum inductarum possunt discuti ad sermonis dilatationem.[49] Cum ergo uerba thematis uel alterius auctoritatis inducte uult predicator discutere, [1] primo quidem debet attendere quot clausulas habeat auctoritas illa; [2] secundo, ordinem clausularum seu etiam uerborum; [3] tercio uero singula uerba consideret secundum modum infra scriptum.

[1] Quando ergo auctoritas habet plures clausulas, adaptet predicator si potest numerum clausularum ad numerum uirtutum uel

49. dilatationem] B.E.O; dilationem M.

agree verbally, for this way is more convenient. We should also know that, if there is something vague in the thema, the sermon may be expanded by authorities that make the thema more specific. For example, take as thema what is written in Ecclesiasticus 37: *He who abstains shall prolong his life.*[67] Then add:

> What a man should abstain from, the apostle Peter shows when he says, in 1 Peter 2: *I beseech you as strangers and pilgrims to abstain from carnal desires.*[68] Paul also shows the same in 1 Thessalonians 4, where he says: *This is the will of God, your sanctification, that you abstain from fornication,* etc.[69]

Thus, what in the thema was indistinct [i.e., *abstains*] is made specific through the quoted authorities with which the sermon is expanded.

We should not conceal that regarding the agreement between authorities there is some diversity among modern preachers. For some establish agreements for as many words in the thema as there are parts into which they divide it. Others establish, in their entire sermon, an agreement with just one word. Though the second way may seem more elegant, either one can be used as the preacher finds it more useful for the souls' benefit, which he should have in mind in his preaching first of all.

[IX]
Chapter 9: Expanding the sermon by discussing words.

The preacher must pay much attention to the discussion of words, for this way is of the greatest use in his sermon making. We must know, then, that not only the words of the thema but also those of the quoted authorities can be discussed in order to expand the sermon. So, when the preacher wants to discuss the words of his thema or of another quoted authority, [1] he must first examine how many phrases that authority has; [2] next he must examine the order of these phrases as well as of the words; [3] and thirdly he must reflect on the single words, as will be described further on.

[1] Now, when an authority contains several phrases, the preacher should, if possible, adapt their number to the number of the virtues

67. Sir 37:34.
68. 1 Pt 2:11.
69. 1 Thes 4:3.

uiciorum, uel ad partes penitentie, et ad similia. Uerbi gratia: Sancti *per fidem uicerunt regna, operati sunt iusticiam, adepti sunt repromissiones.* Hec auctoritas habet[50] tres clausulas. Prima clausula potest adaptari ad fidem credentium, secunda ad spem, tercia ad caritatem, sic:

Sancti per fidem uicerunt regna, idest grauissimas persecutiones tyrannorum uirtute fidei superauerunt; *operati sunt iusticiam,* idest opera iusta propter spem eterne beatitudinis peregerunt; *adepti sunt repromissiones,* idest diuinam beatitudinem, que debetur caritati, perceperunt.

Si autem auctoritas habeat duas clausulas, conetur predicator, si potest, adaptare ipsas ad duas uitas, scilicet actiuam et contemplatiuam;[51] uel ad duas [f. 280rb] stolas, scilicet anime et corporis; uel ad duas partes caritatis, scilicet amorem Dei et amorem proximi; uel ad duo testamenta, scilicet uetus et nouum; uel ad duo necessaria ad salutem, scilicet fidem et opera; et sic de aliis que secundum binarium excrescunt. Si autem auctoritas habeat tres clausulas, conetur predicator adaptare eas ad tres uirtutes theologicas (scilicet fidem, spem, et caritatem), uel ad tres uires anime (scilicet rationalem, irascibilem, et concupiscibilem), vel ad tres partes penitentie (scilicet contritionem cordis, confessionem oris, et satisfactionem operis), uel ad tres status hominum (scilicet incipientium, profiscientium, et perfectorum), uel ad tria uicia que regnant in mundo (scilicet concupiscentiam carnis, concupiscentiam oculorum, et superbiam uite); et sic de aliis que per ternarium numerum multiplicantur. Si uero auctoritas habet quatuor clausulas, adaptentur quatuor uirtutibus cardinalibus (scilicet prudentie, iusticie, fortitudini, et temperancie), uel quatuor passionibus principalibus (de quibus dicit Boetius in fine primi libri *De consolatione:*

> Gaudia pelle,
> pelle timorem,
> spemque fugato,
> nec dolor assit),

50. hec auctoritas habet] B.E; hee auctoritates habent M.O. *The three quoted clauses are part of one and the same authority.*

51. contemplatiuam] B.E.O; exemplatiuam M.

or vices, or to the parts of penitence, and similar groups. For example: The saints *by faith conquered kingdoms, wrought justice, and obtained promises.*[70] This authority has three phrases. The first can be adapted to the faith of the faithful, the second to their hope, and the third to their love, in this fashion:

> The saints *by faith conquered kingdoms,* that is, they overcame the most painful persecutions of tyrants by their virtue of faith; they *wrought justice,* that is, they performed just deeds out of hope for eternal bliss; and they *obtained promises,* that is, they received the divine bliss that is owed to love.

But when an authority has two phrases, the preacher must try, if possible, to adapt them to the two kinds of life, that is, the active and the contemplative life; or to the two garments, that is, soul and body; or to the two parts of charity, that is, the love of God and love of neighbor; or to the two Testaments, the Old and the New; or to the two things that are necessary for salvation, that is, faith and works; and thus with other notions that come in twos. But if an authority has three phrases, the preacher should try to adapt them to the three theological virtues (faith, hope, and love), or to the three powers of the soul (rational, irascible, and concupiscible), or to the three parts of penitence (contrition of heart, confession by mouth, and satisfaction in deed), or to the three states of humans (beginners, those in progress, and the perfect), or to the three vices that rule in the world (concupiscence of the flesh, concupiscence of the eyes, and pride of life[71]); and similarly to other groups that come in threes. But if the authority has four phrases, these may be adapted to the four cardinal virtues (prudence, justice, fortitude, and temperance), or to the four main passions (of which Boethius speaks at the end of the first book in his *De consolatione:* "Away with passing joys! away with fear! put vain hopes to flight! and grant no place to grief!"),[72] or to the four gifts of the glorified body (impassibility, lightness, agility, and clarity). And in the same way the preacher must establish an adaptation to other numbers.

70. Heb 11:33.

71. Cf. 1 Jn 2:16.

72. Boethius, *De consolatione Philosophiae,* 1, metrum 7.5; translation by W. V. Cooper (London: Aldine House, 1902).

uel quatuor dotibus corporis gloriosi (scilicet impassibilitati, subtilitati, agilitati, et claritati). Et secundum hunc modum debet predicator adaptationem facere de aliis numeris.

[2] Secundo debet attendi ordo clausularum seu uerborum. Uerbi gratia, II Thimothei iiii[52] scribitur: *Tu uero uigila, in omnibus labora, opus fac euangeliste.* Dicatur ergo sic:

Bene premittitur *Tu uigila et labora* ac deinde subiungitur *opus fac euangeliste,* quia prius homo debet uigilare ad custodiam sui et laborare in operibus penitentialibus, et postmodum aliorum fieri doctor, quod pertinet ad opus euuangeliste.

Et sicut in hac auctoritate consideratur[53] ordo clausularum, ita potest attendi ordo singulorum uerborum. Puta si dicatur sic: "Mathei v scribitur: *Qui fecerit et docuerit hoc, hic magnus uocabitur in regno celorum.* Bene premittitur *facere* et subditur *docere,* quia prius exigitur in predicatore bona uita et postea recta doctrina."

[3] Tercio debet predicator singula uerba thematis uel auctoritatis inducte discutere, scilicet quare hoc et non aliud, quare sic et non aliter dicatur. Uerbi gratia, in Psalmo scribitur: *Ecce quam bonum et quam iocundum habitare fratres in unum.* Dicatur ergo sic:

Bene dicit *Ecce,* quia humanitas[54] et concordia fratrum lucet proximis in exemplum edificationis. Item bene dicit *bonum,* quia est ipsismet in commodum conuersationis. Item bene dicit *iocundum,* quia est in solatium consolationis uel societatis. Item conuenienter utrique istorum addit *quam,* quia uix potest ex\is/timari [f. 280va] utilitas utriusque. Item bene dicit *habitare,* non salutare uel loqui, quia facile est hominem etiam insolentem ad modicum loqui dulcia, sed non facile est ipsum diucius *in unum* cum sociis cohabitare. Item bene dicit *fratres,* non dominos, quia equalitas multum ualet ad pacem cohabitantium.

Et sic potest alias dictiones thematis uel alterius auctoritatis discutere.

52. iiii] *add* uero M.
53. consideratur] E.O; consideratus est B; *add* est M.
54. humanitas] M.E; unitas B; humilitas O.

[2] Second, the order of the phrases or words must be examined. For example, in 2 Timothy 4 it is written: *But be you vigilant, labor in all things, do the work of an evangelist.*[73] One can then say as follows:

> The Apostle fittingly says first *Be vigilant and work* and then adds *do the work of an evangelist,* because a man must first be vigilant in guarding himself and work in deeds of penance, and afterwards become a teacher for others, which is part of the work of an evangelist.

And just as we have observed the order of phrases in this authority, so can we pay attention to the order of the single words, as for instance: "In Matthew 5 it is written: *He who has done and taught this will be called great in the kingdom of heaven.*[74] Quite rightly it says *has done* first and then adds *taught,* because in a preacher a good life is required first, and afterwards right teaching."

[3] Third, the preacher must discuss the single words of his thema or the quoted authority, namely, why this and not that is said, why thus and not otherwise. For example, in a Psalm it is written: *Behold, how good and how pleasant it is for brethren to dwell together in unity.*[75] Let the preacher say:

> *Behold* is well said, because the kindness and concord among brethren shines forth for others as an example for their own edification. Likewise, *good* is said rightly, because it is for the benefit of their living together. Also, *pleasant* is said rightly, because it leads to the solace of comfort or of social life. And the text adds *how* to both these words, because the usefulness of either can hardly be measured. And it rightly says *to dwell,* not "to greet" or "to speak," because even an insolent person can easily say something sweet, but it is not easy for him to live for a long time *together in unity* with his companions. And likewise it says *brethren,* not "masters," because equality helps a great deal to insure the peace of those who dwell together.

And in this fashion the preacher can discuss the other words of his thema or of some other authority.

73. 2 Tm 4:5.

74. Mt 5:19.

75. Ps 132:1 (133:1).

Ad hunc autem modum dilatandi sermonem reducitur cum predicator considerat uerbum a quo dependet sententia tocius auctoritatis, et secundum quod uerbo competit dilatat sermonem per quatuor causas uel per pauciores. Nam causa efficiens respicit uerbum actiuum ex parte suppositi; causa uero materialis ex parte appositi; causa autem formalis ex parte modi agendi uel actionis quam uerbum importat; causa uero finalis est propter quam agens agit. Si ergo uelit predicator dilatare sermonem ex parte cause agentis, consideret diligenter illa quibus solet uel quibus potest competere actio importata per uerbum in themate uel in alia auctoritate exponenda positum, et secundum similitudinem ad illa dilatet sermonem. Uerbi gratia, Malachie i scribitur: *Dilexi uos, dicit Dominus.* Ecce quod uerbum principale in hac auctoritate est *dilexi.* Consideret igitur predicator quibus competat diligere. Siquidem competit diligere benigno domino, pio patre, fideli amico, potest itaque ex dicta auctoritate sermo dilatari hoc modo: "Dilexit nos Deus sicut dominus benignus, item sicut pater pius, item sicut fidelis amicus." Et cum adducte fuerint auctoritates ad singula membra huius similitudinis, poterit sermo dilatari sufficienter. Quod si uelit sermonem extendere ex parte cause materialis, consideret illa in que actio importata per uerbum in auctoritate positum solet transire, et per similitudinem ad illa dilatet sermonem. Uerbi gratia, quia dilectio solet transire in filios, in seruos, in amicos, potest sermo dilatari per similitudinem ad istos hoc modo: "Dilexit nos Deus sicut filios, sicut seruos, sicut amicos." Si autem ex parte cause formalis uelit predicator dilatare sermonem, consideret modos qui solent—aut saltem qui debent—competere actioni importate per uerbum in auctoritate positum, et secundum illos dilatet sermonem. Uerbi gratia: "Dilectio debet esse uera, firma, et fructuosa, quia illis quos diligimus bonum uolumus." Ex predicta ergo auctoritate potest sermo dilatari hoc

It also comes down to this way of expanding the sermon when the preacher focuses on the verb[76] on which the meaning of his entire authority depends and then expands the sermon according to what that verb implies with the four causes or fewer. For the efficient cause belongs to an active verb in its subject; the material cause, to its direct object; the formal cause, to the quality of acting or of the action which the verb indicates; and the final cause to the end for which the agent acts. If, then, the preacher wants to expand his sermon from the agent cause, he should carefully consider those things with which the action that is indicated in the word that occurs in the thema or in another authority that is to be explained, usually is or can be associated, and then he may expand his sermon through some comparison to those things. For instance, in Malachy 1 it is written, *I have loved you, says the Lord.*[77] Now, the main verb in this authority is *I have loved.* Hence the preacher should consider for whom it is natural to love. Since it is natural to do so for a benign master, a caring father, and a faithful friend, the sermon can be expanded from the quoted authority as follows: "God has loved us as a benign master, and also as a caring father, and likewise as a faithful friend." And after authorities for the single members of this comparison have been quoted, the sermon can be expanded further. But if the preacher wants to expand the sermon from the material cause, he may think about those things on which the action indicated in the verb of the authority usually impinges, and then he can expand the sermon through a comparison to them. For example, since love is usually directed to children, servants, and friends, the sermon can be expanded in this way: "God has loved us as his children, as his servants, and as his friends." Further, if the preacher wants to expand his sermon from the formal cause, he should think about the qualities that usually accompany—or rather, should accompany—the action indicated by the word in his authority, and then expand the sermon according to them. For example, "Love must be true, firm, and fruitful, because we desire the good for those whom we love." And thus the sermon can be expanded from the quoted authority in this way: "God has loved us

76. Here in the sense of predicate.
77. Mal 1:2.

modo: "Dilexit nos Deus ueraciter, dilexit nos firmiter, dilexit nos utiliter." Sciendum uero est quod modus dilatandi sermonem per aduerbia que determinant modum actionis importate per uerbum facilis est et qui potest decenter [f. 280vb] uulgarizari. Quod si predicator uelit extendere sermonem ex parte cause finalis, attendat illa propter que uel ad que solet talis actio fieri. Verbi gratia: "Solemus homines amare ad diuersa bona, Deus autem omnia bona conferre."[55] Potest ergo ex eadem auctoritate ex parte cause finalis sermo dilatari hoc modo: "Dilexit nos Deus ad bona nature, ad bona gratie, ad bona glorie," et huiusmodi. Potest uero sermo dilatari aliquando per unam causam tantum, aliquando per duas uel per plures, sicut predicatori commodius et fructuosius uidetur.

Considerandum quoque est quod iste modus dilatandi sermonem per diuersas causas potest obseruari non solum quando in auctoritate exponenda est uerbum sed etiam quando in ea est participium, sicut maxime pateret si in auctoritate sepe dicta loco eius quod dicitur *dilexi uos* haberetur *eram diligens uos,* nam omnia illa que gracia exempli dicta sunt de hoc uerbo *dilexi* possent adaptari ad hoc participium *diligens,* ut patet per se. Et sic de aliis.

[X]

Capitulum x:[56] De dilatatione sermonis per interpretationem et per diffinitionem[57] nominis seu descripcionem.[58]

Modus iste dilatandi sermonem, sicut titulus ipse ostendit, bipartitus[59] est. Aliter enim sermo dilatatur per interpretationem nominis[60] atque aliter per diffinitionem uel descriptionem. Qui

55. Deus...conferre] M; deus autem potest omnia bona conferre B; deus autem omnia dona confert E; deus autem omnia bona suffert O.

56. *Chapter XI in* B.

57. diffinitionem] B; distinctionem M.O; *rubric lacking in* E. *See the following text.*

58. descripcionem] B; descripcionis M.O; *rubric lacking in* E. *See the following text.*

59. bipartitus *(or bipertitus)*] B.E.O; bispartitus M.

60. nominis] E.O; noīm (nominum) M.B.

in truth, with firmness, and for our benefit." We should realize that it is easy to expand the sermon through adverbs that qualify the action that is indicated in the verb [of the thema], and that this way can be fittingly used in popular preaching.[78] Lastly, if the preacher wants to expand the sermon from the final cause, he should consider for whose sake or what purpose such an action is usually undertaken. For example, "We usually love people for the sake of different goods, while God confers all goods." Hence, the sermon can be expanded from the same authority on the ground of the final cause thus: "God has loved us in order to confer on us the goods of nature, of grace, and of glory," and the like. Sometimes the sermon can be expanded through only one cause, sometimes through two or more, as the preacher finds it most convenient and useful.

We must also keep in mind that this way of expanding the sermon with the help of different causes can be used not only when in the authority that is to be expounded there is a [finite] verb but also a participle. This is most clearly seen if in the authority I have been using several times instead of *I have loved you* we were to have *I was loving you.* Everything that has been said in illustration about the verb form *I have loved* can be adapted to the participial form *loving,* as is evident. And thus in other cases.

[X]
Chapter 10: Expanding the sermon through interpreting and through defining or describing a noun.[79]

As the chapter title indicates, this way of expanding a sermon is twofold. In one way the sermon is expanded through interpretation of a name, in another through definition or description. If one wants

78. The translation "rendered in the vernacular" is possible.

79. The Latin *nomen* means both "name" (i.e., proper noun) and "noun."

ergo sermonem uult dilatare per nominis interpretationem attendat diligenter an nomen quod in auctoritate ponitur habeat plures interpretationes, et illam que ad suum propositum prosequendum fuerit utilior assumat, obmissis aliis. Uerbi gratia: *Israel* interpetratur "uidens Deum," uel "princeps cum Deo," aut "fortis directio Dei." Si ergo in auctoritate sit nomen *Israel* et predicator uelit loqui de fortitudine, assumat ultimam interpretationem huius nominis et dimittat alias que ad fortitudinem non pertinent. Potest nichilominus duas uel tres interpretationes aut plures assumere, prout oportunum uiderit ad suum propositum prosequendum. Puta si dicatur sic:

> Iste sanctus uere figuratur per *Israel,* quia ipse fuit "uidens Deum" per sublimem contemplacionem. Item, quia fuit "princeps cum Deo" per ecclesiasticam prelationem. Item, quia "fortis directio Dei" per commissi populi regulationem.

Ecce qualiter facta est dilatatio per omnes interpretationes huius nominis *Israel.*

Si uero per diffinitionem aut descriptionem explanare nititur, caueat ne a suo proposito nimis dilabatur. Potest tamen ponere descriptionem uel diffinitionem nominis loco ipsius nominis et dilatare sermonem explanando singulas partes descriptionis. Uerbi gratia: Si fuerit auctoritas[61] exponenda *Beati qui habitant in domo tua, Domine,* subdatur diffinitio beatitudinis sic: "Beatitudo est [f. 281ra] status omnium bonorum congregatione[62] perfectus." Deinde explanetur quomodo in celesti domo Domini—

> perficietur intellectus uisione prime ueritatis;
> item perficietur affectus fruitione[63] summe bonitatis;
> item quietabitur desiderium adeptione omnis desiderabilis.

Ecce qualiter ex diffinitione nominis *beatitudinis* subsecuta est ista dila\ta/tio sermonis.

61. auctoritas] O *ends here.*

62. congregatione] M; aggregatione B.E. *Both terms are used in scholastic definitions, even by the same author.*

63. fruitione] B.E; feruitione M.

to expand one's sermon through interpretation of a name, one must diligently see whether the name one finds in one's authority has several interpretations and then take the one that is the most useful for achieving one's purpose and leave the others aside. For example, *Israel* means "seeing God"[80] or "the prince with God"[81] or "the strong leadership of God."[82] So, if the name *Israel* occurs in his authority and the preacher wants to speak about fortitude, he should choose the third meaning of this name and leave the others aside which have nothing to do with fortitude. Nevertheless, he may take two or three or even more meanings as he sees fit to develop what he intends to say. For instance, if he says:

> This saint is truly prefigured in *Israel,* because he was "seeing God" in sublime contemplation. He also was "a prince for God" through his prelacy in the Church. And he was "a strong leadership of God" by ruling the people committed to him.

In this way a development is made through all the meanings of the name *Israel.*

If, on the other hand, the preacher relies on definition or description, he must take care not to move too far away from his intention. Yet he may use a description or definition of a noun instead of the noun itself and expand the sermon by explaining the individual parts of the definition. For example, if the authority to be explained were *Blessed are they who dwell in your house, o Lord,*[83] a definition of blessedness may be added in this way: "Blessedness is the state of perfection made when all good things come together."[84] Then an explanation may follow of how in the house of the Lord in heaven—

> the intellect will be made perfect by the vision of the first truth,
> the affect will be made perfect by the enjoyment of the highest good,
> and the will will come to rest by the attainment of all that is desirable.

In this way the expansion of the sermon follows from the definition of the noun *blessedness.*

80. Origen, Jerome, and many others.

81. Jerome, *Liber quaestionum hebraicarum in Genesim* (PL 23:988).

82. Cf. Bonaventure, *Sermones dominicales,* sermo 6.

83. Ps 83:5 (84:4).

84. Cf. *Auctoritates Aristotelis,* ed. Jacqueline Hamesse (Louvain: Publications Universitaires, 1974), 289, item 34 (from Boethius).

Attendat autem predicator quod auctoritates quas in sermone adducit consonent uocaliter cum ipso nomine quod diffinitur seu describitur, nec oportet quod concordent cum ipsis diffinientibus. Uerbi gratia: Si fuerit auctoritas *Iusticia ante eum ambulabit,* et diffiniatur uel describatur sic: “Iusticia est uirtus reddens unicuique quod ei debetur. Debemus autem quedam Deo, quedam proximo, quedam nobis ipsis,” non debet predicator concordare cum *debere* uel de *reddere,* per que diffinitur uel describitur iusticia, <sed de *iustitia*>, que est ipsum diffinitum. Debet quoque predicator cauere ne indifferenter uelit omnia diffinire aut describere, cum hoc non tam pertineat ad theologum quam ad philosophum. Poterit autem conuenienter diffinire uirtutes, uicia, et peccata et species ipsorum, beatitudinem, et alia que solent frequencius a theologis in predicationibus pertractari. Plus tamen et minus debet se in diffinitionibus dilatare secundum capacitatem auditorum. Caueat etiam ne posita alicuius nominis diffinitione uelit assignare genera et differencias uel aliquid simile. Hoc enim plus pertinet ad disputantem quam ad predicantem.

[XI]

Capitulum xi:[64] De dilatatione sermonis per multiplicationem expositionum et sensuum. Rubrica.

Circa[65] multitudinem uero sensuum diuine scripture tria sunt predicatori scienda. [1] Quorum primum est quot et quibus sensibus sacra scriptura possit exponi; [2] secundum est in quibus sui partibus potest exponi multis sensibus; [3] tercium est qualiter per huiusmodi multiplicationem expositionum sermo ualeat dilatari.

[1] Circa primum autem sciendum est quod scriptura sacra sub una littera habet multiplicem sensum, scilicet litteralem, moralem, allegoricum, et anagogycum. Quorum distinctio sic potest accipi. Cum enim actor sacre scripture sit Deus, in cuius potestate est non solum uoces accommodare ad significandum sed etiam res ipsas, potest in sacra scriptura ueritas aliqua duppliciter manifestari,

64. *Chapter X in* B.

65. Circa] M *written* Cjirca, *with enlarged C.*

But the preacher must pay attention that the authorities he quotes in his sermon agree verbally with the noun that is defined or described; they need not agree with the terms that define them. For example, if the authority is *Justice shall walk before him,*[85] and it is defined or described as, "Justice is the virtue that renders to each what is owed to him. We owe some things to God, some to our neighbor, and some to ourselves," the preacher must [in his proof texts] not use words that agree with *owe* or *render,* which define or describe justice, but with *justice,* for that alone is the term defined. And he must also take care not to define or describe everything indiscriminately, for that is not so much the business of a theologian as of a philosopher. Nonetheless he could fittingly define the virtues, vices, sins and their species, blessedness, and other things that are frequently dealt with by theologians in their sermons. He must, however, be more or less diffuse in developing his definitions according to his audience's capacity. He must further beware, after he has given the definition of a noun, not to detail genera and differences and the like, for that, too, is the business of one who disputes rather than a preacher.

[XI]

Chapter 11: Expanding the sermon by giving multiple explanations and meanings.

Regarding the multiple meanings of Holy Scripture the preacher must know three things. [1] First, in how many and which senses Holy Scripture can be explained; [2] second, in which of its parts it can be expounded in several senses; [3] and third, how the sermon can be expanded through this multiplication of meanings.

[1] About the first we must know that Holy Scripture contains in one and the same word a multiple sense, namely the literal, moral, allegorical, and anagogical. Their difference can be understood as follows. Since the author of Holy Scripture is God, who has the power to assign meaning not only to words but also to things themselves, some truth can be manifested in Holy Scripture in two ways, literally by words and figuratively by things. Manifestation through words establishes the his-

85. Ps 84:14 (85:13).

scilicet per uerba et per rerum figuras. Manifestatio autem que est per uerba facit sensum ystoricum seu litteralem. Vnde patet quod ad sensum litteralem pertinet totum illud quod ex ipsa significatione uerborum directe accipitur. Manifestatio autem ueritatis quam sacra scriptura tradit [f. 281rb] per figuras rerum ordinatur ad duo, scilicet ad recte credendum et ad recte operandum. Si ad recte operandum, sic est sensus moralis, qui alio dicitur nomine tropologicus. Si autem ad recte credendum, sic[66] secundum ordinem credibilium oportet distingui diuersos sensus. Cum enim status presentis Ecclesie sit medius inter statum synagoge et statum triumphantis, sicut uetus testamentum fuit figura noui, ut docet Apostolus primo Corinthiorum x, ita uetus simul et nouum sunt figura celestium. Sensus ergo traditus per figuras rerum qui fundatur[67] in illo modo figurandi quo uetus testamentum figurat nouum vocatur sensus allegoricus seu tipicus, sicut docet Apostolus Galatarum iiii, exponens per duos filios Habrahe duo testamenta. Et generaliter, quando ea que in ueteri testamento contigerunt exponuntur de Christo uel Ecclesia militante, sensus allegoricus uel typicus dicitur. Si uero sensus traditus per figuras fundatur in illo modo figurationis quo nouum simul et uetus testamentum figurant Ecclesiam triumphantem, sic est sensus anagogicus. Ex dictis itaque patet quod sensus litteralis narrat id quod est gestum; sensus uero allegoricus signat[68] quod est credendum de Christo et Ecclesia; sensus moralis docet quod est nobis agendum; sed sensus anagogicus docet quid nobis credendum sit de Ecclesia triumphante ad quam debemus tendere. Vnde facti sunt de hoc uersus:

Littera gesta docet, quid credas allegoria,
Moralis quid agas, quo tendas anagogia.

[2] Circa secundum uero sciendum quod licet quatuor predictis sensibus exponatur scriptura sacra, non tamen in qualibet sui parte recipit omnes quatuor predictos sensus, sed quandoque omnes quatuor, quandoque uero tres, quandoque uero duos, quandoque autem unum

66. sic] B.E; *add* est M.

67. qui fundatur] B.E, *and see the following explanation of the anagogical sense;* que fundantur M.

68. signat] *here and in the following,* M *usually writes* signat, *while* B *and* E *have* significat.

torical or literal sense. Thus it is clear that to the literal sense belongs everything that one understands directly by the meaning of words. But the manifestation of truth which Holy Scripture furnishes figuratively through things has two aims, namely, right belief and right action. If it aims at right action, it is the moral sense, otherwise called tropological. If it aims at right belief, we need to distinguish between different senses according to the order of things that can be believed. The state of the present Church[86] is intermediate between that of the synagogue and that of the Church Triumphant, just as the Old Testament was a figure of the New, as the Apostle teaches in 1 Corinthians 10. Thus, both the Old and the New Testament are figures of heavenly things. Therefore, the sense furnished figuratively by things that rests on that mode of figuration by which the Old Testament prefigures the New is called allegorical or typical, as the Apostle teaches in Galatians 4, where by the two sons of Abraham he indicates the two testaments. And in general, whenever things that happened in the Old Testament are applied to Christ or the Church Militant, we speak of the allegorical or typical sense. But if the sense furnished figuratively rests on that mode of figuration by which the Old and the New Testament together prefigure the Church Triumphant, then it is the anagogical sense. From what has been said, therefore, it is clear that the literal sense reports what happened, while the allegorical sense indicates what is to be believed about Christ and the Church; the moral sense teaches what we must do; and the anagogical sense, what we must believe about the Church Triumphant, which we should strive to reach. Thus have been composed these verses:

> The letter teaches events, allegory what to believe,
> Morality what to do, and anagogy where to go.[87]

[2] About the second point we should know that, although Sacred Scripture may be expounded in these four senses, it does not contain all four of them in every single part—sometimes all four apply, sometimes three, sometimes two, and sometimes only one. In Holy Scripture earlier things prefigure later ones. Hence, what in the literal sense con-

86. The present Church: also called Church Militant. The Church Triumphant is the community of the faithful in heaven.

87. A ubiquitous memory verse; see Walter *Proverbia* 13,899.

tantum. In scriptura namque sacra priora sunt figura posteriorum. Et ideo quod secundum sensum litteralem dicitur de priori potest aliquando exponi spiritualiter de posteriori, sed non conuertitur. Inter ea uero que in sacra scriptura narrantur, prima sunt illa que pertinent ad Uetus Testamentum. Vnde ea que spectant ad gesta Ueteris Testamenti secundum litteram possunt exponi quatuor sensibus. Uerbi gratia: II Regum v dicitur quod *Dauid regnauit in Ierusalem*. Quod quidem uerbum secundum litteralem sensum narrat[69] quomodo ille homo regnauit in illa terrena ciuitate in qua fuit postmodum edificatum templum Domini. Secundum autem sensum allegoricum signat quod Christus, qui per Dauid signatur, regnat per fidem credentium in Ecclesia militante. Secundum uero moralem sensum signat quod Christus regnat in anima sancta per caritatem. Secundum autem anagogicum signat quod Christus per Dauid signatus est rex Ecclesie triumphantis in celo. Post illa uero que pertinent ad gesta Ueteris Testamenti sunt illa que[70] pertinent ad statum presentis Ecclesie, in quibus [f. 281va] illa que pertinent ad capud, scilicet[71] Christum, sunt priora respectu eorum que pertinent ad membra, quia ipsum uerum corpus Christi et ea que in ipso gesta sunt, sunt figura corporis[72] mistici et eorum que geruntur in ipso.

Iterum[73] ex ipso Christo debemus sumere exemplum uiuendi, quia "omnis ipsius actio nostra est instructio." In ipso quoque est nobis premonstrata figura glorie. Ea igitur que de Christo dicuntur possunt exponi quatuor sensibus, scilicet sensu litterali secundum id quod uerba de ipso Christo sonant, et allegorico,[74] referendo ad corpus ipsius misticum, et morali, referendo ad actus nostros qui debent informari secundum ipsum, et anagogico in quantum in eo est nobis regnum glorie premonstratum. Verbi gratia: Mathei ix dicitur quod *ascendens Iesus in nauiculam transfretauit et uenit in ciuitatem suam*. Que quidem uerba secundum[75] sensum litteralem narrant quomodo Christus ascendit in[76] quamdam nauiculam materialem et transfretauit et uenit de terra Gerasenorum in Capharnaum, que dicebatur ciuitas eius et erat in prouincia Galilee. Secundum autem sensum allegoricum per naui-

69. narrat] E; *add* uel M; *add* nobis B.
70. pertinent...que] B; *om.* M.E.
71. capud scilicet] B; *om.* M.E.
72. corporis] B; *om.* M.E.
73. Iterum] M; item B.E.
74. allegorico] B; allegorice M.E.
75. secundum] B.E; *om.* M..
76. in] B.E *and quoted source; om.* M.

cerns something earlier can sometimes be expounded spiritually about something later, but not the reverse. Now, of the things narrated in Sacred Scripture, the first are those of the Old Testament. Therefore, what concerns literally the deeds of the Old Testament can be expounded by the four senses. For example, in 2 Kings 5 it is said: *David ruled in Jerusalem.*[88] In the literal sense, these words report how that particular human being ruled in that earthly city where later the temple of the Lord was built. But in the allegorical sense these words indicate that Christ, who is indicated in David, rules by the faith of his believers in the Church Militant. In the moral sense, however, they indicate that Christ rules through love in a holy soul. And in the anagogical sense they indicate that Christ, indicated by David, is king of the Church Triumphant in heaven. After those things that pertain to the deeds of the Old Testament, however, come those that pertain to the state of the present Church, and in these, things that pertain to its head, that is, Christ, are prior to those that pertain to its members, for the very body of Christ and things that have occurred in it are figures of his mystical body and what occurs in it.

Again, from Christ himself[89] we should take an example of how to live, because "every action of his is for our instruction."[90] In him also we have been shown in advance the figure of glory. Therefore, what is predicated about Christ can be expounded in the four senses, that is: in the literal sense according to what the words say about him; allegorically, in reference to his mystical body; morally, in reference to our actions that should be formed in his likeness; and anagogically insofar as in him we have been shown the reign of glory in advance. For example, in Matthew 9 it is said that *entering a boat Jesus passed over the water and came into his city.*[91] These words, in their literal sense, report how Christ entered some boat and passed over the sea and came from the land of the Gadarenes to Capernaum, which was called *his city* and lay in the province of Galilee. Now, according to the allegorical sense,

88. 2 Sm 5:4.

89. That is, from the historical figure presented in the gospels.

90. Another commonplace, found in many sermons and devotional writings.

91. Mt 9:1.

culam intelligimus Ecclesiam militantem, in quam Christus ascendit quando uirtute fidei humana corda inhabitauit, iuxta illud Ephesiorum iii: *Habitare Christum per fidem in cordibus nostris.* Tunc autem *uenit in ciuitatem suam,* quia ex omni multitudine credentium quasi unam sibi ciuitatem constituit per uinculum caritatis, quia *multitudinis credencium erant cor unum et anima una,* ut dicitur Actuum iiii. Moraliter uero per nauiculam intelligimus quamlibet sanctam personam, que debet portare Christum per fidem et opera bona, iuxta illud primo Corinthiorum vi: *Glorificate et portate Deum in corpore uestro.* Et tunc *uenit* Christus *in ciuitatem suam,* quia unit in sancta anima uirtutes et dona Sancti Spiritus. Dicitur enim Spiritus ciuitas, quasi "ciuium unitas." Anagogice autem per istam ciuitatem intelligimus celestem patriam, que ueraciter dicitur ciuitas Christi, quia gloriam celestis patrie, quam sancti participant per diuinam gratiam, Christus secundum quod Deus ab eterno possidet per naturam. Christus ergo *ascendit in nauiculam,* idest crucem in passione, sed *transfretauit* in morte et *uenit in ciuitatem suam,* idest patriam celestem in ascensione. Patet itaque quod ea que de Christo dicuntur possunt quatuor sensibus exponi, sicut per[77] ciuitatem Christi intelligimus ciuitatem terrenam Capharnaum, et Ecclesiam militantem, et hominem seu animam sanctam, et patriam celestem.

Nec tamen credendum est quod omnia que de Christo dicuntur istis quatuor sensibus exponantur, sed quedam quidem sic, quedam [f. 281vb] uero non, secundum diuersas materias. Quando enim scriptura dicit Christum felle et aceto potatum, non potest hoc anagogice exponi, cum in celesti patria non sit amaritudo uel dolor. Et simile potest inueniri in multis aliis. Si uero secundum sensum litteralem dicitur aliquid de Ecclesia militante, illud potest exponi tribus sensibus, scilicet litterali, morali, and anagogico. Uerbi gratia: Primo Thimothei iiii uocat[78] Apostolus Ecclesiam militantem domum[79] Dei, dicens: *Si tardauero, scias quomodo oporteat te in domo Dei conuersari, que est Ecclesia Dei uiui.* In quibus uerbis secundum litteralem sensum per domum Dei intelligimus Ecclesiam militantem, ut maxime patet. Secundum uero sensum moralem intelligere possumus per domum Dei

77. per] B.E; *om.* M.
78. uocat] B.E; notat M.
79. domum] B.E; donum M. *Thus also in the three following instances.*

by the boat we understand the Church Militant, into which Christ entered when through the virtue of faith he has dwelled in men's hearts, according to Ephesians 3: *For Christ to dwell by faith in our hearts.*[92] He then came *into his city,* for through the bond of love he made for himself, as it were, one city out of the whole multitude of believers, for *the multitude of believers had but one heart and one soul,* as is said in Acts 4.[93] Morally, however, we understand by the boat any saintly person, who must carry Christ through faith and good works, after the words of 1 Corinthians 6: *Glorify and bear God in your body.*[94] And then Christ comes *into his city,* for in a saintly soul he unites the virtues and gifts of the Holy Spirit. For the Spirit is called a city, as it were "citizens' unity."[95] But anagogically we understand by this city our celestial home, which is truly called the city of Christ, because the glory of our celestial home, which the saints share by divine grace, Christ possessed by his nature, since he was God from eternity. Hence, Christ *entered the boat,* that is, the cross in his passion, but *passed over* in his death and *came into his city,* that is, his heavenly home, in his ascension. Thus it is clear that what is said of Christ can be expounded in the four senses, as by *his city* we understand the earthly city of Capernaum, and the Church Militant, and man or a saintly soul, and our heavenly home.

However, we must not believe that everything that is said about Christ can be expounded in these four senses, but some things can, others cannot, according to different subject matters. For when Scripture says that Christ drank gall and vinegar, this cannot be expounded anagogically, for in our heavenly home there is no bitterness or pain. And similar matter can be found in many other passages. But when something is said about the Church Militant in the literal sense, that can be expounded in three senses—literal, moral, and anagogical. For example, in 1 Timothy 4 the Apostle calls the Church Militant the house of God when he says, *If I tarry long, you should know how you must behave yourself in the house of God, which is the Church of the living God.*[96] In these words according to their literal sense, by *the house*

92. Eph 3:17.

93. Acts 4:32.

94. 1 Cor 6:20.

95. *Civium unitas* is the "etymology" of *civitas.*

96. 1 Tm 3:15.

animam uiri iusti, iuxta illud primo Petri ii: *Superedificamini domos spiritales.* Secundum autem sensum anagogicum, per domum Dei possumus intelligere Ecclesiam triumphantem, iuxta illud Psalmi, *Beati qui habitant in domo tua, Domine,* in qua uiri sancti couersantur in presenti non corporaliter sed per contemplationem, iuxta illud Philippensium iii, *Nostra conuersatio in celis est.* Sciendum tamen quod quando illa que in scriptura sacra dicuntur de primitiua Ecclesia exponuntur de futuro statu Ecclesie presentis, tunc[80] potest dici sensus allegoricus, non quod primitiua Ecclesia sit alia a presenti, sed ratione diuersorum statuum. Si uero aliquid dicitur in scriptura moraliter secundum sensum litteralem, illud exponi consueuit duobus sensibus tantum, scilicet litterali, qui etiam mores instruit, et[81] anagogico, licet raro. Illa uero que secundum sensum litteralem pertinent ad statum glorie in nullo alio sensu consueuerunt exponi, quia ipsa non sunt signa aliorum sed ab omnibus aliis figurata.

[3] Circa tercium uero sciendum quod sermo potest dilatari multipliciter exponendo thema duobus modis: vno quidem modo exponendo eandem auctoritatem diuersis sensibus, puta litterali et morali, uel litterali et allegorico, uel morali et allegorico, et huiusmodi. Qualiter autem una auctoritas possit exponi pluribus sensibus patet in exemplis in hoc capitulo positis. Alio modo potest sermo dilatari exponendo eandem auctoritatem secundum eundum sensum, puta moralem, diuersimode, ut in bonum et in malum. Uerbi gratia: Luce viii scribitur, *Exiit qui seminat seminare semen suum.* Potest ergo uerbum hoc moraliter exponi in bonum, ut dicatur quod penitens *exiit* de statu et carcere peccati ad libertatem gratie, et tunc seminat semen suum, idest bona opera, que perducunt ad fructum uite eterne, iuxta illud Psalmi, *Euntes ibant et flebant mittentes semina*

80. tunc] B.E; tamen M.

81. et] B.E; *om.* M.

of God we understand the Church Militant, as is quite obvious. But according to their moral sense, by *the house of God* we can understand the soul of a just person, after 1 Peter 2: *Be you built up as spiritual houses.*[97] According to the anagogical sense, by *the house of God* we may understand the Church Triumphant, after the Psalm *Blessed are they who dwell in your house, Lord,*[98] where holy men live in the present not bodily but by contemplation, after the words of Philippians 3, *Our life is in heaven.*[99] But we should know that when things that in Scripture are said of the early Church are expounded about the future state of the present Church, then this can be called the allegorical sense, not because the early Church was different from the present one, but by reason of different states. But if something in Scripture has a moral meaning in its literal sense, it is usually expounded in only two senses, namely the literal—which already teaches morals—and the anagogical, although this happens rarely. But things that according to their literal sense belong to the state of [future] glory are usually not expounded in any other sense, because they are not signs of other things but themselves are prefigured by all others.

[3] About the third point we must know that the sermon can be expanded variously by expounding its thema in two ways. One is to expound the same authority in different senses, such as the literal and moral, or the literal and allegorical, or the moral and allegorical, and so on. How a single authority can be expounded in several senses can be seen in the examples given in this chapter. The other way is to expound the same authority according to one sense, say the moral one, in different ways, as for instance in a good and an evil sense. For example, in Luke 8 it is written, *The sower went out to sow his seed.*[100] This verse can be expounded morally in a good sense by saying that a penitent person *has gone out* from the state and bonds of sin to the freedom of grace, and then he *sows his seed,* that is, good works, which lead to the fruit of eternal life, after the Psalm *Going they went and wept, casting their seeds, but coming they shall come with joy carrying their sheaves.*[101]

97. 1 Pt 2:5. The Vulgate uses the singular, *domus spiritalis.*
98. Ps 83:5 (84:4).
99. Phil 3:20.
100. Lk 8:5.
101. Ps 125:6–7 (126:5–6).

sua, venientes autem [f. 282ra] *uenient cum exultatione portantes manipulos suos.* Item potest exponi in malum, ut dicatur quod peccator *exiit* et quasi extra seipsum labitur quando iudicium rationis relinquit; et tunc seminat semen suum, idest iniquitates, quibus peruenitur ad malam messem, iuxta illud Prouerbiorum xxii, *Qui seminat iniquitatem metet mala.* Ecce quomodo eadem auctoritas in bonum et in malum est exposita moraliter.

[XII]

Capitulum xii:[82] De dilatatione sermonis per comparationes et diuersas compositiones.

Hic quoque modus quo dilatatur sermo per comparationes et compositiones geminus est.Aliter enim per comparatiua et superlatiua,[83] atque aliter per uarietates compositionum sermo dilatatur.

[1] Per comparatiua enim et superlatiua potest sermo dilatari quando in auctoritate est aliquod nomen adiectiuum uel aduerbium, quia ista sola recipiunt comparationem. Si ergo sit in auctoritate exponenda nomen positiuum, discurratur per comparatiuum et superlatiuum dummodo materia patiatur. Uerbi gratia, in Psalmo scribitur: *Magnus es tu et facis mirabilia.* Dicatur ergo sic: "Magnus apparuit Deus in rerum creatione,[84] maior apparuit in hominis recreatione, sed maximus apparebit in sanctorum glorificatione." Ecce quomodo de positiuo factus est discursus[85] ad comparatiuum et superlatiuum. Et in eodem modo, si fuerit in auctoritate comparatiuum, poterit quandoque, licet raro, sumi positiuum eius et inde per ipsum comparatiuum quod est in auctoritate transitum facere ad superlatiuum. Verbi gratia: Iohannis xix scribitur, *Qui tradidit me tibi maius peccatum habet.* Dicatur ergo sic: "Habuit Iudas peccatum magnum quia precium concupiuit; habuit *peccatum maius* quia dominum suum tradidit; sed habuit peccatum maximum quia de misericordia Dei desperauit." Ecce

82. *Chapter XII in* B.

83. superlatiua] B.E. M *here and in the following writes consistently* suppellatiua *(or related forms), which I have silently corrected to* superlatiua *etc.*

84. creatione] B.E; citatione M.

85. discursus] B.E. *Here and in the following lines* M *writes* decursus.

The verse can likewise be expounded in an evil sense by saying that the sinner *has gone out* and lives as it were outside himself when he relinquishes the judgment of his reason, and then he *sows his seed,* that is, sins, through which he comes to an evil harvest, after the words of Proverbs 22, *He who sows iniquity shall reap evils.*[102] Behold how the same authority has been morally expounded in a good and in an evil sense.

[XII]

Chapter 12: Expanding the sermon by comparison and by various compound words.

This way, in which the sermon is expanded by means of comparisons and word composition, is twofold. In one the sermon is expanded by comparative and superlative degrees, in the other by different compound words.

[1] By means of comparatives and superlatives a sermon can be expanded when the authority contains an adjective or adverb, since these alone can have comparative degrees. Thus, when the authority to be explained contains an adjective in the positive degree, one may employ the comparative and superlative, as long as the subject matter allows it. For example, in a Psalm it is written: *You are great and do wonderful things.*[103] Therefore one can say thus: "God has appeared great in the creation of things, he has appeared greater in man's re-creation, but he will appear greatest in the glory of the saints." Thus there has been a development from the positive degree to the comparative and to the superlative. In the same way, if the authority contains a comparative, one can sometimes—although it is rare—take its positive form and from there through the comparative that is in the authority pass on to the superlative. For example, in John 19 it is written: *He who has delivered me to you has the greater sin.*[104] One may therefore say: "Judas had a great sin because he lusted for money; he had a *greater sin* because he handed over his lord; but he had the greatest sin because he despaired of God's mercy." In this way, by taking the positive degree, the development has

102. Prv 22:8.

103. Ps 85:10 (86:10).

104. Jn 19:11.

quomodo preassumpto positiuo factus est discursus usque ad superlatiuum mediante comparatiuo quod est in auctoritate.

Sciendum est autem quod quando in auctoritate est positiuum uel comparatiuum, non potest fieri talis discursus adeo bene sicut fit quando in auctoritate est[86] superlatiuum. Tunc enim talis dilatatio sermonis est ualde decens et oportuna. Uerbi gratia, scribitur Ephesiorum v: *Estote imitatores Dei sicut filii karissimi.* Dicatur ergo sic: "Bene dicit *karissimi,* quia cari propter ymaginem creatoris,[87] cariores propter precium redemptionis, sed *karissimi* propter hereditatem celestis beatitudinis." Item Ephesiorum ii scribitur: *Propter nimiam caritatem qua dilexit nos Deus,* etc. Dicatur ergo sic: "Bene dicit *propter nimiam,* quia Dei caritas fuit erga[88] nos[89] magna in creatione, fuit maior in gubernatione, fuit maxima in redemptione, sed erit nimia in glorificatione."

Sicut autem potest fieri discur- [f. 282rb] sus a positiuo usque ad superlatiuum respectu eiusdem, ut patet in exemplis iam positis, ita potest fieri idem discursus respectu diuersorum. Verbi gratia, II Regum xxiii scribitur: *Dauid sedens in cathedra sapientissimus inter tres.* Dicatur ergo sic: "Quidam sunt sapientes, illi scilicet qui habent experienciam agendorum; quidam sunt sapientiores, illi scilicet qui habent scientiam humanorum; sed iste fuit *sapientissimus* quia habuit sapientiam diuinorum." Ecce quomodo factus est ingressus a superlatiuo[90] quod est in auctoritate, per positiuum et comparatiuum, tam in eodem quam in[91] diuersis.

[2] Per uarias autem compositiones fit dilatatio sermonis hoc modo. Luce ii scribitur: *Accepit eum Symeon in ulnas suas.* Dicatur ergo sic: "Symeon accepit Iesum in brachio, Maria concepit in utero, Martha excepit in domo, Pater recepit in celo." Uel sic: Primo Machabeorum ii scribitur: *Intendite in preceptum legis.*

86. est] B; fit E; *om.* M.

87. creatoris] E; saluatoris siue creatoris B; creationis M.

88. erga] B; circa E; ergo M.

89. nos] B.E; *add* et M.

90. ingressus a superlatiuo] E; regressus ad superlatiuum B; ingressus per suppellatiuum M.

91. in] B.E; *om.* M.

led to the superlative through the comparative which is in the quoted authority.

But we should know that when the authority contains a positive or comparative degree, such development cannot be made as well as when the authority contains a superlative. In the latter case such expansion of the sermon is truly elegant and opportune. For example, in Ephesians 5 it is written: *Be imitators of God as his dearest children.*[105] Thus one may say: "It says well *dearest,* because they are dear on account of the image of their creation, dearer for the price of their redemption, but *dearest* for their heritage of heavenly bliss." Likewise, in Ephesians 2 it is written: *For his exceeding charity with which God has loved us,* etc.[106] Then one may say: "*For his exceeding* is well said, because God's love for us was great in creation, greater in ruling us, greatest in our redemption, but it will be *exceeding* in our glorification."

Just as one can make a progression from the positive degree to the superlative with respect to the same thing, as has been shown in the examples given, so can one use the same progression with respect to different things. For example, in 2 Kings 23 it is written: *David sitting in the chair was the wisest among the three.*[107] Then one may say: "Some are wise, namely those who have the experience of what ought to be done; others are wiser, namely those who have knowledge of human things; but this one was *the wisest* because he had the wisdom of divine things." In this fashion a progression has been established from the superlative that is in the authority through the positive and the comparative, both with respect to the same and to other things.

[2] By means of different compound word forms the sermon can be expanded as follows. In Luke 2 it is written: *Simeon took him into his arms.*[108] One can then say: "Simeon took Jesus into his arms, Mary conceived him in her womb, Martha received him into her house, and the Father received him into heaven."[109] Or else, in 1 Maccabees 2 it is written: *Take heed to the precepts of the Law.*[110] Then one may say:

105. Eph 5:1.

106. Eph 2:4.

107. 2 Sm 23:8.

108. Lk 2:28.

109. The wordplay created by combining different prefixes with the verb form *-cepit* cannot be imitated in English.

110. 1 Mc 2:68.

Dicatur ergo sic: "Quidam in precepta Dei intendunt per contemplationem; quidam attendunt propter sollicitudinem; quidam pretendunt per simulationem; quidam contendunt[92] per elationem." Sciendum autem est quod iste modus dilatandi sermonem pulcrior est in latino quam in uulgari, eo quod compositiones melius pandunt diuersitatem sententiarum et consonantiam uocum in latino quam in uulgari.

Pertinet etiam ad hunc modum dilatatio sermonis per uarias prepositiones.[93] Uerbi gratia, Iohannis viii scribitur: *Multa habeo de uobis loqui.* Dicatur ergo sic: "Christus loquitur de nobis[94] tanquam iudex; loquitur pro nobis tanquam aduocatus; loquitur in nobis tanquam inspirator; loquitur cum nobis seu nobiscum tanquam doctor," et sic de similibus.

Ad hunc quoque modum reducitur quando manente eodem fine multiplicantur ea que sunt ad finem. Uerbi gratia: Ad istum finem qui est manere in peccato diuersi diuersimode se habent. Quidam enim proponunt remanere in peccato; quidam autem[95] partim uidentur penitere et partim non; quidam uero cauent a committendis sed non agunt penitentiam de commissis; quidam et de commissis non penitent et committenda non abhorrent. Sumatur igitur hec auctoritas que scribitur Romanorum vi: *Quid dicemus, fratres? Permanebimus in peccato ut gratia habundet? Absit.* Deinde dicatur sic:

> Quidam in peccato permanent seu stant, a futuris quidem abstinentes sed de preteritis non satisfacientes. Quidam autem in peccato sedent, partim quidem in peccato remanentes, partim uero ab ipso surgentes. Quidam in peccato iacent omni tempore in ipso[96] remanere proponentes. Quidam quoque in peccato seu in peccatis ambulant de peccato in peccatum labentes.

Et cum ad singula horum adducte fuerint auctoritates, erit sermo non modicum dilatatus. Hic autem modus tam in latine quam in uulgari pulcer est, nec oportet tunc [f. 282va] quod omnes auctoritates concordent uocaliter cum themate, sed sufficit quod consonent realiter cum ipsis membris distinctionis.

92. contendunt] E; contempnunt M.B.
93. prepositiones] B.E; propositiones M.
94. nobis] B; malis E; uobis M.
95. autem] B.E; enim M.
96. ipso] B; ipsis M.E.

"Some take heed to God's precepts by contemplation; others attend to them in their solicitude; others pretend to do so by simulation; and yet others contend through pride."[111] But we must realize that this way of expanding the sermon is more elegant in Latin than in the vernacular, because in Latin compound words provide a greater diversity of meaning and of sound than in the vernacular.[112]

To this way of expanding the sermon also belongs the use of different prepositions. For example, in John 8 it is written: *Many things I have to speak of you.*[113] One may then say: "Christ speaks of us as judge, for us as our advocate, in us as one who inspires, and with us as our teacher," and so in other similar cases.

To the same kind [of expansion] amounts the practice of multiplying ways to an end while the end remains the same. For example, with respect to the end "remaining in sin," different people act in different ways. Some propose to remain in sin; some seem partially to repent and partially not to; some stay clear of committing sins but do not do penance for what they have committed; and some neither repent what they have done nor abhor doing it. Let the preacher then take the authority written in Romans 6: *What shall we say, brethren? Shall we remain in sin, that grace may abound? God forbid.*[114] And then he can say:

> Some remain or stand in sin, abstaining from future sins but not doing penance for past ones. Others sit in sin, partially remaining in sin and partially rising up from it. Others lie in sin, proposing all the time to remain there. And yet others walk in sin or sins, going from one to another.

And when authorities are added to the single parts of this, the sermon will be greatly expanded. This way is elegant in Latin as well as in the vernacular, nor is it then necessary that all authorities agree with the thema verbally, but it is enough for them to agree in meaning with the members of the distinction.

111. Again, the Latin wordplay cannot entirely reproduced in English. Here the preacher puns by combining different prefixes with *-tendunt*.

112. In the Italian of the author (Fusignano) as well as in the English of his translator.

113. Jn 8:26.

114. Rom 6:1–2.

[XIII]

Capitulum xiii:[97] De ornatu et dilatatione sermonis per synonima.

Sicut autem per uarias compositiones et diuersas prepositiones dilatatur interdum sermo, sic etiam nonnunqum per synonima decoratur. Dicuntur uero synonima quando manente uno significato uoces diuersificantur. Quod contingit fieri duobus modis. Vno quidem modo per incomplexa, ut "gladius," "ensis," "mucro"; alio modo per complexa, ut "frustra niteris," "in uanum conaris," "incassum laboras." Et licet utroque modo possit interdum predicator uti, precipue tamen complexis synominis predicatio decoratur. Quod in materia querula et in materia laudatiua et exhortatiua est specialiter faciendum. In materia quidem querula, ut si pertractantes uerbum beati Iob quo dicitur: *Homo natus de muliere breui uiuens tempore repletur multis miseriis* dilatemus nos per synonima hoc modo: "Homo repletur miseriis, quia premitur angustiis, circumdatur erumpnis, molestatur aduersis, anxiatur in periculis." Et sic in similibus. Laudando quoque possumus conuenienter uti synonimis ad nostri sermonis ornatum, vt si laudantes aliquem sanctum doctorem dicamus: "Uere iste sanctus erat lux errantibus, lumen ignorantibus, lucerna deuiantibus"; uel si laudantes aliquam uirtutem dicamus: "Uirtus hec mentem decorat, animam ornat, conuersationem honestat, graciam manifestat." In exhortationibus quoque conuenienter multiplicantur synonima, puta si alios adhortantes ad imitandum exempla maiorum dicamus sic: "Emulemur bonos, imitemur iustos, sequamur sanctos, consideremus patrum exempla." Hoc exhortationis modo usus uidetur fuisse propheta in Psalmo cum dixit: *Exultemur Domino, iubilemus Deo salutari nostro, preocupemus faciem eius in confessione, et in psalmis iubilemus ei.*

Sciendum quoque est quod cum in locutione uel predicatione ingeminantur synonima, non oportet predicatorem discutere sigil-

97. *Chapter missing in* B.

[XIII]

Chapter 13: Adorning and expanding the sermon through synonyms.

Just as the sermon is sometimes expanded with the help of compound words and different prepositions, so is it also very often adorned by the use of synonyms. We speak of synonyms when different words are used while the meaning remains the same. This happens in two ways. One is by single words, such as "sword," "knife," "dagger"; the other is by phrases, such as "you waste your time," "you are trying in vain," "your labor is futile." While the preacher may use either way at times, it is synonymous phrases that adorn his preaching above all. This should be done especially in complaints, in praises, and in exhortations. In complaints, as when in drawing on the words of Job who says: *Man born of a woman, living for a short time, is filled with many miseries,*[115] we amplify through synonyms in this way: "Man is filled with miseries because he is oppressed by anxiety, surrounded by tribulations, troubled by adversity, and fearful in dangers," and similarly in other cases. Also when we praise we can conveniently use synonyms to decorate our sermon, as when we praise a saintly teacher we may say: "Truly this saint was a light to those who wander in the dark, a beam to the ignorant, and a candle to those who go astray;" or else, if we praise a virtue we may say: "This virtue embellishes the mind, adorns the soul, dignifies our behavior, and makes grace manifest." In exhortations, too, are synonyms conveniently multiplied. If for instance we exhort others to follow the examples of our elders, we may say: "Let us emulate good men, imitate the just, follow the saints, and meditate on the examples of our fathers." This way of exhortation the prophet manifestly used when he said in the Psalm: *Let us praise the Lord, let us joyfully sing to God our savior; let us come before his presence with thanksgiving and make a joyful noise to him in psalms.*[116]

We should also know that, when in a speech or sermon synonyms are multiplied, the preacher must not discuss them one after another

115. Jb 14:1.
116. Ps 94:1–2 (95:1–2).

latim singula repetendo uel ad partes singulas auctoritates adducendo, sed sufficit inculcatis synonimis pertransire. Ne autem ex synonimorum multiplicatione fastidium auditoribus generetur, non expedit plus quam semel uel interdum exigente materia bis per singula membra predicationis synonimis habundare. Hic autem modus in latinis sermonibus maxime ostendit hominem copiosum.

[XIV]
Capitulum xiiii:[98] De dilatatione sermonis per rerum proprietates.

Per rerum proprietates potest sermo dilatari quando in themate uel in auctoritate exponenda est [f. 282vb] aliqua res naturalis uel artificialis cuius proprietates adaptari possint[99] ad laudes sancti de quo predicatur uel ad mores. Verbi gratia, in Psalmo <scribitur>: *Vnxit te Deus Deus tuus oleo leticie.* Dicatur ergo sic:

> Conuenienter per oleum designatur gratia, quia oleum habet uirtutem sanatiuam; sic gratia uulnera anime sanat peccata delendo. Item oleum habet uirtutem mittigatiuam; sic gratia[100] pressuras mundi mittigat in tribulatione consolando. Item oleum habet uirtutem illuminatiuam qua profunda aquarum illuminat; sic gratia illuminat mentem de diuinis edocendo. Item oleum habet uirtutem dulcoratiuam, quia est condimentum ciborum; sic facit gratia labores penitentie alleuiando.

Ecce qualiter per proprietates olei adsimilatas effectibus gratie facta est dilatatio sermonis. Et eodem modo potest dilatatio fieri quando in themate uel in auctoritate exponenda est res artificialis, puta domus uel tabernaculum aut aliquid huiusmodi.

Ad hunc modum pertinet dilatatio sermonis per ea que solent rem de qua agitur comitari. Verbi gratia, iudicium concomitantur iudex, testis, accusator,[101] reus, et similia. Si ergo in themate agatur de iudicio, conuenienter potest fieri mentio de iudice, de teste, de accusatore,[102] de reo, et de similibus. Sciendum tamen est quod talis dilatatio

98. *Chapter* 13 *in* B.

99. possint] M; possunt B.E.

100. gratia] B.E; ergo M. *The same in the next two sentences.*

101. accusator] B; actor M.E.

102. accusatore] B.E; actore M..

by repeating them or by adducing authorities for each of them; it is enough just to mention the synonyms in a row. In order not to bore the listeners by multiplying synonyms, it is good if the parts of the sermon do not have synonyms more than once or occasionally twice when the matter requires it. This way shows a well-provided speaker, above all in Latin sermons.

[XIV]
Chapter 14: Expanding the sermon with the properties of things.

The sermon can be expanded with the properties of things when the thema or the authority that is to be explained contains some natural or man-made object whose properties can be adapted to the praise of the saint that the sermon is about or to our morals. For example, in a Psalm it is written: *The Lord has anointed you with the oil of gladness.*[117] Then the preacher may say as follows:

> *Oil* fittingly designates grace, for oil has power to heal; so does grace heal the wounds of the soul by deleting sins. Also, oil has the power to mitigate; so does grace mitigate the pressures of the world by consoling us in tribulation. Further, oil has the power to illumine deep water; so does grace illumine the mind by teaching us about divine matters. And oil has the power to make things sweet, for it is a condiment in food; so does grace by alleviating the labors of penance.

In this way the sermon has been expanded by likening the properties of oil to the effects of grace. Such expansion can be made in the same way when the thema or the authority to be expounded contains a man-made object, such as a house or tabernacle or something of this kind.

To the same way belongs the expansion of the sermon with things that usually accompany the object of which one speaks. For example, a judgment comes with a judge, a witness, the accuser, the accused, and so on. If, therefore, the thema deals with judgment, one can conveniently mention the judge, the witness, the accuser, the accused, and so on. But one should heed that such expansion is used more fittingly

117. Ps 44:8 (45:7).

conueniencius fit quando res cuius proprietates queruntur ponitur in themate, quam si agatur de ea in aliqua auctoritate inducta, licet sub breuitate possint tangi huiusmodi proprietates etiam in expositione auctoritatum. Caueat predicator, ne rerum proprietates inuestigare conetur in sermone ad sciencie ostentationem magis quam ad auditorum edificationem. Ad cognoscendum autem rerum proprietates multum ualet noticia librorum qui dicuntur *De proprietatibus* et *De naturis rerum,* et similium.

[XV]
Capitulum xv:[103] De dilatatione sermonis per similitudines.

Nonnunquam autem et per similitudines sermo dilatatur. Quod quidem potest fieri tribus modis.

[1] Interdum enim adducuntur similitudines illorum qui habuerunt uirtutes illas quas persuadere intendimus, uel uicia a quibus auditores intendimus reuocare. Et tales similitudines exempla uocantur. Puta si predicantes de penitentia adducamus in exemplum beatam Mariam Magdalenam, que tam perfecte penituit, uel Dauid, qui confestim ad uocem Nathan prophete causa penitentie respondit "peccaui"; aut si predicantes de uirtute[104] paciencie adducamus[105] in exemplum beatum Iob uel sanctum Thobiam. Et sic de aliis uirtutibus. Similiter quando predicamus contra aliquod uicium, possumus adducere in [f. 283ra] exemplum dampna[106] illorum qui propter tale uicium perierunt. Verbi gratia, quando predicamus contra luxuriam, possumus adducere in exemplum periculum Sansonis, cui non profuerunt immense uires quin periret per mulierem,[107] vel Salmonem, cui non profuit sapiencia tanta quin per mulieres infatuaretur,[108] uel Dauid, qui, cum esset propheta sanctus, tamen propter mulierem Deum offendit grauiter. Hic autem modus dilatandi sermonem est ualde utilis auditoribus et specialiter rudibus.

Possunt autem sumi huiusmodi exempla non tantum de canone

103. *Chapter* 14 *in* B.
104. uirtute] B.E; ueritate M.
105. adducamus] B.E; adducimus M.
106. dampna] B; dona M.E.
107. mulierem] B.E; mulieres M.
108. infatuaretur] B; infatuabatur E; infamaretur M.

when the object whose properties are sought appears in the thema than when it appears in an authority that is brought in, although such properties may also be briefly touched on in explaining authorities. But the preacher must beware of investigating the properties of things in his sermon in order to show off his knowledge instead of edifying his audience. In order to learn the properties of things it is very helpful to know books that are called *On the properties* or *On the nature of things,* and the like.[118]

[XV]
Chapter 15: Expanding the sermon through exemplification.

Many times the sermon is expanded through exemplification. This can be done in three ways.

[1] Sometimes we cite the example of people who possessed the virtues to which we intend to persuade our listeners, or the vices from which we intend to call them back. Such examples are called exempla. For instance, if in preaching about penitence we cite as an example blessed Mary Magdalene, who did such perfect penance, or David, who when he heard the prophet Nathan, at once remorsefully responded *"I have sinned";*[119] or if in preaching about the virtue of patience we bring in as an example blessed Job or saintly Tobias. And in the same way about other virtues. Similarly, when we preach against some vice, we can exemplify it with the ill fate of those who perished through that vice. For example, when we preach against lechery, we can cite as an example the danger to Sampson, whose immense strength did not save him from perishing through a woman; or Solomon, whose great wisdom did not keep him from becoming a fool through women; or David, who, though he was a holy prophet, yet offended God grievously on account of a woman. This way of expanding the sermon is very useful to our listeners, especially to those of little education.

Such *exempla* can be taken not only from the books of the Bible

118. Standard works of this kind, often quoted in medieval sermons, are Bartholomaeus Anglicus (died 1250), *Liber de proprietatibus rerum;* Alexander Neckam (died 1217), *De naturis rerum;* Thomas of Cantimpré (died 1272), *De naturis rerum;* or John of San Gimignano (died 1333), *Liber de exemplis.*

119. 2 Sm 12:13.

Biblie sed etiam de aliis libris qui ab Ecclesia recipiuntur, scilicet de *Uitis sanctorum patrum*, de *Dyalogo* beati Gregorii, et de aliis legendis sanctorum quibus Ecclesia utitur. Hunc[109] modum in suis predicationibus tenuit Saluator noster, sicut apparet in exemplo de Lazaro et de diuite[110] epulone. Et ad istum modum reducuntur parabole euuangeliorum, que etsi non fuerunt sicut littera sonat, habent tamen[111] omnimodam ueritatem secundum sensum parabolicum. Ad hunc etiam modum dilatandi sermonem pertinet narratio miraculorum, que recitantur tum ad honorem sanctorum, tum ad utilitatem audientium.

[2] Interdum autem adducuntur similitudines <sumpte a rebus naturalibus uel artificialibus, quas similitudines> quidam *motetos* uocant. Puta, si uolentes ostendere quod omnis qui se humiliat exaltabitur, adducimus exemplum de arbore, que ad hoc quod in altum cacumen erigat, prius in imo radicem[112] figit. Uel exemplum de aqua, que ad hoc quod ad alta conscendat, prius descendit ad yma. Uel si uolentes uituperare auariciam, adducimus exemplum de spongia, que aquas quidem faciliter et quasi sitibunde inbibit sed non refundit nisi ab alio prematur; sic auarus quidem bibit diuicias sed non refundit eas nisi cum prematur[113] morte. Istum etiam modum predicandi Saluator noster seruasse uidetur in exemplo sagene misse in mari et aliquibus aliis. Circa huiusmodi autem *motettos* debet predicator cauere ne proponat obscuras proprietates et innotas similitudines, quas forsan auditores difficilius caperent quam id quod principaliter persuadere intendit. Debet quoque tales similitudines accuratius et cum quadam excitatione et sollicitudine auditorum proponere, ut ex ipso modo proponendi auditores deprenhendant quod similitudo est conueniens proposito.

[3] Interdum quoque adducuntur similitudines sumpte ex quibusdam gestis confictis et fabulosis, puta cum inducuntur aues loquentes uel arbores aut bruta. Verbi gratia, si predicantes contra eos qui uaniis[114] laudibus extolluntur, dicamus quod—

109. Hunc] B.E; hic M.
110. diuite] B.E; *add* et M.
111. tamen] B.E; *om.* M.
112. radicem] E; radices B; radice M.
113. prematur] E; *eyeskip* B; *corrected from* premittitur M.
114. uanis] B; uariis M.E.

but also from other books that are accepted by the Church, such as *The Lives of the Holy Fathers,* or the *Dialogue* of Blessed Gregory, or other legends of saints which the Church uses. Our Savior himself used this way in his preaching, as can be seen in his example of Lazarus and the rich man who feasted sumptuously.[120] To this mode belong the parables of the gospels, too; though they are not literally true, they are fully so according to their parabolic meaning. This way of expanding the sermon also includes the telling of miracles, which are narrated both for the honor of the saints and the benefit of our audience.

[2] Sometimes we also cite similes taken from natural or artificial things, which some call "motets."[121] For instance, when we want to show that everyone who humbles himself will be exalted, we bring in the example of a tree, which in order to raise its top high first sinks his roots low. Or the example of water, which in order to rise up high first falls down low. Or else if we want to vilify avarice, we cite the example of the sponge: it soaks up water easily and as it were greedily but does not release it unless it is squeezed by someone; in the same way, a greedy person takes in riches but does not return them unless he is pressed by death. This way our Savior, too, can be observed to have used in the example of the net cast into the sea[122] and in some others. But concerning such "motets" the preacher must be careful not to present obscure properties or unfamiliar comparisons, which his listeners might perhaps understand less easily than what he chiefly intends to preach about. He must also present such comparisons with care and with a certain rousing solicitude for his audience, so that from his very manner of presentation his listeners may understand that his exemplification fits his purpose.

[3] Sometimes examples are also taken from fictive narratives and fables, as when birds or trees or brute animals are presented as speaking. For example, if in preaching against people who get puffed up by vain praises we say:

120. Lk 16:19–31.

121. Evidently the Italian word *mottetto,* diminutive of *motto,* meaning "a brief and sharp saying" (Dante) or "a brief sententious phrase" (Brunetto Latini); see Manilio Cortelazzo and Paolo Zolli, *Il nuovo etimologico DELI: Dizionario etimologico della lingua italiana* (Bologna: Zanichelli, 1999), 1013; and Salvatore Battaglia, *Grande dizionario della lingua italiana,* 11:19 (Turin: Unione tipografico-editrice torinese, 1981).

122. Mt 13:47.

Coruus tenens ore caseum ramo alte arboris insidebat. Cui uulpis uanis laudibus eum uolens decipere [f. 283rb] sic ait: "O corue, quis similis tui? Pennarum tuarum magnus decor. Quantus decor tibi esset[115] si uocem claram haberes!" Ac coruus dum adulatrici[116] uulpi uoce placere cupit, in altum uocem extulit et ore patefacto caseum oblitus deiecit, quem dolosa uulpis celerius rapuit. Tunc dolens coruus ingemuit et se uanis deceptum laudibus[117] post dampnum cognouit. Sic qui uanis laudibus extolluntur faciliter adulantium uocibus decipiuntur.

Ecce qualiter ex fabula Esopi sumpta est moralis instructio. Fabulis tamen huiusmodi rarissime uti debet predicator et cum cautela, ne auditores in errorem ducat. Nam et Saluatorem nostrum nusquam has fabulosas parabolas legisse me memini populo predicasse. Potest uero uti predicator aliquo tali fabuloso exemplo quando deprehenderit auditores sompnolentos uel attediatos, ad excitandum eos et alleuandum[118] tedium ipsorum. Tunc quoque debet aliquid subdere per quod auditores aduertant illa non fuisse sic realiter. Sciendum quoque quod huiusmodi fabulose similitudines conueniencius recipiuntur in collocutionibus priuatis quibus aliquid persuadere uolumus quam in publicis predicationibus.

[XVI]

Capitulum xvi:[119] De dilatatione sermonis per assignationem oppositi.

Sicut autem sermo dilatari potest assignando similia, sic potest dilatari tangendo contraria seu opposita. Attendat igitur predicator an uirtus quam persuadere intendit sic maxime[120] consistat in medio quod utrumque extremum patenter[121] relinquat uiciosum, quia tunc poterit dilatare sermonem suum loquendo de utroque extremo. Verbi gratia: Fortitudo tenet medium inter audaciam et timiditatem. Si ergo in themate aut in auctoritate exponenda tangatur de fortitudine et uelit

115. esset] B.E; est M.

116. adulatrici] E; adulatiue B; adulatrice M.

117. laudibus] B.E; *om.* M.

118. alleuandum] M; ad subleuandum B; ad leuandum E.

119. *Chapter* 15 *in* B.

120. maxime] M.E; manifeste B. *Here and elsewhere* M's maxime *may be a scribal error for an abbreviated form of* manifeste *in his exemplar; cf. note* 123.

121. patenter] B.E; patent M.

A crow was sitting on a branch of a tall tree with a piece of cheese in his beak. A fox wanted to deceive him with vain praise and said to him: "O crow, who is like you? Your feathers are so beautiful. How beautiful you would be if you had a clear voice." The crow wanted to please the flattering fox with his voice; so he raised his voice, and as he opened his beak, he forgot the cheese and let it fall, and the cunning fox quickly grabbed it. Then the crow sighed in sorrow and after his loss knew he had been deceived by vain praises. Thus, people who are boosted by vain praise are easily deceived by the words of flatterers.

Thus moral instruction is derived from a fable by Aesop. Yet the preacher must use such fables very rarely and with caution, lest he lead his audience into error. I do not remember ever having read that our Savior preached such fables to the people. However, the preacher may use such an exemplary fable to rouse his audience and relieve their tedium when he notices them nodding or getting bored. In that case he must add something to alert them that what he narrates did not really happen. We must also understand that such exemplification through fables is used more fittingly in private conversations in which we want to persuade someone, rather than in public sermons.

[XVI]
Chapter 16: Expanding the sermon by stating the opposite.

Just as the sermon can be expanded by speaking of something that is similar, so can it be expanded by touching on contrasts or opposites. The preacher must check whether the virtue he wants to inculcate is so obviously the mean that either extreme clearly represents a vice, for in that case he can expand his sermon by talking about either extreme. For example, fortitude stands as the mean between audacity and timidity. If, then, the thema or authority that is to be explained mentions fortitude, and the preacher wants to talk about it, his sermon could be expanded by mentioning the audacity of presumptuous people (which is contrary to fortitude by its excess) and the timidity of people who are needlessly afraid (which is contrary to fortitude by its lack). In the same fashion, if he wants to speak about generosity, he can mention

predicator loqui de ipsa, poterit sermo dilatari tangendo de audatia presumptuosorum (que opponitur fortitudini per excessum) et[122] de timitidate frustra timentium (que opponitur ei per defectum). Et eodem modo, si uelit loqui de liberalitate, potest tangere de prodigalitate (que opponitur liberalitati per excessum) et de auaricia (que opponitur ei per defectum). Et simili modo, si intendat uituperare aliquod uicium, potest dilatare sermonem commendando uirtutem oppositam. Quod si uirtus de qua predicator loqui intendit consistit quidem in medio rationis sed non adeo maxime[123] quod a simplicibus auditoribus faciliter possit capi (ut patet de uirtute uirginitatis), tunc sufficiat predicatori quod tangat tantum uicium illud quod manifestius uirtuti opponitur. Puta si loquatur de castitate, sufficit quod tangat de opposito uicio, scilicet de luxuria, et e conuerso si loquatur[124] [f. 283va] contra luxuriam, sufficit quod laudet castitatem.

Ad hunc modum dilatandi sermonem pertinet cum ostendimus effectus gratie uel alicuius uirtutis quam persuadere intendimus contrariari effectibus peccati uel alicuius uicii. Verbi gratia, si dicamus sic:

> Peccatum obcecat hominis intellectum, inquinat hominis affectum, debilitat hominis uirtutem. Sed e conuerso gratia intellectum illuminat, quia lux est; affectum purificat, quia lauacrum seu aqua munda est; potenciam corroborat, quia uirtus Dei est.

Ecce quomodo dilatatus[125] est sermo ostendendo effectus gratie contrariari[126] effectibus peccati. Et eodem modo potest ostendi quomodo effectus castitatis contrariantur[127] effectibus luxurie, et similiter in aliis uirtutibus et uiciis oppositis. Pertinet quoque ad modum istum quando predicantes de aliquo sancto qui prius fuit peccator ostendimus qualiter species peccatorum mutauit in species uirtutum, uel numerum peccatorum in numerum uirtutum. Sic facit beatus Gregorius in omelia beate Magdalene. Et eodem modo quando uituperantes eos qui de bono conuertuntur ad malum ostendimus quod numerum bo-

122. et] B.E; *om.* M.
123. maxime] M.E; manifeste B. *Cf. above, note* 120.
124. loquatur] B.E; loquitur M, *repeating* -tur *on f.* 284*va*.
125. dilatatus] B.E; dilatus M.
126. contrariari] B; contrarios E; contraria M.
127. contrariantur] E; contrarietur M.B.

prodigality (which is contrary to generosity by its excess) and avarice (which is its contrary by its lack). And in a similar way, if he wants to disparage some vice, he can expand his sermon by praising the opposite virtue. Now, when the virtue the preacher wants to talk about consists in a logical mean, but not to the extent that simple people can easily understand it (as it happens with the virtue of virginity), then it is enough for the preacher to mention only the vice that is most clearly the opposite of the virtue. For instance, if he speaks about chastity, it will sufficient for him to mention the opposite vice, lechery; and vice versa, if he speaks against lechery, it will be sufficient to praise chastity.

This way of expanding the sermon includes the practice of showing that the effects of grace or of some virtue that we intend to inculcate are the opposite of the effects of sin or of some vice. For example, if we were to say:

> Sin blinds man's mind, stains man's will, and weakens man's virtue. But in contrast, grace illumines the mind, for it is light; it purifies the will, for it is a bath or clean water; and it firms up one's strength, for it is the power of God.

Thus the sermon has been expanded by showing that the effects of grace are contrary to those of sin. And in the same way one can show how the effects of chastity are contrary to the effects of lechery, and likewise with other virtues and their opposite vices. This way of expansion further obtains when, preaching about some saint who earlier was a sinner, we show how he changed his individual sins into individual virtues, or the number of his sins into a number of virtues. Blessed Gregory does this in his homily on Blessed Magdalene.[123] And we can do the same if by reproving those who turned from good to evil we show how they changed the many good things they had into so many evils. For instance, if we were to say that Judas, who had left everything

123. Perhaps Gregory, *Homiliae in Evangelia* 2.25 (PL 76:1544).

norum mutauerunt[128] in numerum malorum. Puta, si dicamus quod Iudas, qui sequendo <Deum> reliquerat omnia, postmodum per auariciam perdidit seipsum; qui doctus fuerat inimicos diligere, proprium Dominum in mortem tradidit; qui cum aliis apostolis demones eiecit, postea peccando seipsum receptaculum dyaboli[129] fecit. Et sic de aliis.

Cum autem minus bonum comparatur ad maius bonum, sicut imperfectum ad perfectum,[130] constat quod ad istum etiam modum pertinet cum maius bonum laudando preferimus minori. Puta, si laudantes uitam contemplatiuam preferamus ipsam actiue, et cum laudamus uirginitatem preferamus eam statui coniugali. Caueat autem predicator ne preferendo <in laude> maius bonum uideatur minus bonum reprobare. Ex hoc enim quibusdam daretur occasio superbiendi et quibusdam forsan desperandi aut minus bonum contempnendi, utpote si[131] tantum laudaret uirginitatem quod dampnare uideretur[132] statum coniugalem.

[XVII]

Capitulum xvii:[133] De dilatatione sermonis per diuisiones tocius in partes.

Dilatari quoque potest sermo per diuisionem tocius in partes quatuor modis: aut enim in auctoritate exponenda est totum uniuersale, aut totum integrale, aut totum collectiuum, aut totum potestatiuum. Et sub quolibet horum potest predicator loqui de partibus eius.

[1] Verbi gratia, de toto uniuersali Canticorum ii scribitur: *Ego flos campi.* Dicatur ergo sic: "Iste sanctus similatur flori, quia fuit [f. 283vb] uelut rosa succensus ardore caritatis; fuit uelut lilium candidus nitore puritatis; fuit uelud uiola ymus uirtute humilitatis." Ecce quomod facta est diuisio tocius uniuersalis, scilicet floris, in aliquas suas species, scilicet rosam, lilium, et uiolam. Item in Psalmo scribitur: *Multiplicabis in anima mea*[134] *uirtutem.* Dicatur ergo sic: "Multiplicat Deus in anima nostra uirtutem fidei, qua cognoscamus; uirtutem spei, qua confortemur; uirtutem caritatis, qua diligamus," et sic de aliis.

128. mutauerunt] B; mutauit E; mutauerit M.

129. dyaboli] *add* se M.

130. imperfectuam ad perfectum] B; perfectum et imperfectum E; perfectum ad imperfectum M.

131. si] B.E; sed M.

132. uideretur] B.E; u'r M.

133. *Chapter* 16 *in* B.

134. anima mea] B.E; animam meam M.

and followed God,[124] afterwards lost himself through greed; who had been taught to love his enemies, handed his own Lord over to death; who with the other apostles had driven out devils, afterwards through sin made himself a vessel for the devil. And similarly in other cases.

But when a lesser good is compared to a greater one, as something imperfect to the perfect, it is clear that this mode also includes our practice of preferring the greater good to the lesser by praising it. For instance, if in praising the contemplative life we set it above the active life, and if by praising virginity we set it above marriage. But the preacher must be cautious that in praising the greater good he does not appear to demean the lesser. For in doing so he might give some listeners occasion to be proud and others perhaps occasion to despair or to despise the lesser good, as when he praises virginity so much that he would seem to condemn marriage.

[XVII]

Chapter 17: Expanding the sermon by dividing a whole into its parts.

The sermon can also be expanded by dividing a whole into its parts, and this in four ways: when the authority contains a whole that is universal, or integral, or collective, or potential. In each of these cases the preacher can speak of its parts.

[1] For example, a universal whole appears in Canticles 2: *I am the flower of the field.*[125] One may then say as follows: "This saint is likened to a flower, for he was like a rose aflame with the ardor of love; he was like a lily white in the brightness of his purity; and he was like a violet lowly in the virtue of his humility." Thus we have made a division of a universal whole, namely *flower,* into some of its species, that is, rose, lily, and violet. Likewise in a Psalm it is written: *You will multiply strength in my soul.*[126] Then we can say: "God multiplies in our soul the virtue of faith, by which we understand; the virtue of hope, by which we are comforted; and the virtue of charity, by which we love," and thus in other cases.

124. Cf. Mt 19:27.

125. Sg 2:1.

126. Ps 137:3 (138:3).

[2] Per diuisionem autem tocius integralis in partes potest sermo dilatari loquendo de partibus quibus integratur totum illud quod ponitur in auctoritate, hoc modo: In Psalmo scribitur: *Domine, dilexi decorem domus tue.* Dicatur ergo sic:

> *Domus* Dei, scilicet sancta Ecclesia, decora est, quia eius fundamentum sunt apostoli et prophete, iuxta illud Ephesiorum ii, *Superedificati super fundamentum apostolorum et prophetarum.* Item quia eius muri sunt uiri contemplatiui, qui dum mente terrena deserunt sese in alta tollunt. Item eius tectum sunt uiri sanctis actionibus dediti. Ex quibus omnibus miri decoris domus resultat.

Et sic dici potest de aliis partibus quibus domus componitur uel ornatur, etiam si non integratur ex ipsis, puta de fenestris, de ostio, et picturis, et huiusmodi. Item Romanorum xii scribitur: *Multi unum corpus sumus in Christo.* Dicatur ergo sic: "Huius mistici corporis capud est Christus, oculi sunt uiri contemplatiui, os sunt sancti predicatores, manus sunt boni actiui," et sic potest dilatari sermo per alia membra ex quibus corpus integratur.

[3] Per diuisionem uero tocius collectiui in partes potest dilatari sermo loquendo de partibus ex quibus colligitur totum collectiuum de quo agitur in auctoritate, hoc modo: Apocalipsis v scribitur: *Fecisti nos Deo nostro regnum.* Dicatur ergo sic: "In regno Christi et Dei ipse Christus est rex, assessores iudices sunt apostoli, milites sunt martires, precones sunt sancti doctores et predicatores," et sic de aliis officialibus ex quibus solet regnum colligi.

[4] Totum autem potestatiuum dicitur quod nec ex hiis que potestatem continent[135] quasi ex partibus integralibus componitur, nec ex eis colligitur sicut totum collectiuum \ex/[136] partibus suis, nec de eis sic proprie predicatur sicut totum uniuersale. Sed ideo dicitur totum potestatiuum quia comprehendit sub se diuersas potentias, sicut anima comprehendit sub se intellectum, memoriam, uoluntatem, et alias potentias suas, vnde anima est

135. potestatem continent] B.E; potestatiue continet M.
136. ex] *interlinear, replacing* in *canc.* M.

[2] By a division of an integral whole into its parts the sermon can be expanded when we speak of the parts that form integrally a whole that appears in the authority, such as: In a Psalm it is written, *Lord, I have loved the beauty of your house.*[127] We can then say:

> The *house* of God, that is, holy Church, is beautiful because its foundation is the apostles and prophets, after the word of Ephesians 2, *Built upon the foundation of the apostles and prophets.*[128] Also, because its walls are the contemplative, who while in their mind they abandon what is earthly raise themselves on high. And because its roof is people dedicated to holy deeds. All these make up a house of marvelous beauty.

And in the same way one can speak of the other parts that form or adorn a house, even if they are not essential to it, such as windows, the door, pictures, and so on. Further, in Romans 12 it is written, *We being many are one body in Christ.*[129] We can then say: "The head of this mystical body is Christ, its eyes are contemplative men, its mouth the holy preachers, and its hands the good active men," and thus the sermon can be expanded with the help of the other members of which a body is integrally composed.

[3] By a division of a collective whole in its parts can the sermon be expanded when we speak about the parts that form a collective whole that is mentioned in the authority, as in the following: In Revelation 5 it is written, *You have made us a kingdom to our God.*[130] We can then say: "In the kingdom of Christ and of God, Christ himself is the king, his assistant judges are the apostles, his soldiers the martyrs, his messengers the holy teachers and preachers," and so on concerning other officers of which a kingdom is collectively made up.

[4] We speak of a "potential whole" when its parts, which contain power, neither form an integral whole, nor are collected into one (as a collective whole is formed by its parts), nor can be said to form a universal whole. Rather, a "potential whole" is thus called because it comprises different powers, as the soul comprises intellect, memory, will, and other powers that belong to it, whence the soul is a "potential whole" with respect to its powers. Now, when the authority that is to

127. Ps 25:8 (26:8).
128. Eph 2:20.
129. Rom 12:5.
130. Rv 5:10.

quoddam totum potestatiuum respectu suarum potentiarum. Quando igitur in auctoritate [f. 284ra] exponenda ponitur ipsum totum potestatiuum, potest sermo dilatari per ea que sub toto potestatiuo continentur hoc modo: Deuteronomii vi scribitur: *Diliges Dominum Deum tuum ex toto corde tuo, et ex tota anima tua,* etc. Dicatur ergo sic:

Ex tota anima Deum diligere precipimur[137] ut ipsum cognoscamus toto intellectu sine errore, amemus tota uoluntate sine contradictione, meditemur tota memoria sine obliuione.

Ecce quomodo facta est dilatatio sermonis per diuersas potencias anime que sub anima continentur sicut sub quodam toto potestatiuo. Et eodem modo potest predicator loqui de irascibili, concupiscibili, et rationabili, et de aliis potenciis.

[XVIII]

Capitulum xviii:[138] De dilatatione sermonis per assignationem seu considerationem causarum et effectuum.

Quia uero secundum testimonium Domini in Mattheo vii *Arbor bona fructus bonos facit, mala autem arbor fructus malos facit,* ideo cum de bonitate alicuius uirtutis uel de malicia alicuius uicii loquimur, potest sermo per causas et effectus eorum conuenienter dilatari. Puta, si loquentes de caritate qua Deum iubemur diligere assignemus causas ad hoc mouentes et effectus inde consequentes, hoc modo: Deuteronomii vi scribitur: *Diliges Dominum Deum tuum,* etc. Dicatur ergo sic:

Ad diligendum Deum debent nos mouere multe rationes seu cause. Quarum prima est eius bonitas infinita, secunda est eius pulcritudo maxima, tercia est causa erga nos beniuolencia immensa. Effectus quoque dilectionis qua Deum diligimus est quia per eam diuinam legem adimplemus; item, quia per eam Deo unimur; item, quia per eam uitam eternam acquirimus,

et sic de aliis effectibus caritatis. Et eodem modo loquentes de aliquo uicio loqui possumus de occasionibus propter quas solent homines in illud uicium cadere, et de effectibus ipsius uicii. Verbi gratia, si uolentes loqui contra luxuriam, dicamus quod—

137. precipimur] B.E; precipimus M.
138. *Chapter* 17 *in* B.

be explained contains such a "potential whole," the sermon can be expanded by those things that are included in the "potential whole" in the following way: In Deuteronomy 6 it is written: *You shall love the Lord your God with your whole heart, with your whole soul,* etc.[131] Then you may say:

We are commanded to love God *with our whole soul* so that we may know him with our whole mind without error, love him with our whole will without contradiction, and meditate on him with our whole memory without forgetting.

Thus the sermon has been expanded with the help of different powers of the soul, which belong to the soul as to a "potential whole." In the same fashion the preacher can speak of the irascible, concupiscible, rational, and other powers.

[XVIII]

Chapter 18: Expanding the sermon by indicating or considering causes and effects.

Since after the testimony of the Lord in Matthew 7 *a good tree brings forth good fruit, but an evil tree brings forth evil fruit,*[132] if we speak of the goodness of a virtue or the evil of a vice, our sermon can be fittingly expanded by their causes and effects. For instance, if in speaking about the love with which we are enjoined to love God we were to specify the causes that lead us to it and the effects that follow from it, [we quote] as follows: In Deuteronomy 6 it is written, *You shall love the Lord your God,* etc.[133] Then we may say:

Many reasons or causes should lead us to love God. The first is his infinite goodness, the second his outstanding beauty, the third his immense benevolence toward us. Equally, the effects of our loving God are that through it we fulfill God's law; we are united with God; and we gain eternal life,

and similarly about other effects of love. In the same fashion, in speaking about some vice, we can speak of the occasions through which people fall into it, and about the effects of the same vice. For example, if we want to speak against lechery, we can say:

131. Dt 6:5.
132. Mt 7:17.
133. Dt 6:5.

Debet homo cauere ab aspectibus mulierum; item a familiaritatibus earum; item ab excessu cibi et potus; item ab ocio nimio et a ceteris huiusmodi que occasionem prestare solent cadendi in peccatum luxurie.

De effectibus autem loqui possumus dicendo quod peccatum luxurie facit hominem infamem mundo,[139] et sic de aliis effectibus eiusdem uicii.

Circa hunc autem modum dilatandi sermonem duo sunt obseruanda. Quorum primum est quod predicator non conetur assignare causas et effectus omnium rerum indifferenter, sed tantum illarum quarum noticia est utilis ad informandum mores uel ad laudem sancti de quo predicatur. Huiusmodi autem sunt uirtutes, [f. 284rb] uicia, et actus ipsorum, ut oratio, elemosina, ieiunium, et hiis similia. Secundum est quod huiusmodi cause et effectus non tam assignari debent ad ostendendum quot sint uirtutes et uicia quam ad persuadendum actus uirtutum, et ad retrahendum a peccatis et uiciis. Finis enim moralis sciencie est opus et non sola noticia uirtutum et viciorum.

[XIX]

Capitulum xix:[140] De dilatatione sermonis per ratiocinationem. Rubrica.

Ratiocinando[141] potest sermo dilatari multis modis. [1] Vno quidem modo emptimemando latenter ex auditorum iudicio; [2] secundo modo utendo confutationibus quasi ad tacitas questiones respondendo; [3] tercio modo comparando bonum meliori; [4] quarto modo laudando bonum et confutando malum oppositum. Sed quia de duobus modis ultimis in precedentibus actum est, ideo hiis obmissis[142] de duobus prioribus est dicendum.

[1] Primus itaque modus ratiocinationis[143] est iudicio ab auditoribus postulato occulte inferre quod intendimus. Puta si dicamus sic:

139. mundo] B *adds* odiosum Deo, effeminatum in seipso.
140. *Chapter* 18 *in* B, *calling it* undecimus modus.
141. Raciocinando] *thus in* M, *against its usual practice (see note* 41*)*.
142. obmissis] B (*with* b *expuncted*).E; submissis M.
143. ratiocinationis] B; raciocinandi E; rationationis *corr from* ratiocinationis M.

A man must beware of the looks of women and of their familiarities; likewise, of eating and drinking in excess; also of too much leisure and of other things that usually furnish an occasion to fall into the sin of lechery.

And about the effects of lechery we can say that this sin deprives a man of his good reputation in the world, and so on about other effects of this vice.

With respect to this way of expanding the sermon two things must be kept in mind. One is that the preacher must not try to specify the causes and effects of just everything at random, but only of those things whose knowledge is helpful in one's moral formation or in praise of the saint whom he is preaching about. Such are the virtues, vices, and their acts, such as prayer, almsgiving, fasting, and the like. Second, such causes and effects should not be specified in order to indicate how many virtues and vices there are but rather to persuade the audience to engage in virtuous deeds and to withdraw them from sins and vices. For the end of moral knowledge is virtuous action and not just getting to know what virtues and vices there are.

[XIX]
Chapter 19: Expanding the sermon through reasoning.

By reasoning the sermon can be expanded in various ways. [1] One way is by means of a hidden enthymeme appealing to the audience's judgment. [2] Another is by providing refutations as if one were answering silent questions. [3] A third way is by comparing something good to something better. [4] And a fourth way is by praising something that is good and refuting its evil opposite. Of the last two ways we have dealt before; thus we omit them and deal with the first two.

[1] The first way of reasoning, then, is to silently present what we intend to say by asking for the audience's judgment. For instance, we can say thus:

Nonne stultus esset qui propter quamcumque delectationem[144] sumeret cibum in quo non dubitaret latet uenenum? Stultus est ergo peccator, qui propter modicam carnis delectationem committit peccatum, in quo latet uenenum eterne mortis. Item, nonne sapientissimus mercator diceretur qui daret denarium ut lucraretur magnum thesaurum? Sapientissimus est ergo qui dat pro Deo temporalem elemosinam ut recipiat eternas et infinitas diuicias.

Hoc modo usus est Saluator noster Mathei xxi et Marci xii in parabola de agricolis qui occiderunt heredem. Hoc etiam modo usus fuit Nathan propheta, II[145] Regum xii, redarguens Dauid de peccato commisso in Uriam.

[2] Secundus modus ratiocinationis est utendo confutationibus quasi respondendo ad tacitas questiones que ex uerbis predicatoris possent suboriri. Puta si predicator in sua predicatione dicat quod dampnatis debetur supplicium eternum, deinde ratiocinando subdat sic:

Sed diceret aliquis, cum peccatum sit temporale, cur ei debetur pena eterna et non pocius pena temporalis? Sed dicendum quod qui per impenitentiam finem sibi in peccato mortali constituit, uoluntatem habuit in eternum peccandi, et ideo iustum est ut qui in suo eterno peccauit, in eterno ipsius Dei puniatur.

Debet autem predicator cauere ne forte mouendo dubitationem quam intendit soluere utatur paralogismo pro uera argumentatione. Et iterum caueat ne etiam in uera et bona argumentatione uelit assignare maiorem et minorem propositionem, et postea inferre conclusionem. Hoc enim non tam est[146] [f. 284va] predicantis quam disputantis. Attendat quoque diligenter ne dum confutationibus uti intendit, graues et difficiles questiones rudibus proponat auditoribus. Et iterum ne in soluendo dubitationes quas mouerit sit obscurus.

Explicit libellus artis predicatorie.[147]

144. propter quamcumque delectationem] B; quantumcumque delectabilem E.M.
145. II] *add* et M.
146. est] repeated on f. 284va M.
147. Explicit...predicatorie] M; explicit libellus de doctrina predicandi deo gratias amen B; *om.* E.

Wouldn't it be stupid if for the sake of some delight one were to consume food that one knew without doubt hid some poison? Thus a sinner is stupid, who for a little pleasure of the flesh commits a sin, which hides the poison of eternal death. Likewise, wouldn't you call that man a most skillful merchant who gives a single penny in order to gain tremendous wealth? Thus that person is most skillful who gives some temporal alms for God's sake in order to gain eternal and infinite riches.

This way our Savior used in Matthew 21 and Mark 12, in the parable about the husbandmen who killed the heir.[134] The prophet Nathan, too, used this way, in 2 Kings 12,[135] when he reproved David of the sin he had committed against Uriah.

[2] The second way of reasoning is by giving refutations as if one were answering silent questions that might arise from the preacher's words. For instance, if the preacher says in his sermon that the damned deserve eternal punishment, he may then reason and say:

Now, someone might say that since a sin is temporary, why does it deserve eternal punishment rather than only a temporary one? To that we must reply that if through his impenitence someone has made mortal sin his end, he had the desire to sin forever, and thus it is just that a person who has sinned forever is to be punished by God forever.[136]

But the preacher must take heed that by bringing in a doubt that he wishes to solve he does not use a false syllogism instead of true argumentation. And further, he must take heed that even in a true and good argument he does not state a major and a minor proposition and then draw the conclusion, for this belongs to disputation rather than to preaching. And he also should take diligent care that, when he intends to use confutations, he does not propose to an uneducated audience grave and difficult questions. Nor must he be obscure when he lays the doubts he has raised to rest.

Here ends the little book about the art of preaching.

134. Mt 21:33–39; Mk 12:1–8.

135. 2 Sm 12:1–6.

136. Cf. Aquinas, *Summa theologiae* 1–2, qu. 87, a. 3, with a reference to (pseudo-?) Gregory.

II
QUAMVIS

THIS AND THE NEXT two works are anonymous. All three appear together in sequence in two manuscripts from England, where only the first has been noticed by previous scholars. That they are in fact different and separate works is clear from their preservation as individual treatises elsewhere, as well as from differences in overall conception, style, and even vocabulary.[1]

1. Technical terms that would distinguish the three treatises from one another are *manuduccio* and *impaccio* (in *Quamvis*), or *pedis posicio* (in *Vade*).

Quamvis presents itself as a short treatise *(notula)* on the art of preaching. It announces as its three parts (I) the introduction of the thema, (II) the division of the thema, and (III) the development of the parts. The parts are dealt with in order and fully illustrated with a number of examples. The work pays comparatively more attention to its third part, as is at once shown by the latter's relative length as well as by the author's explaining (and partly rejecting) such highly artificial structures as the *sermo pyramidalis* and others.[2] Moreover, part III, perhaps using material from various sources, has a more complicated structure than parts I and II, which caused the scribe(s) some manifest difficulty. An outline may help to guide readers through its complexity:

III. Opening statement: nowadays, the members of the sermon can be developed in two ways ("Modo videndum").
  1. By subdividing the members.
    Procedure to be followed, with special attention to developing a member (here the first, virginity) by its opposite ("Quando enim" and "Iste autem").
    Developing the second member, possibly with correspondence to the first ("Similiter eciam").
    Developing the third member, in the same way ("Similiter tercium").
    Subdivision may be introduced in the same ways as the main division ("Et sicut d dictum est").
    Finding a single proof text for the three members ("Subtilitas eciam foret").
    Two ways of developing the members of the subdivision:
      (a) By going through them in regular fashion (i.e., 1.a-b-c, 2.a-b-c, 3.a-b-c; ("Quando autem singulum . . . Primus").
      (b) By more refined ways, for instance: 1.a, 2.b, 3.c ("Alius eciam modus"). Other possibilities are discussed in the next paragraphs:

2. This and other structures (*linearis, circularis,* etc.) are also discussed by Higden (p. 57). Basevorn, too, discusses complicated structures of this kind, but in different terms (e.g., *circulatio,* pp. 301–2). Both authors voice some disapproval, as does *Quamvis.*

Further subdividing the subdivision ("Item aliqui nimis curiosi").
Various structures achieved by multiple division ("Quidam eciam").
Using a final connection of the divided members with a proof text that contains all of them ("Solent aliqui").
Connecting the members of a division ("Augetur enim curiositas").
Another way of connecting members of a division ("Alie eciam sunt").
Summary of the recommended way of building a sermon ("Vnde breuiter").

2. By adducing a proof text and subdividing it:
   Exemplified ("Alius est modus procedendi" and "Eodem modo").
   Evaluation ("Iste modus predicandi").

The treatise has been attributed to Thomas Penketh, an Augustinian friar who studied at Oxford and Cambridge in the 1460s, became prior provincial of England and a professor at Padua, and died in 1487.[3] The attribution goes back to Bale, who evidently knew Cambridge, Corpus Christi College, MS 423, and it has been repeated by recent scholars including Richard Sharpe.[4] But Jeremy Catto points out that the script of *Quamvis* in University College 36 is too early.[5] So is that of Utrecht, University Library, MS 317. In addition, material from *Quamvis* is referred to and used in the treatise *Fecunda* by Geoffrey Schale, another Augustinian friar, who apparently died in or shortly after 1421 (see below in the section on CUL Gg.6.20 and further in appendix B). Lastly, as will be shown in appendix C, *Quamvis* furnished material used by Ranulph Higden, who wrote his *Ars componendi sermones* around 1340.

A different and more probable indication of authorship appears in manuscript U, which ascribes the work to an English Dominican by

3. Jeremy Catto in the online *Oxford Dictionary of National Biography* (2004), "Penketh, Thomas" (http://www.oxforddnb.com./view/article/21844).

4. Sharpe 674.

5. Catto, "Penketh, Thomas."

the name of Johannes de Gwidernia: "Explicit tractatus introductorius et breuis de modo predicandi editus a fratre Johanne de gwidernia de prouincia anglie ordinis predicatorum." About the identity of this friar nothing seems to be known.

It should also be noted that in the treatise the author of *Quamvis* refers to his own *collationes,* so far not identified, which he says exemplify a rather artificial sermon structure.

SOURCES

Quamvis has been preserved in the following manuscripts:

Lincoln, Cathedral Library, MS 234 (L).[6] Parchment, fifteenth century, 185 folios. A composite volume made up of five originally separate parts. The entire volume contains material to help medieval preachers: the *Dieta salutis* by the Franciscan William of Lavicea, with sermon outlines; a *Speculum sacerdotis* (Bloomfield 5269); articles on moral topics labeled A–V with excerpts from the Bible, the Fathers, and medieval theologians, including Grosseteste and Wyclif;[7] sermons including some extracts from the Franciscan *Fasciculus morum*; and finally, in part V, three *artes praedicandi*:

(1) *De sermonibus pertractandis uel etiam collationibus,* "Quamvis de sermonibus faciendis," ff. 171–176v, beginning with an enlarged and flourished initial. Caplan 144 and Caplan Suppl 144. Heavily annotated in the margins by a very late fifteenth- or sixteenth-century hand.
(2) Without title but beginning with an enlarged initial: "Hic docet Augustinus," ff. 176v–179.

6. For a more detailed description see R. M. Thomson, *Catalogue of the Manuscripts of Lincoln Cathedral Chapter Library* (Woodbridge, Suffolk; Wolfeboro, N.H.: D. S. Brewer, 1989), 193–95.

7. Thomson's catalogue entry needs to be corrected. There is no indication that this section of the manuscript, ff. 145 (not 146!)–154v, is imperfect, and the presence of Grosseteste and Wyclif (quoted several times as "doctor euangelicus") excludes its being "another version of *Dieta salutis.*" Very likely it is a series of excerpts from a work like the *Floretum* or *Rosarium.* After these excerpts, on f. 154v, follows a partial outline of *Dieta salutis* (chapters 1–6 out of 10), which does not seem to have any connection with the preceding excerpts.

(3) Without title but beginning with an enlarged initial: "Vade in domum," ff. 179v–182v.

Artes praedicandi (2) and (3) have not been recognized as separate works by earlier scholars, including Caplan and Thomson.

London, British Library, MS Additional 24361 (A).[8] Parchment, fifteenth century, eighty-nine folios, written in various hands. Contents:

(1) *Tragedia de Flauio et Affra,* "A cubice denum," in hexameters, ff. 2–4v.

(2) Richard de Bury, *Philobiblon,* ff. 4v–21.

(3) Alanus of Lille, *De planctu Nature,* ff. 21v–44v.

(4) Thomas Merke, O.S.B., *Regule dictaminis,* ff. 44v–51v. Sharpe 668–69. Critical edition in Martin Camargo, *Medieval Rhetorics of Prose Composition: Five English Artes Dictandi and Their Tradition* (Binghamton, N.Y.: Medieval and Renaissance Texts and Studies, 1995), 105–47.

(5) [*Q*]*uamvis,* ff. 52–57v, followed immediately by:

(6) [*H*]*ic docet,* ff. 57v–60, followed immediately by:

(7) [*V*]*ade,* ff. 60–63. The three treatises begin a new quire and are written in a mixed Anglicana hand which differs from the preceding Secretary. All three treatises begin with a blank space for an enlarged initial and a small guide letter. They bear neither title nor author's name.

(8) Alexander de Villa Dei, *Versus secundum Bibliam,* ff. 63v–70.

(9) "Biblia versificata per libros et capitula, quod Walterus Hothom monachus," ff. 70–89v. An expansion of the memory words of item (8). For both see Friedrich Stegmüller, *Repertorium Biblicum Medii Aevi* (Madrid, 1950–), nos. 1175–82,3, vol. 2, 77–79.

Oxford, University College, MS 36 (O). See above under Fusignano. *Quamvis* here occurs alone, entitled *Alius modus tractandi seu compilandi sermones,* ff. 120ra–124va, and is followed by Jacobus de Fusignano.

8. *Catalogue of Additions to the Manuscripts in the British Museum 1854–1875,* vol. 2 (London: Trustees of the British Museum, 1877), 59.

Utrecht, University Library MS 317 (U).[9] Parchment and paper, an irregularly constructed[10] composite volume written in various hands of the late fourteenth and early fifteenth century, probably a Dominican preacher's book from Germany (see item 6); 149 numbered folios. Contents:

(1) *De regimine principum vel Secreta secretorum,* "Domino suo excellentissimo... Dignum fuit," ff. 1–17.

(2) Articles on religious and moral topics, some in verse, "De misse gracia. Augustinus in libro de diuitate dei enumerans multiplices fructus," ff. 17v–46, in the same hand and layout as (1).

(3) Innocent III, *De miseria condicionis humane,* "Qvare de wlua matris egressus sum," ff. 47–68v, in the same hand and layout as (1).

(4) *Meditationes Bernardi,* "Multi multa sciunt," ff. 70–84.

(5) *Questio de peccato originali,* "Vtrum Beata Virgo si ante filium decessisset protinus euolaret," ff. 85–88v. Among medieval authors are quoted Anselm, Durandus, Peter Lombard, Franciscus de Mayronnes, St. Thomas of Aquinas, Magister Herueus, and "Olivus."

(6) Verses against the wiles of women[11] and simony,[12] ff. 89r–v. Some lines are in German or macaronic. At the top of f. 89: "Fratris g^{e}othzonis vus broetelin ordinis fratrum predicatorum conuentus Argentinensis deo gracia," evidently an owner's note.

(7) An abbreviated version of Albertanus of Brescia, *Tractatus super dicendo et tacendo breuis,* "Quis, quid, cui dicas \vel facias/, cur quomodo, quando requiras," ff. 90–91.

(8) Notes, ff. 96–98v, 103v, 105v–107, including a chapter outline of *Tractatus de libro posteriorum* (ff. 96v–97) and astronomical matters; on f. 103v a prognostication ("erit") of solar eclipses from 1366 to 1386.

9. *Catalogus codicum manu scriptorum Bibliothecae Universitatis Rheno-Trajectinae,* vol. I [comp. P. A. Tiele] (Utrecht, 1887), 103; and vol. II [by A. Hulshof] (Utrecht: Kemink, 1909), 43.

10. I am grateful to Dr. Jaski of the Utrecht University Library for providing me with a scan, and to Sr. Gimbrère and Grace Swart for a codicological description of the manuscript.

11. Walther *Initia* 12,293 and 14,018.

12. Walther *Initia* 18,562.

(9) Johannes de Gwidernia, *Notala*[13] [*sic*] *de modo predicandi breuis et vtilis* (inc.) or *Tractatus introductorius et breuis de modo predicandi* (expl.), "Quamuis de predicacionibus et sermonibus faciendis," ff. 99–103. This version, listed as Caplan 78 and 143, contains all the substance of the edited text of *Quamvis* but with stylistic differences that in general show a tendency to abbreviate. For example: U writes "exemplificare" for "exemplum adducere," "modus iste vltimus subtilis difficilis est" for "et reuera modus iste vltimus subtilis est et commendabilis et difficilis," "in Deuteronomio" for "in Deuteronomio dicitur," etc. Items (6)–(9) are in the same hand; (10) perhaps also but with somewhat larger lettering.

(10) *Tractatus de modo predicandi,* "Ad habendum[14] materiam" (Caplan 1 and Suppl. 1), ff. 104–105.

(11) Seven sermons, ff. 108–117v. Of the first, on St. Cecilia, the beginning is missing. The last two are academic speeches in praise of logic and philosophy, the last incomplete.

(12) Robert Holcot, *Moralitates,* "Nota quod multi sunt in Ecclesia rectores . . . Narratur in *Gestis Romanorum* quod cum Romulus cinxerat ciuitatem Romanam muro," ff. 119–149.

Cambridge, University Library, MS Gg.6.20 (G).[15] Paper and some parchment, written in several Anglicana hands of the fifteenth century, 143 folios. It contains:

(1) Thomas Waleys, *De modo componendi sermones,* "Reverendo . . . Theobaldo . . . Cum predicacionis officium sit pocius," parts i and ii, ff. 1–101v, Caplan 32 and Charland 94–95; edited in Charland 328–403 (part i only).

13. The word clearly is *notala,* with an elongated *l*; it surely is a scribal mistake for *notula,* the term used at the end of the first sentence. The scribe of this section uses a peculiar and characteristic form of *o*: he often pens its right loop as a straight line, thus giving the letter a great similarity to *a*. His own *a* frequently but not always has the two-compartment form. Charland, Caplan, and Sharpe give the incorrect reading *notata* and compound the error by transcribing *incipit* as incipiunt; the former is clearly thus written out in the manuscript.

14. *Habendum* is clearly written and not abbreviated. Caplan and others record this word as *habendam,* which in this context is classical but not characteristically medieval usage.

15. *A Catalogue of the Manuscripts Preserved in the Library of the University of Cambridge,* 5 vols. (Cambridge: Cambridge University Press, 1856–67), 3:233–34.

(2) *Ars faciendi sermonem,* "Circa artem[16] faciendi sermonem sive collationem," ff. 101v–104v, Caplan Suppl. 23a. Also preserved, with a slightly different incipit, in Oxford, Bodleian Library, MS Bodley 5, ff. 102v–108, see Charland 97; listed as Caplan Suppl. 24.

(3) *Alia doctrina componendi sermonem,* ff. 104–106v, beginning "Tria vero sunt in arte predicandi principaliter attendenda," that is, the second sentence of *Quamvis* as edited below. Here the text is considerably shorter but can be considered logically and syntactically complete. It ends in part III.1 (beginning "Modus autem noster procedendi"), where it deals with the subdivision of *virginitas* into three kinds and, avoiding *impactio* as well as the complicated sermon structures discussed in III.2, comes to a genuine end, though without a characteristic closing formula ("Et postea debent concordancie literales adduci, et sic consequenter est procedendum," f. 106v). But G also contains an interesting addition, in which it introduces the term *stipes,* not otherwise found in the *artes praedicandi* that have been studied; see note 19 to the translation.

(4) Geoffrey Schale, O.S.A., *De modo sermocinandi,* "Fecunda gratia Salvatoris," ff. 107–111v, Caplan Suppl 17a ("Assecunda" is a misreading). Also preserved in Brno, University Library, MS A.88. In the final paragraph, the author asks his reader to correct what he may find faulty in it ("corrigat emendanda mee ignorancie aut nesciencie") and to thank God for what may be there to please him, and finally to pray for Friar Geoffrey Schale ("pro me insuper fratre Galfrido Schale . . . quod preces pie porrigat"). Schale apparently was a master in theology at Cambridge and preached a sermon at the Council of Constance in 1417.[17] He probably died in or shortly after 1421. For the relation of this treatise to *Quamvis* see appendix B.

16. The text has "Circa autem artem . . ." with *autem* expuncted.

17. See Charland 37, and Adolar Zumkeller, O.S.A., "Unbekannte Konstanzer Konzilspredigten der Augustiner-Theologen Gottfried Shale and Dietrich Vrie," *Analecta Augustiniana* (1970): 5–74, esp. 6–7. Also, A. B. Emden, *A Biographical Register of the University of Cambridge to 1500* (Cambridge: Cambridge University Press, 1963), 510–11.

(5) Sermon: "Redde quod debes, Mathei 18. Ne in extremo examine crudeliter extorqueatur," ff. 111v–115.
(6) Treatise on the vices and virtues, "De superbia. Vesica inflata dum vngitur," ending imperfect, ff. 117–128v. Bloomfield 1464.
(7) Alphabetical articles on the properties of things, *Angelus–Vultur,* "Angelus purus in natura," in three columns, ff. 129–144v. A copy or version of Ps.-Hugh of Folieto, *De bestis et aliis rebus,* book IV: "De proprietatibus et epithetis rerum," PL 177:135–64.

Cambridge, Corpus Christi College, MS 423 (C).[18] Parchment and paper. A composite volume of three parts, written at the end of the fifteenth and the beginning of the sixteenth century, comprising a total of 153 folios. Part 1 contains a letter collection, part 2 several *artes praedicandi,* and part 3 the sermons of Michael of Hungary.

Part 2 contains:

(1) Without title or author's name, "Quamuis vnica et certa ars sermocinandi tradi non solet," pp. 99–118, followed by several model prothemes, etc., to p. 124. A compilation of material from several *artes praedicandi* that elsewhere survive as individual treatises. After copying the initial sentences of *Quamvis,* which announce the three parts, the anonymous compiler, in speaking of thema, switches to the treatise *Predicacio est thematis assumptio,* a short *ars praedicandi* sometimes attributed to John of Wales and edited by Ross (see above, p. 6). He follows this text to its very end, but not without enriching it with a good deal of relevant material, including another definition of thema from Huguiccio[19] and several illustrative examples. After the closing words of *Predicacio est,* he returns to *Quamvis* and, after a blank line and an enlarged initial, follows it to its next-to-the-last sentence, "ad principale propositum et ad diuisiones sequentes, etc." (103–15). Then, instead of closing his copy with the

18. M. R. James, *A Descriptive Catalogue of the Manuscripts in the Library of Corpus Christi College, Cambridge,* 2 vols. (Cambridge: Cambridge University Press, 1912), vol. 2, 322–28, at 327.

19. As in Uguccione, *Derivationes,* ed. Enzo Cecchini et al. (Firenze: SISMEL, 2004), vol. 2, 1199.

normal ending of *Quamvis,* he continues after a blank line with some more illustrative sermon material, part of which comes from another very popular art of preaching, the *Ars concionandi* sometimes attributed to Bonaventure.[20] After three blank lines this is followed by further illustrative material for sermons (118–24).

(2) *Ars sermocinandi tractatus secundus* (in a modern hand), "Ad, quare, per, propter," 125–38. Elsewhere attributed to Simon Alcok (died 1459; Caplan 8 and 9).

THE TEXT

For base text, C cannot be a serious candidate because of its nature as a compilation. Similarly, G cannot serve as base text because of its incomplete state and other peculiarities noted above. Of the remaining copies, OU frequently run together against LA and preserve readings that make better sense and may be original. But neither is free of clear scribal errors and eyeskips. Particularly in the difficult sections of part III, O's text is often grammatically incomplete and hence incomprehensible. One can also find in O what I have called the "dropping-penny phenomenon" (p. 8). And both O and U differ from LA in presenting the subject matter in a shorter, crisper style which on the whole strikes me as an abbreviation of the archetype against the fuller and altogether smoother style of L and A. Moreover, since L and A preserve the three treatises (*Quamvis, Hic,* and *Vade*) together and part of my aim in presenting these three *artes* is to call attention to their different approaches, the choice of L as the base text is preferable. I have compared it closely with A, O, and U and emended it in the light of paleographical and logical reasons. I have generally neglected C, which usually—but by no means always—agrees with O, although in one or two debatable cases I have recorded its readings. Similarly I have recorded readings from the other manuscripts in a few cases that are of bibliographical importance (title and colophon) or may shed some light

20. Caplan 114. Printed in *Opera Sancti Bonaventurae,* ed. Patres Collegii S. Bonaventurae, 9 vols. (Quaracchi: Patres Collegii S. Bonaventurae, 1864–71), vol. 9, 8–21.

on the history of the text. Therefore, the edited text represents L with emendations that seem to me to be required by the logic or grammar of its exposition and are usually supported by one or more of the other three manuscripts (AOU).

QUAMVIS

TEXT

Lincoln Cathedral MS 234.

[*f. 171*]

<De sermonibus pertractandis vel eciam collacionibus>[1]

Quamuis de sermonibus faciendis certa ars tradi non possit, eo quod predicandi facultas diuina gracia inspiratur, studio roboratur, et consuetudine confirmatur, tamen propter leuiorem aliqualem ingressum in vsum et graciam predicandi hanc notulam annotaui. Tria igitur sunt in presenti notula principaliter videnda:

[I] primum est de thematis introduccione,
[II] secundum de thematis diuisione,
[III] et tercium de menbrorum prosecucione.

[I]

Quantum ad primum ergo est notandum quod primo eligendus est thema non nimis strictum sed cuius vocabula in biblia multociens et in aliis libris sunt contenta et replicata, et quod thema alico modo tempori vel sancto de quo fit sermo aproprietur. Verbi gracia: Si quis haberet predicare de Annunciacione et acciperet hoc thema *Concha plena rore*,[2] proprium esset sed non

1. De sermonibus... collacionibus] L; *om.* A; alius modus tractandi seu compilandi sermones O; incipit notala de modo predicandi breuis et vtilis U.

2. plena rore] A.O; plenarie L; plena roris U.

QUAMVIS

TRANSLATION

How to build sermons or collations

Although no definitive[1] technique about sermon making can be given—because the ability to preach is inspired by grace, strengthened by study, and firmed up by practice—yet I have put together this short note to facilitate an easy entrance to the practice and grace of preaching. Thus, in this note three main things are to be considered:

[I] first, the introduction of the thema;
[II] second, its division;
[III] and third, the development of its members.

[I]

Regarding the first section, we must note that first a thema must be chosen that is not too narrow, but whose words occur often in the Bible and are contained and repeated in other books, and that this thema is in some fashion appropriate to the [liturgical] time or the saint that the sermon deals with. For example: If one had to preach on the Annunciation and took as one's thema *A vessel full of dew*,[2] it would be appropri-

1. Definitive, Lat. *certa:* cf. *vnica et certa* in Cambridge, Corpus Christi College, MS 423, p. 99.

2. Cf. Jgs 6:38; the Vulgate reads *concam rore complevit.*

fecundum saltem quantum ad primum vocabulum, quia vix alibi in biblia inuenitur, vel si inuenitur, non tamen crebro. Si enim acciperetur hoc thema *Dilectus meus candidus et rubicundus,* improprium quidem festo foret, in materia licet amplum. Sed si acciperetur hoc thema *Habitabit iuuenis cum virgine,* vel *Ecce virgo concipiet et pariet filium,* simul esset thema proprium et fecundum.

Habito ergo competenti themate, introducatur vel per aliquam propriam manuduccionem, vel per simile in natura, vel per aliquam sacram scripturam, vel per auctoritates sanctorum vel philosophorum. Verbi gracia: Si accipiatur hoc thema *Habitabit iuuenis cum virgine,* posset introduci tali manuduccione:

> Si inter duo regna esset iugis guerra et periculosa contencio, non posset meliori modo et firmiori concordia stabiliri quam, si vnus rex haberet filium iuuenem et decentem et alius filiam virginem pudore et decore pollentem qui possent matrimonii vinculo copulari, mergerentur. Sed post primum peccatum continua fuit guerra inter regem terrenum et celestem, et continua pugna, que sedari nullo pacto potuit donec filius regis celestis eam sibi coniungeret federe sempiterno. Ista coniunccio fuit hodie celebrata, sed diu ante preconizata per prophetam dicentem *Habitabit enim iuuenis cum virgine.*

Et sic introducitur per manuduccionem.

Sed per simile in natura introducitur sic:

> Animalia fortissima et ferocissima, cuiusmodi sunt elephas et vnicornis, hoc modo feritatem dimittere dicuntur: Elephas ad cantum virginis et ad [f. 171v] ostensionem vberum eius que lambet suauiter mitescit. Vnicornis cum sit eciam animal ferocissimum et nullo modo vel arte posset eius ferocitas edomari, tandem adducta virgine in eius gremio mansuescit. Sic Filius Dei fortissimus, ostensis illis vberibus Virginis de quibus[3] scriptum est: *Beatus venter qui te portauit et vbera que suxisti,*[4] vbera illa lambens et suggens, prius tamen

3. quibus] O.U; quo L.A.
4. suxisti] A.U; succisti O; etc. L.

ate but not fruitful,[3] especially with regard to its first word [i.e., *vessel*], for this is hardly found anywhere else in the Bible, and if it is found at all, not frequently. And if one were to take as one's thema *My beloved is white and red,*[4] this would be inappropriate for the feast [of the Annunciation] even if it provides much matter. But if one were to take as one's thema *The youth shall dwell with the virgin,*[5] or *Behold, a virgin will conceive and bear a son,*[6] that would at once be appropriate and fertile.

So, when a fitting thema has been found, it is to be introduced either by an appropriate lead-in, or by a simile found in nature, or by a scriptural quotation, or by authorities from the saints or philosophers. For example, if *The youth shall dwell with the virgin* is chosen as the thema, it could be introduced with the following lead-in:

If there were continual war and dangerous strife between two kingdoms, peace could not be established in a better and firmer way than, if one king had a young and noble son and the other a virgin daughter outstanding in virtue and beauty who could be joined in marriage, they were indeed thus joined. Now, after the first fall there was continual war between the earthly king and the heavenly one, and a continual strife, which could not be settled by any truce until the son of the king of heaven joined her [i.e., human nature] to himself in an eternal bond. That joining was celebrated today, but it had been foretold long ago by the prophet saying, *The youth shall dwell with the virgin.*

In this way the thema is introduced by a lead-in.

By a simile from nature it is introduced as follows:

Very strong and ferocious animals, such as the elephant and the unicorn, are said to abandon their ferocity in the following way. The elephant becomes pleasant and mild when a virgin sings and shows him her breast that he will lick. The unicorn also is a most fierce animal, and its ferocity cannot be tamed by any way or skill, yet when you bring a virgin to him, he grows mild in her lap. In the same way, when the very strong Son of God was shown the breasts of that Virgin of whom is written, *Blessed is the womb that bore you and the breasts that nursed you,*[7] and when he sucked those breasts after he had been

3. *Fecundum,* "fruitful" or "fertile," in the sense of leading to or providing much material for the sermon's development. The adjective *facundus (-um),* "eloquent," has a similar connotation, and scribes sometimes confused the two.

4. Sg 5:18.

5. Is 62:5.

6. Is 62:5.

7. Lk 11:27.

adductus per cantum Virginis que cecinit *Magnificat anima mea Dominum,* etc., mitis effectus est. In huius eciam gremio ille vnicornis fortissimus Dei, qui angelum et hominem sibi resistentem, idest sapienciam appetentem que[5] sibi apropriatur, cornu vindicte interemit, mansuetissimus est effectus quando *edificauit sicut vnicornis sanctificium suum in terra quam fundauit in secula,* scilicet in gremio virginis, implens illud vaticinium Ysaie dicentis: *Habitabit iuuenis cum virgine.*

Per sacram autem scripturam introducitur thema sic:

In Lege precepit Dominus quod summus sacerdos non acciperet viduam repudiatam aut meretricem sed virginem de stirpe sua. Modo autem Filius Dei est summus sacerdos. Quod patet quia ei dictum est: *Tu es sacerdos in eternum secundum ordinem Melchisedech.* Debet igitur Filius Dei sibi matrimonio virginem copulare incorruptam. Et licet hoc mistice verificetur de Christo et Ecclesia (vnde dicit Apostolus: *Dispondi enim vos vni viro virginem castam exhibere Christo*), hoc tamen ad literam verificatum fuit de Christo Filio Dei et Virgine gloriosa, cum qua tanquam cum matre, tanquam cum sponsa et sorore, hodierna die incepit habitare, sicut preuidit Ysaias dicens: *Habitabit iuuenis cum virgine.*

Per scripturam sanctorum introducitur sic thema sicut predictum:

Nichil ita discordes reconciliat vel amoris fedus confirmat sicut vinculum matrimoniale. Vnde cum nostra natura diuinam inimiciciam[6] quam incurrerat non poterat tollerare (quia penam mortis pro ista[7] quilibet incurrrebat), necesse habuit de aliqua virgine speciosa sibi prouidere, cuius matrimonio hec inimicicia posset tolli et nos secure ad eum tanquam ad generum nostrum (quia ad sponsum sororis nostre), ymmo pocius ad hominem de nostro genere (quia ad filium sororis nostre) possemus accedere. Vnde Augustinus 4 *Confessionum* dicit: "Descendit huc ipsa vita et tulit mortem nostram, et occidit eam, et de habundancia vite sue intonuit clamans vt [f. 172] redeamus hinc ad eum, idest in illud secretum vnde processit ad nos, idest in ipsum purum virginalem vterum, vbi ei nupsit humana creatura, caro mortalis, ne semper esset mortalis. Et inde tanquam sponsus processit de talamo[8] suo." Ista sponsalia preuidit Ysaias dicens: *Habitabit iuuenis cum virgine.*

5. que] O; qui L.A; *longer omission* U.
6. inimiciciam] A.O.U; inimiciam L.
7. pro ista] L.A; per illam O; per euam U.
8. talamo] tab' L; tabernaculo A; *om.* O; thalamo C.U *and in source.*

drawn by the Virgin's song as she sang *My soul does magnify the Lord,* etc.,[8] he became mild. In her lap, too, that most ferocious unicorn of God, who killed with his horn of vengeance both angel and man when they resisted him by wanting the knowledge that belonged only to him, became most meek when *like a unicorn he made his sanctuary on the earth he had established forever,*[9] that is, in the Virgin's womb, and thereby fulfilled the prophecy of Isaiah who said, *The youth shall dwell with the virgin.*

With a biblical quotation the thema can be introduced in this way:

In the Old Law, God commanded that the high priest should not marry a widow, divorcee, or defiled woman, but a virgin of his own people.[10] Now, the Son of God is the high priest. This is manifest because it was said to him: *You are a priest forever according to the order of Melchizedek.*[11] Therefore the Son of God ought to marry an undefiled virgin. And although this mystically refers to Christ and the Church (since the Apostle says, *I have espoused you to one husband, that I may present you as a chaste virgin to Christ*),[12] yet it applies literally to Christ and the glorious Virgin, with whom he began to live today as with his mother, bride, and sister, just as Isaiah had foreseen it when he said, *The youth shall dwell with the virgin.*

With a quotation from the saints the quoted thema is introduced thus:

Nothing reconciles warring parties or strengthens mutual love as much as the bond of marriage. Hence, since our nature could not endure God's hostility which it had incurred (for everyone suffered the pain of death for it), it had to find a fair virgin, through whose marriage that enmity might be lifted and we might have safe access to God as to our brother-in-law (since he became the husband of our sister), nay even as a member of our own family (since he became the son of our sister). Hence Augustine says, in book 4 of his *Confessions:* "Life itself came down and took away our death and killed it, and from his abundant life he sounded forth and called that we should return from here to him, that is, to that secret place from which he came to us, namely to that pure virginal womb where he married human nature, our mortal flesh, to himself, so that it would not be mortal forever. And from there he came forth as a bridegroom comes out of his bridal bed."[13] This marriage Isaiah foresaw when he said, *The youth shall dwell with the virgin.*

8. Lk 1:46.
9. Ps 77:69 (78:69).
10. Lv 21:14.
11. Heb 5:6, quoting Ps 109:4 (110:4).
12. 2 Cor 11:2.
13. Augustine, *Confessions* 4.12 (PL 32:701); cf. Psalm 18:6 (19:4–5).

Auctoritate philosophica vel poetica introducitur thema sic:[9]

Dicit Sen\e/ca in quadam epistula ad Lucillum: "Miraris homines ad Deum ire, Deus ad homines, ymmo quod melius est, in homines venit." Certum est quod in nullum hominem magis quam in hominem cuius se filium vocat, dicens: *Filius hominis venit querere et saluum facere quod perierat,* etc. Ipse enim solus vere est filius hominis, quia solius matris, non alterius hominis, quia non habet hominem patrem eius sicut ceteri homines, eo quod ipse de sola intemerata virgine generatus est, sicut preuidit Ysaias propheta dicens: *Ecce virgo concipiet et pariet filium.* De hac virgine intelligitur illud poeticum:

Virgo decora nimis Dauid de semine regis.

Et de ipsa et prole sua illi versus poetici possunt intelligi:

Iam redit et virgo, redeunt Saturnia regna,
Nam noua progenies celo dimittitur alto.

Et hoc quia isto die noua progenies dimittitur in vterum virginalem, vt impleatur Ysaie prophete vaticinium dicens: *Habitabit iuuenis cum virgine.*

Istis igitur modis potest thema introduci, vel singulis per se, vel omnibus simul. Hoc tamen semper est conueniens quod, siue per manuduccionem, siue per exemplum, siue per simile in natura, siue per scripturam sanctorum vel philosophorum seu poetarum fiat, semper sacra scriptura adiungatur; et hoc vel auctoritas ad literam vel figuratiuum signum, quod magis est decens.

[II]

Modo dicendum est de thematis diuisione. Cauendum est igitur ne in thematis diuisione accipiatur vel idem vocabulum quod debet esse menbrum diuisionis, vel sinonomum, vel penitus extraneum vel repugnans. Verbi gracia:

9. sic] A.O. U; sicut L.

With a quotation from philosophy or poetry the thema is introduced thus:

Seneca says in a letter to Lucilius: "You are astonished that men go to God, that God comes to men. Indeed, what is even better, he comes into men."[14] It is certain that God comes into no man more than he came into the human being whose son he calls himself when he said, *The Son of Man has come to seek and to save that which was lost,* and so on.[15] He alone is truly the "Son of Man," because he was son only to his mother and not to any other man, for he did not have a human father as all other humans have, since he was born of an inviolate virgin alone, as Isaiah foresaw when he said, *Behold, a virgin shall conceive and bear a son.*[16] This virgin is understood by the poetic verse:

> A virgin most sublime of David the king's line.[17]

And of her and her offspring may be understood the poet's verses:

> Now the Virgin returns, and Saturn's rule comes back,
> For a new offspring is sent us from high heaven.[18]

And that is because today a new offspring is sent into the Virgin's womb, so that the prediction of the prophet Isaiah will be fulfilled who said, *The youth shall dwell with the virgin.*

In these ways, then, can the thema be introduced, either with any one of them or with all of them together. But it is always fitting that—whether the thema is introduced with a lead-in, or an exemplum, or a simile from nature, or a quotation from the saints, the philosophers, or the poets—a quote from Holy Scripture should always be added, and that either as a literal citation or as a figurative sign, which is more fitting.

[II]

Now we must speak of the division of the thema. One must take care, in the division of the thema, not to use the same word that is part of the text that is to be divided, or a synonym for it, or something totally strange or repugnant. For example:

14. Seneca, *Ep.* 73.15.
15. Lk 19:10.
16. Is 7:14.
17. Unidentified.
18. Virgil, *Eclogues* 4.6–7.

Habitabit iuuenis cum virgine. Hic tria notantur in hoc themate, scilicet Filii Dei habitacio familiaris, quia *habitabit;* secundo, Dei coniunccio[10] singularis, quia *iuuenis;* et tercio, matris condicio puellaris, quia *cum virgine.*

In hac diuisione[11] est triplex defectus. In primo enim menbro ponitur ipsa diccio que est diuisionis menbrum, scilicet *habitabit.* In secundo menbro ponitur aliquid impertinens, quia *coniunccio*[12] in nullo notificat iuuenem plus quam quodcumque aliud. In tercio menbro ponitur nomen sinonomum, quia *puella* et *virgo* sunt quasi sinonoma. Debet ergo diuisio dari per alia nomina seu vocabula, exprimencia tamen aliqua propria vel apropriata illi dic- [f. 172v] cioni que debet esse menbrum diuisionis. Verbi gracia:

Habitare est morari per aliquod magnum tempus in vno loco. Condicio eciam apropriata *iuueni* est species vel pulcritudo vel leticia, quia iuuenis est letus, sicut senex tristis, et similiter iocundus, sicut senex iracundus. Condicio autem *virginis* est mundicia mentis et corporis.

Videatur eciam quod condicio que debet poni in diuisione aliqualiter reluceat in auctoritate per quam debet menbrum diuisionis confirmari, sicut verbi gracia requies vel mora, que est condicio habitacionis, aliqualiter relucet in hac auctoritate *Habitabit in tabernaculo tuo, requiescet,* etc. Potest ergo thema in verbis propositis diuidi sic:

Primo iocundamur de Dei venientis ad nos morosa requie et iocunda, quia *habitabit;* in Psalmo: *Habitabit in tabernaculo tuo, requiescet,* etc. Secundo, letamur ex nascentis formosa facie et letabunda, quia *iuuenis;* in Psalmo: *Introibo ad altare Dei, qui letificat iuuentutem meam.* Tercio, admiramur de parentis graciosa specie atque munda, quia *cum virgine;* Ad Corinthios 7 dicitur: *Virgo cogitat que Dei sunt, vt sit sancta mente et corpore.*

10. coniunccio] L.A.U; cognicio O.
11. diuisione] dīone O; diccione L.A; *om.* U.
12. coniunccio] L.A; cognicio O; *longer omission* U.

The youth shall dwell with the virgin. In this thema three things are indicated, namely, the Son of God's dwelling with us, in the words *shall dwell;* second, God's singular connection, in *the youth;* and third, his mother's maidenly condition, in *with the virgin.*

In this division are three defects. For in its first member occurs the same word as in the thema to be divided, namely *dwell.* In the second member appears something irrelevant, for *connection* in no way means *youth* more than anything else. And in the third member appears a synonym, for *maiden* and *virgin* are fairly synonymous. But the division must be made with different nouns or words which however express the same as, or something appropriate to, the word in the thema to be divided. For example:

To *dwell* means to live in the same place for a long time. The proper condition of a *youth* is his status or handsomeness or joyfulness, for a young man is joyful, just as an old man is sad, and similarly he is agreeable, while an old man is irascible. But the condition of a *virgin* is to be pure in mind and body.

It should further be seen to that the attribute that must be given in the division should be somehow reflected in the authority with which this member of the division is to be confirmed. For instance,[19] the [attribute of] resting or living for a long time that is proper to "inhabiting" is somewhat reflected in the verse [*Who*] *shall dwell in your tabernacle,* [*who*] *shall rest* [*on your holy mountain*]? etc.[20] Thus the thema with the words as stated can be divided as follows:

First, we take delight in God's coming to us for his lasting and joyful rest, for *he shall dwell;* as stated in the Psalm, *He shall dwell in your tabernacle, he shall rest,* etc.[21] Second, we rejoice in the beautiful and gladdening face of him who is born, for he is a *youth;* as in the Psalm, *I will go to the altar of God, who gives joy to my youth.*[22] Third, we regard with wonder his mother's grace and purity,

19. At this point G has a longer insertion, which calls this shared attribute *stipes* and illustrates it with: "Three things proclaim and extol the blessed incarnation of Christ, the Son of God." The three things are those given in the example of the edited text ("delight in God's coming," etc.). They are here—in G—(a) listed and then (b) illustrated with proof texts, as in the edited text. Between these two sections (a-b), G speaks of the "secondary division," which in the edited text *follows* upon section b. In other words, the edited text lacks section (a).

20. Ps 14:1 (15:1).

21. Ps 14:1 (15:1).

22. Ps 42:4 (43:4).

Solet eciam aliunde ob[13] decorem ad diuisionem principalem addi vna secundaria diuisio sic:

Primum facit amiciciam, scilicet habitacio cum alio; in Deuteronomio dicitur: *Amantissimus Domini habitabit confidenter;*

secundum mouet ad leticiam; in Ecclesiaste dicitur: *Letare, iuuenis, in adolescencia tua;*

tercium habet[14] status preeminenciam;[15] I Corinthiorum dicitur: *Qui dat virginem suam matrimonio bene facit, et qui \non/ dat, melius facit.*

Verumtamen quando fit talis duplex diuisio, non oportet ad vtramque adducere auctoritates, sed sufficit ad primam vel secundam cui magis consonant vel congruunt[16] auctoritates.

Videndum est eciam quod in singulis menbris diuisionis sit vna diccio vel due vel tres dicciones quasi rithmice[17] correspondentes vocabulis in aliis menbris, sicut sunt in diuisione supra dicta.

Item ad decorem sermonis multum foret si in auctoritate per quam confirmatur menbrum diuisionis non solum esset illa diccio thematis secundum vocalem concordanciam sed eciam vna illarum diccionum que ponuntur in menbro diuisionis, sicut verbi gracia in menbro diuisionis supra posite *requies* tanquam proprietas habitacionis et in auctoritate qua probatur[18] primum menbrum non solum ponitur *habitabit* sed *requiescet.* In aliis autem menbris non oportet quod sit sic, quia nec in primo menbro est necessarium sed solum ad decorem. Sufficit enim quod auctoritas habeat cum ipsa [f. 173] diuisione concordanciam[19] realem, licet non vocalem; sed cum diuisione thematis semper debet habere concordanciam[20] vocalem.

13. ob] O; *om.* L.A; ad U.
14. habet] A.O; *add* inter L*(interlin.)*.U.
15. preeminenciam] A.U; preiminenciam O; preminenciam L.
16. congruunt] O; congruant L.A (*om.* consonant vel); competunt U (*om.* consonant vel).
17. rithmice] O.U; ritmice A; ritnice *or* ritmce L.
18. probatur] O.U; ponitur L.A.
19. concordanciam] O.U; concordiam L.A.
20. concordanciam] O.U; concordiam L.A.

for [he dwells] *with the virgin;* as is said in 1 Corinthians 7: *She thinks on the things that are God's, that she may be holy in mind and body.*[23]

Sometimes for the sake of ornamentation preachers add a second division to the first, as in the following example:

The first, that is, dwelling with someone else, makes for friendship; in Deuteronomy it is said, *The best beloved of God shall dwell confidently;*[24]

the second moves to rejoicing; Ecclesiastes says, *Rejoice, young man, in your youth;*[25]

and the third holds a preeminent status;[26] in 1 Corinthians it is said, *He who gives a virgin in marriage does well, and he who does not, does better.*[27]

However, if one uses such a double division, it is not necessary to adduce authorities for each, but it is enough to do so for either the first or the second only, whichever the authorities echo or agree with better.

One should also see to it that the individual members of the division contain one or two or three words that rhyme with the corresponding words in the other members, as is the case in the division above.[28]

Further, it would enhance the beauty of the sermon if in the authority with which a member of the division is confirmed were not only the respective word of the thema in verbal agreement, but also one of the words that have been put in the respective member of the division. For instance, in the member of the division given above, the word *rest* appears as an attribute of dwelling, and in the authority that confirms the first member appears not only *dwell* but also *rest.* In the other members this does not need to be done, because it is not necessary even in the first member but only a matter of elegance. It is sufficient that the authority have some notional agreement with the [second] division even if it is not verbal. But with the division of the thema it must always have verbal agreement.

23. 1 Cor 7:34.
24. Dt 33:12.
25. Eccl 11:9.
26. Since virginity is considered a higher status than marriage (and widowhood).
27. 1 Cor 7:38.
28. I.e., amiciciam, leticiam, preeminenciam.

Notandum eciam quod multum foret ad decorem sermonis si per aliquod dictum sancti vel philosophi vel per pulcram manuduccionem non solum thema sed eciam ipsa diuisio posset introduci. Verbi gracia, si accipiatur hoc thema *Butirum et mel comedet vt sciat reprobare malum et eligere bonum,* et esset introductum aliquo istorum modorum predictorum, postea ad inducendam diuisionem diceretur sic:

Eligere bonum non est nisi per virtutem, quia secundum Philosophum 2 *Ethicorum* "virtus est habitus electiuus in medietate[21] consistens," et certum est quod \est/ electiuus boni, quia secundum eundem "virtus est que[22] bonum facit habentem et opus eius bonum reddit." Nam virtus consistit in medio, secundum eundem. Modo ad inueniendum medium docet Aristoteles primo *Priorum* ad tria respicere, scilicet ad antecedens, consequens, et repugnans, et secundum hec, tria in verbis propositis exprimuntur.[23] Primo enim docetur habere illud quod virtutem precedit,[24] ibi *Butirum et mel comedet,* idest pinguedinem et dulcorem sancte meditacionis; in Deuteronomio dicitur: *Vt suggeret mel de petra, oleumque de saxo durissimo, butirum de armento,* etc. Secundo docetur cauere quod virtuti obest et quod virtuti non obedit, ibi *vt sciat reprobare malum;* et Psalmo dicitur: *Declina a malo et fac bonum.* Tercio docetur fauere ei quod virtuti succedit, ibi *et eligere bonum;* in Matheo: *Eligerunt bonos in vasa sua,* etc.

Tantum dictum sit de secundo, scilicet de diuisione.

21. in medietate] O; immediate L.A; in medio U.
22. que] O.U; qui L.A.
23. exprimuntur] O.U; exprimitur L.A.
24. precedit] C.U; pretendit L.A; precipit O.

Notice also that it would make the sermon very beautiful if not only its thema but also its division could be introduced with some saying of a saint or a philosopher, or with an elegant lead-in. For example, if you choose as your thema *He shall eat butter and honey that he may know to refuse the evil and to choose the good,*[29] and you introduce it in any of the just mentioned ways, you might then, in presenting the division, say this:

> To choose the good requires virtue, for according to Aristotle in book 2 of his *Ethics,* "virtue is a state of character concerned with choosing the mean,"[30] and it certainly chooses what is good, for according to the same philosopher, "virtue makes him who has it good, and makes his deed good."[31] For virtue consists in the mean, according to the same.[32] Now, in order to find the mean, Aristotle teaches in book 1 of the *Prior Analytics* to look at three things, namely at what comes before, what follows, and what is opposed to it.[33] And accordingly, in the quoted words [of the thema] are three things expressed. For first it teaches us to have what precedes virtue, in the words *He shall eat butter and honey,* that is, the fat and sweetness of holy meditation; Deuteronomy says, *That he might suck honey out of the rock and oil out of the hard stone, butter of the herd,* etc.[34] Second, it teaches us to beware of what is opposed to virtue and offends it, in the words *that he may know to refuse the evil;* and the Psalm says, *Decline from evil and do good.*[35] And third, it teaches us to embrace what follows upon virtue, in the words *and to choose the good;* Matthew says, *They selected the good ones into their vessels,* etc.[36]

This much about the second section, that is, the division.

29. Is 7:15.

30. Aristotle, *Nicomachean Ethics* 2.6 (1107a).

31. Ibid. (1106a).

32. Ibid. (1107a).

33. There seems to be some confusion, or at least a shift, in this passage. Moral virtue as the mean between two extremes is discussed in the *Nicomachean Ethics* 2.6–9. The *Prior Analytics* discusses syllogistic argument, in which a "middle term" occurs. *Virtus* as the middle term in a syllogism is used as illustration in book 2 of Boethius's *De syllogismo categorico* (PL 64:809–832). The three "things" mentioned in *Quamvis—antecedentia, consequentia,* and *repugnantia*—were also topics in classical rhetoric; see Cicero, *Topics* 53 and *De oratore* 2.40.170. Notice that U here reads *in 2 Posteriorum.*

34. Dt 32:13–14.35. Ps 36:27 (37:27).

36. Mt 13:48.

[III]

Modo[25] videndum est de menbrorum prosecucione. Hoc autem fit istis diebus dupliciter: [1] vno modo per menbrorum subdivisionem, [2] alio modo per auctoritatis adducte exposicionem et subdiuisionem. Primus modus est communior, secundus est subtilior.

[1] Quando enim thema est diuisum, respiciende sunt concordancie pro illo menbro quod predicator vult prosequi, et colligende sunt auctoritates magis pregnantes vel que plus placent predicanti. Si vero forsan voluerit facere impacciones, verbi gracia de primo themate, si voluerit prosequi menbrum de virginitate,[26] in promptu habeat[27] istas auctoritates: primo in Luca, *Missus est Gabriel angelus ad Mariam virginem,* et hanc in Apocalipsi, *Hii sunt qui cum mulieribus non sunt coinquinati, virgines enim sunt,* <et hanc que> habetur in libro Trenorum: *Virgines eius squalide.* Facere ergo subdiuisionem potest sic:

> Ad virginitatem est aduertendum quod [a] quedam est virginitas detestanda, [b] quedam imitanda, et [c] quedam admiranda. [a] Virginitas detestanda est que non [f. 173v] Deo dedicatur sed propter ypocrisim vel vanam gloriam conseruatur; et de tali dicitur in libro Trenorum: *Virgines eius*[28] *squalide.*

Si autem tunc adducatur exemplum vel manuduccio vel auctoritas sancti vel philosophi, magis laudabilis erit.

[b] Virginitas imitanda est illa que Deo dedicatur. Et sicut[29] virgines parentes suos secuntur ad ecclesiam qui istam virginitatem conseruant, sic ille vel illa qui virginitatem Deo dedicant ipsum secuntur vt ab ipso custodiantur. In Apocalipsi dicitur: *Hii sunt qui cum mulieribus non sunt,* etc.; *secuntur agnum quocumque ierit.* Et eciam Jeremie dicitur: *Pater meus dux virginitatis mee,* etc. Ad hoc eciam est auctoritas Augustini *De bono virginitatis,* vbi dicit: “Gaudia virginum

25. Modo] *add* 2m [*sic*] principale est menbrorum prosecucio *marg.* L.
26. virginitate] *add* et *interlin.* L.
27. habeat] A; habet L.O; habeo *or* habeto U.
28. eius] A.U *and source;* eorum O; enim L.
29. sicut] O.U; sic L.A.

[III]

Now we have to see about the development of the members.[37] In our time this is done in two ways: [1] in one way by subdividing the members, and [2] in another way by explaining and subdividing the authority that has been quoted. The first way is more common, the second more subtle.

[1] When the thema has been divided, the preacher must look for quotations that agree with the member that he wants to develop, and he must take up those authorities that are more fruitful or more pleasing to him. Let us assume he wants to use a direct negation,[38] for example of the first thema [i.e., *The youth shall dwell with the virgin*]. If he wants to develop the member on virginity, he should have these authorities to hand: first, *The angel Gabriel was sent to the virgin Mary,* from Luke;[39] and then *These are the ones who were not defiled with women, for they are virgins,* from Revelation;[40] and then, from Lamentations, *Her virgins are wretched.*[41] Now he can make a subdivision as follows:

> Regarding virginity we should notice that [a] one kind is to be detested, [b] another to be imitated, and [c] a third to be admired. [a] The kind of virginity that is to be detested is the one that is not dedicated to God but kept out of hypocrisy or vanity; and of this it is said in the Book of Lamentations, *Her virgins are wretched.*

If one then brings in an exemplum, or a lead-in, or an authority from a saint or philosopher, the development will be more praiseworthy.

[b] The kind of virginity that is to be imitated is the one that is dedicated to God. And as maidens follow their parents to the church who keep this virginity, so he or she that dedicates his or her virginity to God follows him that he or she may be protected by him. In Revelation it is said, *These are the ones who were not defiled with women,* etc.; *they follow the Lamb wherever he goes.* And also in Jeremiah it is said, *My father, the guide of my virginity,* etc.[42] Also the authority of Augustine speaks to this, in his book *On the Good of Virginity,*

37. An outline of this section was given in the headnote above.

38. Direct negation: the Latin *impaccio,* a rare word, is found in Higden but nowhere else in the published *artes.* Dictionaries of medieval Latin gloss it as "the act of striking on," "onslaught," "charge," "attack," "offense," "scandal," etc. Here (as in Higden) it evidently indicates making a strong moral point by pointing out the negative (of a virtue).

39. Lk 1:26–27.

40. Rv 14:4.

41. Lam 1:4.

42. Jer 3:4.

sunt de Christo, in Christo, cum Christo; gaudia aliis alia, sed nullis talia."

[c] Virginitas admiranda est illa que non habet parem, scilicet vt maneat virginitas et assit fecunditas. Nam talia sunt mirabilia et mira que non reperiuntur in natura. Vnde dicit quidam versificator:

> Numquam natura mutauit sic sua iura
> vt virgo pareret nisi virginitate careret.

Hoc tamen in sola Maria habet instanciam, que filium concepit in vtero et permansit virgo. In Ecclesiastico dicitur: *Mulier a virginitate suscepit illum,* et in Luca: *Missus est angelus Gabriel ad Mariam virginem,* etc. Et sequitur: *Ecce, concipies in vtero et paries filium.*

Iste autem est vnus modus prosequendi in sermonibus, scilicet accipere vnum menbrum impactum et secundum bonum vel tercium optimum. Vel aliter potest accipi quodlibet menbrum bonum in prosecucione, et contra[30] quodlibet facere impaccionem per quedam contraria sic:

Virgo debet habere tres condiciones, scilicet—

ornamentum decoris; in Jeremia dicitur: *Numquid obliuisci potest virgo ornamenti sui?* quod est contra illud in Trenis, *Virgines eorum squalide;*

secundo debet habere virgo munimentum pudoris; in Genesi dicitur: *Virgo pulcherrima et incognita viro,*[31] quod est contra illam filiam Iepte, que circumiuit per montes et planxit virginitatem suam, vt habetur in libro Iudicum;

tercio debet virgo habere condimentum amoris, vt in Matheo dicitur de virginibus sapientibus que *acceperunt oleum in vasis suis,* quod est contra illud[32] de virginibus fatuis, ibidem.

Et est iste bonus modus predicandi et largus et fecundus, quia ad virtutes[33] predicandas et ad vicia detestanda equaliter se extendit.[34]

30. et contra] U; econtra L.A.O.
31. viro] O.U; virgo L.A.
32. illud] O; illas L.A; *om.* U.
33. virtutes] O.U; virginitates L.A.
34. extendit] A.O.U; exdendit L.

where he says: "The joy of virgins is from Christ, in Christ, and with Christ. Others have other joys, but none have any like this."[43]

[c] The kind of virginity that is to be admired is the one that has no equal, that is, which remains virginity and at the same time is fruitful. Such virginity is a marvel and miracle and is not found in nature. Whence some poet says:

> Never has nature so changed its course
> that a virgin gives birth without losing her virginity.[44]

But this occurred in Mary alone, who conceived a son in her womb and remained a virgin. In Ecclesiasticus it is said, *She received him as a woman from virginity;*[45] and in Luke, *The angel Gabriel was sent to the virgin Mary,*" etc.; and then follows: *Behold, you will conceive in your womb and bear a son.*[46]

But this is only one way of developing the sermon, that is, to take one member with a negative sense, the second in a good sense, or the third in the best. In a different way, one can take up, in one's development, each member in the good sense, and then adduce a direct negation against each member with something that contradicts [the point of the member], such as:

A virgin must have three qualities, namely—

the ornament of beauty; in Jeremiah it is said, *Will a virgin forget her ornament?*[47] This is contrary to the words in Lamentations, *Their virgins are wretched;*

second, a virgin must have the protection of modesty; in Genesis it is said, *A virgin most fair and not known to man.*[48] This is contrary to the daughter of Jephtha, who went about the mountains and bewailed her virginity, as is related in the Book of Judges;[49]

third, a virgin must have the relish of love, as is said in Matthew of the prudent virgins who *took oil in their vessels.*[50] This is contrary to the foolish virgins in the same passage.

This is a good way of preaching, broad and fruitful, because it touches equally on virginity, which is to be commended, and on the vices that are to be condemned.

43. Augustine, *De sancta virginitate* 27.27.
44. Cf. Walther *Proverbia* 19,275 (cf. *Initia* 12,412).
45. Sir 15:2. The Vulgate has the future tense: "will receive."
46. Lk 1:26, 31.
47. Jer 2:32.
48. Gn 24:16.
49. Jgs 11:37.
50. Mt 25:4.

Similiter eciam debet menbrum secundum[35] principale diuidi [f. 174] in tria. Et si auctoritates permittant quod sic diuidatur secundum quamdam correspondenciam ad primam diuisionem, decencior erit sermo. Verbi gracia, si teneamus primam diuisionem de virginitate (secundum quod alia est detestanda, alia imitanda, alia admiranda), similiter tunc in secundo principali potest dici:

Alius est *iuuenis* dissolutus, alius est iuuenis virtutibus bonis tutus, alius est iuuenis super omnia constitutus. Pro primo in Prouerbiis dicitur: *Audi iuuenem vecordem,* et Apostolus dicit: *Iuuenilia facta deuita;* pro secundo in Tobia dicitur: *Vnde habemus te, bone iuuenis?* pro tercio in Daniele: *Suscitauit Deus spiritum pueri iunioris,* idest Christi, et post dictum est sibi quod sederet in medio et iudicaret, et signat Christum cui omne iudicium datum est. Et sic mala iuuentus correspondet male virginitati, et bona iuuentus bone virginitati, et excellens iuuentus admirande virginitati.

Similiter tercium menbrum potest diuidi correspondenter istis, et hoc si auctoritates permittant, alioquin non est causa, quia talis correspondencia non est nisi vna curiositas.

Et sicut dictum est de principali diuisione—si posset introduci per manuduccionem pulcram vel auctoritatem—ita eciam de subdiuisione dicendum est. Multum nanque esset ad decorem sermonis si eo modo posset decenter introduci. Verbi gracia: Si istud esset thema *Bonum semen seminasti,* et supposita diuisione principali vellem subdiuidere ly *bonum,* dicerem sic:

Secundum Augustinum tria sunt genera bonorum: quedam sunt minima, quedam sunt media, et quedam sunt maxima. Bona minima sunt[36] diuicie et bona exteriora; bona media sunt bona naturalia et interiora; bona optima vel maxima sunt bona gratuita vel superiora. De primo dixit ille diues qui voluit multiplicare horrea sua: *Anima, habes plurima bona reposita,* etc. De secundo in Genesi cum dicitur: *Vidit Deus cuncta que fecerat et erant valde bona.* De tercio dicitur in Exodo:[37] *Ego ostendam tibi omne bonum.*

35. secundum] O.U *(cf. the next paragraph)*; tercium L.A.
36. sunt] O.U; sicut L.A.
37. Exodo] O.U; exodi L.A(?).

In the same fashion the second main member must be divided into three parts. And if the authorities allow that it be thus divided so as to have some correspondence with the first division, then the sermon will be even more beautiful. For example, if we take the first division, of virginity (namely, that one kind is to be detested, another to be imitated, and the third to be admired), we can then in the second division similarly say:

One kind of *youth* is dissolute, another is firm in good virtues, and another is set above all things. About the first it is said in Proverbs, *I have heard a foolish young man,*[51] and the Apostle says, *Avoid youthful deeds;*[52] about the second is said in Tobit, *Where are you from, good young man?;*[53] and about the third in Daniel, *God raised up the spirit of a young boy,*[54] that is, of Christ, and afterwards he is told he should sit in their midst and give judgment,[55] which signifies Christ, to whom all judgment is given.[56]

In this way, bad youth corresponds to bad virginity, and good youth to good virginity, and excellent youth to virginity that is to be admired.

In the same way the third member can be divided in a corresponding fashion, if the quoted authorities permit it—otherwise it does not matter, for such a correspondence is only one kind of elegance.[57]

And as was said about the main division—that it should be introduced with a beautiful lead-in or authority if possible—the same should be said about the subdivision. For it would make a beautiful sermon if the subdivision could be fittingly introduced in this way. For example: if the thema were *You have sown good seed,*[58] and after the main division I wanted to subdivide the word *good,* I could say as follows:

According to Augustine there are three kinds of good things: some are the least, some are of medium value, and some are the greatest. The least good things are wealth and external goods; of medium value are natural and in-

51. Prv 7:7. The Vulgate has *video,* "I behold."

52. Cf. 2 Tm 2:22.

53. Tb 5:6.

54. Dn 13:45.

55. Dn 13:50.

56. Cf. Jn 5:22.

57. Elegance: here in Latin *curiositas.* Medieval *curiosus* and *curiositas,* derived from *cura,* "attention, care," do not have a negative connotation in rhetorical contexts (as *curiosus, curiositas* in the sense of "curiosity" in moral contexts do).

58. Mt 13:27.

Subtilitas eciam foret si posset dari diuisio trimenbris et omnia menbra in vna auctoritate possent reperiri secundum concordanciam. Verbi gracia, in isto themate *Bonum semen seminasti,* si velim diuidere[38] *bonum,* dicam sic:

Secundum Philosophum virtus est que "bonum facit habentem et opus eius bonum reddit." Sed hoc triplex est bonum, scilicet in subiecto quod in habitu virtutis perficitur; in ipso habitu qui in subiecto inducitur; et in operacione que ab habitu elicitur. De hiis tribus simul dicitur in Matheo: *Bonus homo de bono thesauro* [f. 174v] *cordis sui profert bonum—bonus homo* quantum ad bonitatem subiecti; *de bono thesauro cordis sui* quantum ad bonitatem habitus vel virtutis; *profert bonum* quantum ad bonitatem operacionis.

Similiter si velim subdiuidere *Seminasti,* dicam sic:

Seminare spiritualiter non est nisi operari bonum. Hoc autem contingit tripliciter, scilicet: in animi preparacione, in operis execucione, in usus[39] exercitacione. De hiis tribus simul dicitur in Matheo: *Exiit qui seminat,* ecce animi preparacio; *semen suum,* ecce actualis operacio; *et dum seminat,* etc., ecce vsus[40] excercitacio.

Quando autem singulum menbrorum principalium diuiditur <in> tria, tunc potest esse duplex[41] modus prosequendi. [a] Primus:[42] primo prosequendo omnia menbra primi menbri, et secundo omnia menbra secundi, et tercio omnia menbra tercii. Et iste modus est communior et clarior, sicut patet in illo themate antedicto *Habitabit iuuenis cum virgine,* si primo

38. diuidere] O.U; dicere L.A.

39. usus] O.U; vel L.A.

40. vsus] U; *add* vel L.A.O.

41. duplex] O.U; triplex L.A.C, *see also the outline given in the headnote above (p. 98, "Two ways").*

42. Primus] *om.* L.A.O.U. *Perhaps a word or phrase has dropped out in the archetype of all extant manuscripts;* primus *would make good sense, to go with* Alius *at [b].* U *may read* Uel primo.

ternal goods; and the best or greatest goods are goods of grace or goods from above. The first were referred to by the rich man who wanted to increase his barns: *My soul, you have many goods laid up,* etc.[59] Of the second it is said in Genesis: *God saw all the things he had made, and they were very good.*[60] And of the third, in Exodus: *I will show you everything that is good.*[61]

It would also be very subtle if one could establish a division of three members and all members could be found, in verbal agreement, in a single authority. For example, if in the thema *You have sown good seed* I wanted to divide *good,* I could say:

According to the Philosopher, virtue is what "makes him who has it good and renders his work good."[62] But "good" is threefold: in the subject that is perfected by the habit of virtue; in the habit itself that is created in the subject; and in the work that comes out of that habit. Of these three together it is said in Matthew: *A good man, out of the good treasure of his heart, brings forth good things*[63]—*a good man* with respect to the goodness of the subject; *out of the good treasure of his heart* with respect to the goodness of his habit or virtue; and *brings forth good things* with respect to the goodness of his work.

Similarly, if I wanted to subdivide *You have sown,* I could say:

Sowing understood spiritually is nothing but working good. But this consists in three things, namely, in preparing one's mind, in carrying out the work, and in habitual practice. Of these things together it is said in Matthew: *The sower went forth to sow*—the preparation of the mind; *his seed*—the actual work; *and while he was sowing*—his habitual practice.[64]

Now, when one of the main members is divided into three, there is a twofold way of development.

[a] The first is by first developing all parts of the first member, second the same of all parts of the second member, and third the same of all members of the third member. This way is quite commonly used and is quite transparent, as can be seen in the thema used above, *The youth shall dwell with the virgin,* where there was first a development of

59. Lk 12:19.
60. Gn 1:31.
61. Ex 33:19.
62. Aristotle, *Nicomachean Ethics* 2.6 (1106a).
63. Mt 12:35.
64. Mt 13:3–4.

fiat execucio de triplici virginitate, et secundo de triplici iuuentute. Ad decorem tamen foret sermonis si in[43] vltimo menbro primi principalis posset introduci secundum principale quasi per quandam continuacionem siue concathenacionem vel commixtionem, et hoc conuenienter fiet si posset inueniri aliqua alia auctoritas quam thema vbi primum menbrum prenotatur et secundum simul inuenitur. Sicut verbi gracia quando dictum est de triplici virginitate, posset adduci illa auctoritas *Iuuenes et virgines, senes cum iunioribus laudent nomen Domini,* vbi introducitur secundum principale, *iuuenis.*

[b] Alius eciam modus est procedendi in themate sic diuiso per tria menbra quod primo procedatur a primo primi vsque ad secundum secundi et ad tercium tercii.[44] Et iste modus solebat fieri a curiosis vt ostenderetur corespondencia inter tria primi menbri et tria secundi, et tria tercii. Verumtamen iste modus est minus clarus et nimis inuolutus.

Item aliqui nimis curiosi non solebant esse contenti de nouem menbris, ita quod quodlibet principalium diuiderent in tria,[45] sed vlterius quodlibet istorum nouem diuiserunt in tria, vt sic essent in[46] vniuerso viginti septem menbra. Sed hoc reputo nimiam curiositatem et superfluitatem confusam, et ideo non exemplificabo.

Quidam eciam abbreuiantes sermonem primum menbrum diuidunt in tria, secundum in duo, et tercium manet indiuisum, sicut sermo piramidalis. Piramis est enim figura habens basem latam et per medium minus tendens in conum. Si autem sermo habeat duo menbra vel tria que non vlterius diuiduntur, potest dici sermo linearis, sicut numerus binarius [f. 175] vel ternarius sunt linearius numerus dicti, quia ad smilitudinem linee non habent nisi vnam dimensionem. Si[47] autem sermo habeat duo menbra vel tria, et quod quodlibet diuidatur in duo vel tria ita quod sint in vniuerso bis duo vel ter tria menbra,

43. in] O.U; *om.* L.A.

44. a primo . . . tercii] L.A.O, *possibly with an eyeskip; cf.* U: a primo primi usque ad primum secundi et a primo secundi usque ad primum tercii. Deinde fiat reductio ad secundum secundi et ad secundum tercii. Deinde redeat ad primum [*read* tercium] tercii et ad tercium secundi et ad tercium tercii.

45. principalium diuiderent in tria] O; istorum nouem diuiserunt (vltra L) in tria L.A; tercium principale diuidebant in tria U.

46. in] O.U; *om.* L.A.

47. Si] O.U; similiter L.A.

three kinds of virginity and then of three kinds of youth. But it would give the sermon elegance if in the last member of the first principal one could introduce the second principal by some sort of continuation or concatenation or mixture, and this would happen fittingly if one could find a different authority from the thema which mentions the first member and at the same time provides the second. For example, after having spoken of the threefold virginity, one might quote this authority: *Let youths and virgins, old men and youths, praise the name of the Lord.*[65] This already introduces the second principal, youth.

[b] The second way of developing a thema that is thus divided into three members is to go first from the first part of the first member to the second part of the second member and to the third of the third. This way used to be followed by elegant preachers in order to show the correspondence between the three parts of the first member and the three of the second and the three of the third. However, this way of development is less clear and rather convoluted.

Some exceedingly refined preachers were not content with nine members, arrived at by dividing each main member into three, but divided each of these nine further into three more, so that they had all together twenty-seven members. But this I consider[66] far too elegant and superfluously confusing, and therefore I will not give an example.

Some also abbreviate their sermon by dividing the first member into three parts and the second into two and leaving the third undivided, thus forming a "pyramid sermon." A pyramid is a figure with a broad base and a smaller middle leading up to a tip. Now, when a sermon has two or three members that are not divided further, it can be called a "linear sermon," just as a binary or ternary number is called linear, for like a line these have only one dimension. If however a sermon has two or three members and each is again divided into two or three parts, so that altogether there are twice two or three times three members, then this can be called a "plane sermon," just as twice two and three times three are called plane numbers, because like a plane they have two dimensions. But if a sermon has three members that are divided into two

65. Ps 148:12 (148:12).

66. C attributes this evaluation marginally to *Lincolniensis,* i.e., Grosseteste.

potest dici sermo superficialis, sicut bis duo et ter tria dicuntur numeri superficiales, quia ad similitudinem superficiei habent duas dimensiones. Si autem sermo habeat[48] tria menbra diuisa in duo vel tria, et quodlibet istorum foret diuisum in duo vel tria, ita quod forent menbra bis duo bis vel ter tria ter, etc., iam esset sermo cubicus vel solidus vel corporalis, quia ad similitudinem corporis habet tres dimensiones, sicut iste numerus bis duo bis et ter tria ter est numerus cubicus vel solidus vel corporalis, quia ad similitudinem corporis habet tres dimensiones et numeri replicaciones ternas.

Solent aliqui qui tenent communem modum predicandi diuidendo singulum trium menbrorum in tria, si primo exequerentur tria primi menbri per se, secundo tria secundi per se, et tercio[49] tria tercii per se, si inter illa esset correspondencia, in fine colligere et colligare vel epilogare sermonem, ostendendo quomodo singula singulis menbris corresponderent, et per vnam auctoritatem thema totum continentem vel excludentem, si posset haberi, concludere sermonem. Verbi gracia: Si hoc thema *Bonum semen seminasti* diuideretur in tria, quia in hoc themate tria notantur, scilicet creatoris operacio laudanda, ibi *seminasti;* creature incepcio admiranda, ibi *semen;* et eiusdem condicio approbanda, ibi *bonum semen,*[50] scilicet de Dei operacione et seminacione, sciendum est quod triplex est Dei seminacio sicut et eius operacio, scilicet creacio, iustificacio, et glorificacio. Et secundum hoc, opus eius quod incipit et[51] intelligitur per semen[52] triplex est, quia quoddam incipit esse, quoddam incipit bene[53] esse, et quoddam incipit esse feliciter siue beate esse. Et secundum hoc est triplex bonum, scilicet nature, gracie, et glorie. Colligam ergo sermonem sic et faciam vel formabo tales tres processus:

48. habeat] O; habens L.A; habens . . . habeat U.
49. tria secundi per se et tercio] O.U (*om.* et); *om.* L.A.
50. semen] A.O; *om.* L.U.
51. et] O.U; *om.* L.A.
52. semen] O.U; se enim L.A.
53. bene] O.U; bonum L.A; *but see the following division.*

or three, and each of the latter were to be further divided into two or three, so that there were twice two times two or thrice three times three parts, then this would be a "cube" or "solid" or "three-dimensional body sermon," because like a body it has three dimensions, just as the number "twice two times two" or "thrice three times three" is a cubic or solid or three-dimensional number. Like a three-dimensional body it has three dimensions and threefold repetition of its number.[67]

Some preachers who follow the common way of preaching by dividing each of three members into three, if they then develop the three parts of the first member separately, next the three parts of the second member separately, and finally the three parts of the third member separately, and if there is correspondence among them, they usually collect and bind together, or make an epilogue to, their sermon, showing how the single parts correspond to each other. And thus they conclude their sermon with a single authority that either contains or excludes the entire thema, if they can find one. For example, let the thema *You have sown good seed*[68] be divided into three, since three things are indicated in it, namely, the Creator's work, which is to be praised, in the words *You have sown;* the creature's beginning, which is to be admired, in the word *seed;* and the latter's quality, which is to be praised, in the words *good seed,* namely through God's working and sowing. Now, we should know that God's sowing and his work is threefold, that is, creation, justification, and bringing to glory. And accordingly, his work of establishing, which is indicated by *seed,* is threefold: one establishes being itself, another establishes well-being, and the third establishes being in bliss.[69] And accordingly there are three kinds of good, namely that of nature, of grace, and of glory. Now I can bind the sermon together and establish the following three developments:

67. For the number lore of this paragraph see Isidore, *Etymologies* 3.7.

68. Mt 13:27.

69. For these three aspects or degrees of God's creation, see for example John Scotus Erigena, *De diuisione naturae,* 5.

Seminasti per creacionem *semen* quod incipit esse, et ideo *bonum* propter nature condicionem;
seminasti per iustificacionem *semen* quod incipit bene esse, et ideo *bonum* propter gracie infusionem;
seminasti per glorificacionem *semen* quod incipit beate esse, et ideo *bonum* propter tui eternam fruicionem.

Et de toto hoc potest intelligi et exponi illud Mathei: *Simile est regnum celorum homini qui seminat bonum se-* [f. 175v] *men in agro suo.*

Augetur enim curiositas ostendendo conuenienciam vel consequenciam inter menbra diuisionum, sicut si dicerem: "Si bonum est triplex, scilicet nature, gracie, et glorie, secundum presupponit primum, et tercium presupponit primum et secundum." Vel sic potest dici: "Secundum sequitur ad primum, et tercium ad secundum," vel "tercium sequitur ad vtrumque." Quando eciam prosequitur a primo[54] primi ad primum secundi, et sic vsque ad primum tercii, et ab illo reditur ad secundum primi, et sic deinceps, si primum tercii et secundum primi conuertentur[55] in vna auctoritate, et similiter secundum secundi et tercium primi, posset dici sermo circularis,[56] quia quasi in circulo principium et finis conueniunt. Fatuum tamen reputo circa tales curiositates studere.

Alie eciam sunt[57] sermonum curiositates, quia aliqua sunt themata talia[58] quod post diuisionem in tria potest

54. primo] A.U; principio primi L.O.

55. conuertentur] L; committeretur (?) A; O.U *lack the clause;* conueniant C. *Read* conuenirent?

56. Quando...circularis] L.A; O *gives the clause in shorter form:* Quando eciam proceditur a principio primi ad primum secundi, etc., vsque ad primum tercii, et ab illo reditur vsque ad secundum primi, potest dici sermo circularis; U *has:* Quando eciam proceditur a primo primi usque ad secundi primum et sic usque ad tercium primi [*corrected from* primum], et ab illo reditur usque ad secundum primi, et deinceps usque ad primum tercii uel usque ad tercium primi, posset dici sermo circularis.

57. sunt] U; sic L.A; *om.* O.

58. sunt themata talia] O; sit thema L; sint themata A; aliqua themata U.

> *You have sown* through creation *the seed* which establishes being, and therefore it is *good* because of the condition of [created] nature;
>
> *you have sown* through justification *the seed* which establishes well-being, and therefore it is *good* because of the infusion of grace;
>
> and *you have sown* through bringing to glory *the seed* which establishes being in bliss, and therefore it is *good* because of eternally enjoying you.

And all this can be understood and explained in the words of Matthew: *The kingdom of heaven is like a man who has sown good seed in his field.*[70]

The elegance of a sermon can be further enhanced by showing how the members of the divisions agree with or follow each other. Thus, I could say: "If the good is threefold, namely of nature, of grace, and of glory, then the second presupposes the first, and the third presupposes both the first and the second." Or else I could say: "The second follows the first, and the third the second," or "the third follows both." Now, when one proceeds from the beginning of the first member to the first part of the second member, and so on to the first part of the third, and then returns to the second part of the first member, and so forth, if in this case the first part of the third member and the second of the first were to be combined in a single authority, and similarly the second part of the second member and the third of the first, the sermon could be called "circular," because just as in a circle the beginning and the end come together. However, I consider it foolish to devote much attention to such refinements.[71]

There are other sermon refinements. There are some themata where after a division into three one joins the members mutually together, so that one can say: "In the first and the second member, this is shown; in the first and the third, that is shown; in the second and the third, that is shown; and in all three members together, that is shown." Such a procedure can be followed only if authorities can be found that con-

70. This last quotation, Mt 13:24, combines the terms used in the division and thereby "binds up" the entire sermon. Notice that it verbally differs from the chosen thema, Mt 23:27. For this technique of combining the terms of the division in one scriptural quotation other *artes* also use the terms *unitio* or *complexio*.

71. Cf. the exposition of *circulatio* in Basevorn and his similarly negative judgment, 301–2.

fieri conclutinacio menbrorum adinuicem, vt dicitur sic: "In primo et secundo hoc notatur; in primo et tercio hoc notatur; in secundo et tercio hoc notatur; in omnibus tribus simul hoc notatur." Et hoc non potest fieri nisi vbi auctoritates possunt inueniri in quibus simul inuenitur primum menbrum et secundum et tercium, et omnia tria simul. Et talia themata sunt valde rara. Exemplum huius tamen patet in quibusdam collacionibus meis, scilicet de Gregorio vel Katerina, et fuit hoc thema *Requiescet in monte sancto;* et in quadam dominica, et tunc fuit thema *Tu quis*[59] *es.* Nec oportet hic exemplum adducere, quia curiositas est et modica vtilitas.

Vnde breuiter ego consulo quod ad predicandum non alia curiositas fiat[60] nisi pulcra diuisio principalis et subdiuisio ad plus cuiuslibet menbri in tria, quamuis quandoque fiat in quatuor, et hoc maxime est faciendum quando auctoritates ad propositum adducantur. Et primo fiat vna pulcra sentencia[61] per exemplum vel per auctoritatem sancti vel philosophi, et postea adducatur auctoritas sacre scripture que videtur directe dicere quod dixit sentencia[62] precedens. Vnde nunc quantum ad hoc est reperta vna bona curiositas que est, quando menbrum diuiditur vel subdiuiditur et debeat probari, primo probetur per racionem vel manuduccionem, secundo per auctoritatem sancti vel philosophi, tercio per auctoritatem litteralem sacre scripture, et quarto per signum vel figuram. Et ista est vtilis curiositas et pulcra, et iste modus est vt communiter modus bonorum predicatorum. Verumtamen non obstante quod illa curiositas sit vtilis et pulcra, tamen non potest communiter fieri, quia hoc esset nimis laboriosum, sicut patet exemplificando in proximo capitulo.[63]

[2] Alius est modus procedendi [f. 176] per auctoritatis adducte exposicionem et subdiuisionem. Verbi gracia, si accipiatur hoc thema *Surgam et ibo ad patrem meum,* supposita introduccione <diuidatur sic:

59. quis] A.U *and biblical source;* qui L.O.
60. fiat] O; stat L.A; *om.* U.
61. sentencia] U; summa L.A; summa vel sentencia O.
62. sentencia] O.U; summa L.A.
63. Sicut . . . capitulo] L.A; *om.* O.U *(with further confusion).*

tain the first, second, and third member at the same time, and all three together. Such themata are very rare. Yet an example of this procedure can be found in some of my collations, namely, in that on Gregory or Katherine, with the thema *He/she shall rest on the holy mountain,*[72] and in one on some Sunday with the thema *Who are you?*[73] It is not necessary to give an example here, for this procedure is refined and of little use.

I therefore advise that in preaching there should be no other refinement except an elegant main division and a subdivision of no more than three parts for each member, though it may sometimes have four parts, and this especially when relevant authorities are to be quoted. And first there should be a pleasing *sententia*[74] by means of an exemplum or a quotation from a saint or philosopher, and then an authority from Scripture should be introduced that can be seen to say directly the same as the preceding *sententia.* Which regard to this, nowadays a good refinement can be found when a member is divided or subdivided and then must be proven: first it should be proven by rational argument or a lead-in; second, by a quotation from a saint or philosopher; third by a literal quotation from Scripture; and fourth by a metaphor or *figura.*[75] Such refinement is useful and pleasing, and this is the common practice of good preachers. Nonetheless, even if such refinement is useful and pleasing, it cannot be used commonly, for that would be too laborious, as will be shown by an example in the next chapter.[76]

[2] The second way of development is by explaining and subdividing the quoted authority. For example, if the thema is *I will arise and go to my father,*[77] after the introduction let it be divided thus:

72. Ps 14:1 (15:1).

73. Jn 1:19 etc. The collations mentioned are unidentified.

74. *Sententia:* here not in the sense of "sentence" or "meaning," as earlier, but as "a pithy moral saying, proverb, aphorism," etc.

75. *Figura:* a (biblical) person or event that can carry an allegorical meaning.

76. There is no next chapter in this treatise.

77. Lk 15:18.

In verbis istis tria notantur: inchoacio reuertentis, Surgam,>[64] ibi *surgam,* expedicio proficientis, ibi *ibo;* et perfeccio peruenientis, ibi *ad patrem.* De primo dicit Apostolus: *Surge qui dormis et exurge a mortuis et illuminabit te Christus.*

Ista prima auctoritas, que probat menbrum diuisionis, non decet vt diuidatur, sed postea introducatur alia concordans auctoritas aliquo modorum[65] quo introducitur thema, et illa diuidatur sic:

Videmus \quod/ qui multum laborauit profunde dormit, et ideo indiget ex[c]itante qui eum excitet de mane, precipue si debet dietam magnam facere. \Sic/[66] peccator quamdiu exercuit peccata <sua> et actus peccatorum, multum laborauit, quia opera peccatorum sunt valde laboriosa, vnde in Sapiencia[67] dicitur: *Lassati sumus in via iniquitatis.* Et ideo profunde dormit in peccato quasi iam ductus consuetudine peccandi. Indiget igitur ex[c]itante, scilicet predicatore exterius clamante et Deo interius inspirante, et hoc quia habet magnam dietam \ire/ vel facere, scilicet a terra ad celum, a miseria ad beatitudinem.[68] Sed sicut magnam viam aggressurus in mane sumit cibum vt confortetur, sic peccator penitens cibum eukaristie et cibum verbi Dei vel cibum deuocionis accipiat antequam viam penitencie animus profunde ingrediatur. Et hoc est quod dicitur in <3 Regum> per angelum excitantem Helyam: *Surge, comede, grandis enim restat tibi via.*

Ecce quomodo factus est quidam pulcher processus, qui totus includitur in auctoritate <adducta, qua sic introducta diuidatur sic:

In auctoritate peccator excitatur> vt dimittat peccati soporem,[69] ibi *surge;* inuitatur ad celestis cibi saporem, ibi *comede;* certificatur magnum subire laborem, ibi *grandis enim restat tibi via.*

64. diuidatur...Surgam] L.U. *The marginal addition is lacking in* A *(hence clearly leaving an eyeskip);* O *also has a longer eyeskip.*

65. modorum] A.O.U; modo *and blank space,* L.

66. Sic] *interlin.* L; *om.* O.A.U.

67. in Sapiencia] O; ibi L.A; sapiencie U.

68. beatitudinem] L *(marg. to replace* bonitatem, *canc).*O.U; bonitatem A.

69. soporem] O.U; saporem L.A.

In these words three things are indicated: the beginning of a return, in the words *I will arise;* the undertaking of the progress, in the words *will go;* and the completion of arrival, in the words *to my father.* Of the first the Apostle says, *Rise, you who sleep, and arise from the dead, and Christ shall enlighten you.*[78]

This first authority, which confirms the [first] member of the division, should not be subdivided, but after it another authority that agrees with it may be introduced in one of the ways in which the thema is introduced, and that authority may then be subdivided as follows:

We see that someone who has worked hard sleeps deeply and thus needs someone to wake him in the morning, especially if he has a long day ahead. In the same way, a sinner has worked hard as long as he has been carrying out his sins and sinful acts, for sinful deeds are very toilsome. Hence it is said in the book of Wisdom: *We wore ourselves out in the way of iniquity.*[79] And therefore he is profoundly asleep in his sin, as if led by his custom of sinning. He therefore needs someone to wake him, namely a preacher to call him from the outside and God to inspire him from within, and this because he has a long day's work to go or to do, that is, from earth to heaven, from misery to blessedness. Now, a person who is about to go on a long journey eats in the morning so that he may be strengthened. Likewise, a sinner who repents must take the food of the Eucharist or the food of the word of God or the food of devotion before his mind can wholeheartedly set out on the way of penance. And this is what in 3 Kings the angel says to Elijah in exhorting him: *Arise, eat, for you still have a long way to go.*[80]

Lo, how an elegant development has been devised which is entirely included in the quoted authority, which after being thus introduced can then be divided as follows:

In this authority the sinner is awakened that he may shake off the sleep of sin, in the word *Arise;* he is invited to the taste of heavenly food, in the word *eat;* and he is informed that he has to undertake much labor, in the words *for you still have a long way to go.*

78. Eph 5:14.
79. Ws 5:7.
80. 1 Kgs 19:7.

Modo ad quodlibet istorum adducatur auctoritas inducta per racionem quare peccator debet surgere de peccato per simile de dormiente qui est quasi mortuus, quia secundum Philosophum 2 *Ethicorum* secundum mediam vitam, idest sompnum, studiosus non differt a misero, quando scilicet dormit. Consimiliter dum homo iacet in peccato \non differt/[70] a mortuo, idest dampnato. Et propter hoc Christus iuueni mortuo dixit: *Adolescens, tibi dico, surge!* Consimiliter ostendat per racionem quare debet comedere cibum spiritualem sic: "Sicut corpus sine cibo corporali deficit, sic similiter mens sine cibo spirituali." Exemplum enim in natura ad hoc est quod "<quamdiu> radices arboris attrahunt humorem, arbor viuit, et quando non attrahunt <humorem>,[71] moritur. Sic, etc." <Per auctoritatem:> "Vnde Augustinus in *Confessionibus* audiuit vocem de celo [f. 176v] dicentem[72] sibi: 'Cibus sum grandium; cresce et \manducabis/[73] me.'" <Quod> et per figuram: "In Actibus Apostolorum de Paulo dicitur: *Surgens baptizatus est et accepto cibo confortatus est.*" <Per auctoritatem litteralem:> "Auctoritas autem literalis ad hoc est in Ecclesiaste: *Comede in leticia panem tuum quia placent Deo opera tua.*"

Eodem modo ad tercium adducatur auctoritas per omnia ista vel per aliquod saltem istorum vel per plura istorum.

Iste modus predicandi per subdiuisionem auctoritatis facilis est vtique sed non placet curiosis nisi condiatur per multa et pulcra exempla et per pulcras deducciones et auctoritates sanctorum et philosophorum. Et racio est quod in auctoritate diuisa mox receditur a primo themate, sic quod quando peruenitur in auctoritate iam diuisa ad ly *comedo* et illud quod sequitur, iam enim recessum est ab illo primo themate *Surgam et ibo ad patrem meum.* In aliquibus tamen thematibus possibile erit et

70. non differt] L *(interlin.)*.O.U; *om.* A.

71. humorem] L *interlin.*; tunc O; A *garbled with eyeskip; om.* U.

72. dicentem] *the text on f. 176v is very faded, often to the point of being illegible. I have here reconstructed it with the help of A and O, whose scribes however experienced some difficulty.*

73. manducabis] O.U; *interlin. to replace* multiplicabis, L; multiplicabis A.

Now for each of these an authority should be quoted which gives a reason why a sinner must arise from his sin. By way of a simile: a person who sleeps is as it were dead, for according to the Philosopher in book 2 of the *Ethics*, according to the mean, namely sleep, a studious man is not any different from a wretched man, that is, when he is asleep.[81] In a similar way, as long as a person lies in sin he is not different from a dead one, that is, from one who is condemned. And therefore Christ said to the young man who was dead, *Young man, I say to you, arise!*[82] In the same way the preacher must give a reason why one needs to eat spiritual food, thus: "As the body without bodily food languishes, so likewise the mind without spiritual food." An example from nature for the same purpose is: "As long as the roots of a tree draw moisture, the tree lives, but when they do not draw moisture, it dies. In the same way, etc." Or he must prove the part with an authority: "Whence Augustine in his *Confessions* heard a voice from heaven saying to him: 'I am the food of grown men; grow, and you shall eat me.'"[83] With a *figura:* "In the Acts of the Apostles it is said of Paul: *Rising up he was baptized, and when he had taken food, he was strengthened.*"[84] With a literal authority: "But a literal authority regarding this part occurs in Ecclesiastes: *Eat your bread with joy, for your works are pleasing to God.*"[85]

In the same fashion, for the third part[86] an authority should be quoted by means of all these or at least one or several of them.

This manner of preaching by subdividing an authority is quite easy, but it does not please elegant preachers unless it is spiced with many beautiful exempla and with beautiful deductions and quotations from saints and philosophers. The reason for this is that in the divided authority one quickly leaves the original thema behind, so that, when in the already divided authority one comes to the word *eat* and what follows it, one has already left the original thema *(I will rise and go to my father)* behind. But in some themata it will be, and is, possible to find

81. Cf. Aristotle, *Nicomachean Ethics* 1.13 (1102b).
82. Lk 7:14.
83. Augustine, *Confessiones* 7.10.16.
84. Acts 9:18–19.
85. Eccl 9:7.
86. I.e., *to my father.*

est[74] inuenire concordanciam[75] subdiuise auctoritatis et principalis thematis simul, sic verbi gracia: Si ad tercium menbrum huius thematis iam diuisi, *Surgam et ibo,* etc., adducatur ista auctoritas *Pater vester misericors est,* etc., et subdiuidatur sic:

Hic tria notantur, scilicet Dei ad nos attinencia, ibi <*Pater;*> <in reuerencia dicitur: *Amodo voca me, Pater meus es tu.* Secundo notatur eius proba presidencia, ibi *vester;*[76] vt Luca dicitur:> *Pater vester dabit spiritum bonum petentibus se.* Tercio notatur eius grata beneuolencia, ibi *misericors est;* vnde Apostolus dicit: *Benedictus Deus et Pater Domini nostri Iesu Christi, pater misericordiarum et dominus tocius consolacionis nostre.*

Ecce in hiis auctoritatibus semper manet concordancia[77] principalis, quia *Pater,* et concordancia[78] de auctoritate diuisa, scilicet *vester* et *misericors.* Et ideo adducatur talis auctoritas que continet plures proprietates[79] illius diuisionis pro qua adducatur.[80] Et si fiat diuisio \super/ illis proprietatibus non recedetur a principali proposito thematis. Et reuera modus iste vltimus subtilis est et commendabilis et difficilis, quia in paucis thematibus potest inueniri talis concordia auctoritatum que ita sunt fecunde ad principale propositum et ad diuisiones sequentes.

Hec de modo predicandi secundum vsum modernorum ad presens sufficiunt, etc.[81]

74. erit et est] O; est et erit A; erit et *with blank space* L; est et U.

75. concordanciam] O.U; concordiam L.A.

76. vester] U; *om.* L.O; A *has a longer eyeskip.*

77. concordancia] O.U; concordia L.A.

78. concordancia] U; concordia L.A.; concordanter O.

79. proprietates] O; auctoritates L.A. *Notice the following* super illis proprietatibus. U *lacks the sentence.*

80. adducatur] O; additur L.A; U *lacks the sentence.*

81. etc.] L; *add* Amen O.A(?). *Instead of the final sentence* U *has:* Laus Christo, Amen. Explicit tractatus introductorius et breuis de modo predicandi editus a fratre Johanne de gwidernia de prouincia anglie ordinis predicatorum.

agreement between the subdivided authority and the main thema together, as for instance: If to the third member of the already divided thema (*I will rise and go,* etc.) one adds this quotation: *Your father is merciful,* etc., and then subdivides it as follows:

Here are three things indicated, namely, God's close relation with us, in the word *Father;* as it is said reverently: *From this time call to me: "you are my father."*[87] Second, his excellent rule, in the word *your;* as Luke says: *Your father will give a good spirit to those who call upon him.*[88] And third, his gracious benevolence, in the words *is merciful;* whence the Apostle says, *Blessed be the God and Father of Our Lord Jesus Christ, the father of mercies and lord of all our consolation.*[89]

Behold, there is always agreement within these quotations, in the word *Father,* and an agreement between them and the authority that has been divided, namely in the words *your* and *merciful.* In this way let an authority be added that contains several elements of the division for which it is added. And if a division is based on those elements, one will not leave the main proposition of the thema behind. Indeed, this last mode is subtle, commendable, and difficult, because such an agreement between authorities that thus enrich the original proposition and the following divisions can be found in few themata.

This much concerning the way of preaching according to the custom of modern preachers suffices for now, etc.

87. Jer 3:4.
88. Lk 11:13.
89. 2 Cor 1.3.

III
HIC DOCET

THE UNKNOWN AUTHOR of this short treatise begins by distinguishing a *collatio* from a *sermo* and then announces that he will treat four main features of a *collatio:* (I) the introduction of the thema, (II) its division, (III) the subdivision, and (IV) the use of proof texts to confirm the proposed meaning. These topics are dealt with by other *artes praedicandi* as well, but in comparison with the preceding work *(Quamvis),* for example, *Hic docet* pays greater attention to such aspects as the mode of speech that appears in the chosen thema, the form and function of the thema's introduction, details regarding the subdivision (which is the only mode of developing the sermon—or rather collation—dealt with here), and others. It therefore approaches the nature of a limited rather than a complete *ars praedicandi.* After dealing with the announced four topics, the author adds a fifth section (V), in which he deals with the difference between collation and sermon and discusses several additional features peculiar to the latter.[1]

The treatise contains several features that are reminiscent of the first part of the very popular *Ars concionandi* sometimes attributed to Bonaventure (Caplan 114).[2] Both begin with the same quotation from Augustine's *De doctrina christiana* (a work well known to and quoted by most medieval *artes praedicandi*), and then share the next sentence *(Et quia in hiis duobus).* But from that point on, *Hic docet* goes its own way. In discussing the mode of speech that appears in the thema (in part I) it lists a number of modes that occur also in Ps.-Bonaventure, but then adds more of its own, all without illustrations. At its end, in part V, it offers a distinction between *divisio interior* and *exterior,* which corresponds to Pseudo-Bonaventure's *divisio intra* and *extra,* including the appropriateness of the two modes for different audiences.[3] In general, *Hic docet* is nearly devoid of illustrative examples, in stark contrast to Ps.-Bonaventure as well as its two companion pieces in manuscripts L and A. It does, however, pay attention to and name several technical features of the scholastic sermon that are found in other *artes,* such as *claves,*[4] *sufficientia,*[5] *pes,*[6] and *preambulum* for the introductory statement.[7]

1. For the distinction between *sermo* and *collatio* in later-medieval England see Siegfried Wenzel, "A Note on *Collatio* in Late-Medieval Preaching," in *Swedish Students at the University of Vienna in the Middle Ages,* eds. Olle Ferm and Erika Kihlman (Stockholm: Centre for Medieval Studies, Stockholm University, 2011), 235–43.

2. The edited text is a composite of three parts, the third by Richard of Thetford. All three were printed as one work in the edition of Bonaventure, *Opera,* vol. 9 (Quaracchi: Patres Collegii S. Bonaventurae, 1901), 8–21.

3. Ibid., 8b.

4. *Claves* are discussed in Pseudo-Bonaventure (p. 9a), Higden (pp. 50–51), and *Vade* III.3.

5. *Sufficientia* also in Pseudo-Bonaventure (p. 9a–b), the unedited *Ad euidenciam simplicium* (Caplan Suppl b, in the Valencia manuscript), and *Vade* III.3.

6. *Pes* as *pedis posicio* in the anonymous *Dic nobis* (pp. 57–58), *Nota pro arte* (unedited, Caplan 89), and *Vade* III.3.

7. The term *preambulum* occurs also in the *artes* by Alfonso d'Alprão (Caplan Suppl 72), Christian Borgsleben (Caplan Suppl 155a), the anonymous "Ad euidenciam simplicium" (Caplan Suppl b, MS. Valencia 184), and as a variant in *Vade* (below, textual note 78).

The opening word *Hic,* "Here," poses a problem. At face value the word would refer back to something, but in this case it does not have a fitting antecedent—hardly the preceding treatise *Quamvis.* One suspects a scribal error for *Sic* or *Sicut,* a standard way of introducing a quotation. But L clearly begins with an enlarged *H,* while A has left a blank space for the initial with a clear guide letter *h. Hic docet* is manifestly a complete and independent treatise, but no independent treatise with the beginning *Sic(ut) dicit Augustinus* is listed by Caplan.

The treatise is known to exist only in the two manuscripts that preserve the three treatises *(Quamvis, Hic docet, Vade)* together:

Lincoln Cathedral Library, MS 234 (L), ff. 176v–179.
London, British Library, MS Additional 24361 (A), ff. 57v–60.

For more information about both manuscripts, see the headnote to *Quamvis* above.

For the edition I have used L, for the reasons explained in the headnote to *Quamvis.* The relation between L and A is the same as was described there. In the absence of further witnesses, suspected errors in both are emended by editorial suggestions that are based on grammar (at notes 2, 8, 13, etc.) and the context (at notes 6, 11, 14, 16, etc.).

HIC DOCET

TEXT

Lincoln Cathedral, MS 234
[f. 176v]

HIC DOCET AUGUSTINUS 4 *De doctrina Christi:* "Omnis tradicio scripturarum consistit circa modum inueniendi que intelligenda sunt, et circa modum prosequendi que intellecta[1] sunt." Et quia in hiis duobus principaliter predicandi et conferendi versatur negocium, non impertinens est videndum qualiter in istis debet peruigilare studium et intencio predicantis [f. 177] et eciam conferentis. Vbi primo sciendum est quod collacio debet esse materia sermonis, et ideo incipiendum est a modo et arte faciendi collaciones, quia quod[2] exigitur ad collacionem requiritur ad sermonem sed non econtra, quia plura concurrunt ad sermonem quam ad[3] collacionem.

Quantum ad artem faciendi collacionem sciendum est quod intencio conferentis debet versari circa quatuor, quia circa [I] thematis introduccionem, [II] diuisionem, [III] subdiuisionem, et [IV] auctoritatum applicacionem, per quas quidem auctoritates debet confirmari sentencia a conferente proposita.

[I]

Themate autem proposito cum sua cotacione, diligenter inspicienda est intencio principalis auctoris, vtrum scilicet verbum illud dirigatur vni persone vel multis personis, siue vtrum dicatur de vna persona vel de multis, hoc est vel per modum exortantis seu

1. intellecta] *thus source;* intelligenda L.A.
2. quod] *om.* L; igitur A.
3. ad] A; *om.* L.

HIC DOCET

TRANSLATION

HERE AUGUSTINE TEACHES in book 4 of his *The Doctrine of Christ:* "All handing on of Scripture is concerned with the way of finding what must be understood, and with the way of developing what has been understood."[1] And since the task of preaching and of making collations lies chiefly in these two things, it is not irrelevant to investigate how the preacher's as well as the collation maker's study and intention must be watchful in these matters. Hence we must first understand that a collation must be the subject matter of a sermon, and thus we must begin with the way and technique of making collations, because what is necessary for a collation is also required for a sermon, but not the reverse, for in a sermon more things come together than in a collation.

Regarding the technique of making a collation, we must know that the speaker's attention is to be directed to four things, namely: [I] the introduction of the thema, [II] the division, [III] the subdivision, and [IV] the application of authorities through which the topic proposed by the preacher is to be confirmed.

[I]

After a thema has been proposed, together with its source identification, one must diligently examine the main intention of its author, that is, whether that quotation is directed to one person or to many, or whether it is said about a single person or about many, and further if it

1. Augustine, *De doctrina christiana,* 4.1, referring back to 1.1.

ex[c]itantis, increpantis vel detestantis, imperantis, retrahentis vel alienantis, commendantis, alloquentis, promittentis vel terrentis, consolantis vel sub racione condonantis vel irridentis, vocantis[4] vel exoptantis, increpantis[5] vel auxilium postulantis, vel per alium modum quemcumque, forte ne in verbis introductoriis aliquid dicatur quod possit repugnare intencioni principali auctoris. Et quia si auctor principalis intendit commendare,[6] non debet dicere quod ipse increpat vel hortatur. Hoc est ergo principium quod est diligenter aduertendum circa thematis introduccionem.

Secundum notandum circa istam materiam est quod in principio collacionis debet premitti aliquid in quo contineatur et claudatur sentencia tocius thematis, vel aliquod preambulum ad sui sentenciam. Et illud potest fieri vel per verba alicuius sancti exponentis illud quod assumitur pro themate, vel eciam per verba ipsius conferentis et sentenciam sub aliis verbis recolligentis. Et illa sentencia dicitur pes vel fundamentum collacionis. In quo quidem pede latenter contineri debet aliquid vnde elici vel extrahi possit principalis diuisio ipsius thematis. Et vt ita fiat, diligenter debet conferens laborare, quia sicut multitudo presupponit vnitatem, et diuisio est actus integritatis particio, ita in arte conferendi presupponi debet et premitti aliqua sentencia integra. Et postea ex illa debet elici diuisio thematis principalis. Ista dicta sunt ad thematis introduccionem.

[II]

Quantum ad ipsius diuisionem, quod est secundum principale, diligenter probanda[7] est signacio verborum in themate positorum. Quorum [f. 177v] signatio transferri debet et mutari in verba cognate signacionis, idest propinque et consimilis signacionis. Que quidem verba semper voluenda et reuoluenda sunt[8] donec appareat aliqua formalis in qua tota sentencia principalis thematis,

4. vocantis] *nearly illegible,* L; bonantis(?) A; vocantis *appears in Ps.-Bonaventure; see the headnote above.*

5. increpantis] *already listed, a few lines above.*

6. commendare] *see preceding sentence;* comedere L.A.

7. probanda] *suggested emendation for* ponenda L.A.

8. sunt] sic L; sint A.

is said as the words of one who exhorts or incites, warns or repels, commands or withdraws or turns off, commends, addresses, promises or frightens, consoles or condones with reason or derides, calls or desires, warns or asks for help, or in whatever other way, so that in one's opening words one should not say something that perhaps contradicts the chief intention of the author. Thus, when the original author intends to praise, one must not say that he threatens or exhorts. This is the first thing one must carefully attend to with respect to the introduction of one's thema.

The second to be considered in this matter is that at the beginning of one's collation one should put something that contains and embraces the entire meaning of one's thema, or some preamble to its meaning. This can be done with the words of a saint who has expounded what is taken up as one's thema, or also with the words of the speaker himself who expresses that meaning in other words. That expression is called the "foot"[2] or "foundation" of the collation. In this "foot" something should lie enclosed from which the main division of the thema itself can be drawn. And in order to do that, the speaker must labor diligently, for just as a multitude presupposes unity, and a division is the splitting up of some integral matter, so must, in the art of preaching, some integral meaning[3] be presupposed and stated in advance. And after that the main division of the thema must be elicited from it. This much about the introduction of the thema.

[II]

With regard to its division—which is the second main section [of this treatise]—one must diligently examine the meaning of the words that appear in the thema. Their meaning must be transferred and changed into words that have a closely related meaning, that is, a meaning that is close and similar. These words must always be turned over and over [in one's mind] until a form appears in which the entire sense of the main thema finds expression, though divided and in parts. For the division of the thema must exhaust or express everything contained in the thema.

2. Foot: compare the explanation of *pedis positio* in the following treatise, *Vade* III.1.

3. By "integral meaning" and its expression the writer refers to what one might call the theme or topic of the sermon, derived from its thema and leading to the division.

licet diuisim et per partes, exprimi videatur. Nam diuisio thematis debet euacuare vel exprimere totum quod in themate continetur. Et iste partes diuidentes debent esse[9] verba, non tantum[10] propria sed eciam breuia, quia breuitas diuisionis super paucitatem verborum in partibus diuidentibus multum facit ad decorem collacionis. Si vero menbra diuidencia[11] primo non euacuent totam sentenciam thematis, debent apponi aliqua alia menbra per modum diuisionis ad primorum menbrorum[12] declaracionem, quousque totum contentum in themate appareat euacuatum. Et ista menbra sic apposita dicuntur claues, eo quod ad modum clauium apperiunt et reserant sentenciam inuolutam in primis menbris diuidentibus vel in principalibus verbis ipsius thematis. Et si primo diuidencia menbra non sunt in se sufficiencia, idest non diuidant ad vnum immediate, tunc ista menbra habent reduci ad aliqua menbra que vnum tercium immediate diuidere <possunt>. Et ista menbra que \ad/ alia reducuntur dicuntur sufficiencia collacionis.

Et post hec menbra iam diuisa possunt adduci auctoritates confirmantes sentenciam menbrorum diuisionis principalis et partes signari secundum partes diuisionis. Quando[13] vero in themate per aliquam rem corporalem designatur aliqua persona vel aliqua res spiritualis, tunc non debet fieri diuisio per verba cognate et consimilis signacionis, sed per verba exprimencia proprietatem vel condicionem illius persone eciam spiritualis. Verbi gracia: Proposito ad honorem beate Marie isto themate *Egredietur virga de radice Iesse,* potest dici quod ipsa comendatur vel describitur hic quantum ad tria, que sunt sanctitas[14] personalis, nouitas,[15] et dignitas parentalis. Primum notatur ibi, *virga;* secundum ibi, *egredietur;* et tercium ibi, *de radice Iesse.*

[III]

Quantum ad subdiuisionem faciendam: primo repeti debet illa pars thematis super quam cadebat primum menbrum principalis diuisionis, idest diligenter debent attendi proprietates et condiciones

9. debent esse] debent L; essent A.
10. tantum] t*amen* L.A.
11. diuidencia] diuidenda L.A. *See the following sentence.*
12. menbrorum] A; modorum L.
13. Quando] *written* Q L.A.
14. sanctitas] sanctitatis L.A.
15. nouitas] *evidently an adjective ending in* -alis *is missing,* L.A.

And these parts of the division must be words that are not only appropriate but also short, because brevity in the division achieved by few words in the dividing members is an important cause of the collation's elegance. But if the members of the division do not at first exhaust the complete sense of the thema, some further members must be added by way of a [second] division which explain the first members, until everything contained in the thema is clearly extracted. These members that are thus added are called "keys," because like keys they open and close the sense involved in the first members of the division or in the main words of the thema itself. And if the members of the division at first are not self-sufficient, that is, if they do not fully divide at once, then these members must be reduced to some members that can at once divide a third set. And these members that are reduced to others are called the "rationale" of the collation.[4]

After these dividing members, we can quote authorities that confirm the sense of the members of the main division and mark the parts according to the parts of the division. Now, when in the thema something corporeal designates a person or something spiritual, then the division must not be made by means of words of a cognate or similar meaning, but rather by words that express a property or condition of that person or spiritual object. For example: Given that in honor of Blessed Mary this thema is proposed: *A rod shall come forth from the root of Jesse,*[5] one can say that Blessed Mary is here commended or described by three things, namely personal holiness, newness, and and a parent's worthiness. The first is shown in the words *A rod;* the second in *shall come forth;* and the third in *from the root of Jesse.*

[III]

With respect to making a subdivision: first one must repeat that part of the thema which the first member of the main division has divided; that is, one must diligently consider its properties and condi-

4. The notions of "key" and "rationale" in a sermon are more fully explained and illustrated in *Vade,* parts III.3 and IV–V.2.

5. Is 11:1.

ipsius, non solum in se sed in relacione ad alias partes illius thematis. Et si illa particula contineat rem nominaliter signatam,[16] subdiuisio potest fieri per adiec- [f. 178] tiua, vel per genitiuos casus, vel per accusatiuos, vel per casus alios prout requirit materia. Verbi gracia: Si in themate fuerit hoc nomen *Dominus* et dicatur de Deo aut de Christo, dici potest quod "ipse Deus est metuendus, audiendus, diligendus," vt possint hic fieri claues et sufficiencia sicut in diuisione principali sic: "metuendus quia potentissimus, audiendus quia scientissimus, diligendus quia clementissimus." Uel: "Propter potenciam, scienciam, et clemenciam." Et de aliis quere exempla satis.

Si autem illud super quod cadit diuisio fuerit res verbaliter signata, tunc diuisio potest fieri per aduerbia, per gerundiua et per casum talem qualem per eum regi habet, per preposiciones cum suis casualibus, uel eciam aliis modis secundum exigenciam materie. Et eodem modo[17] iudicandum est de aliis. Iste subdiuisiones et eciam claues earum semper fiant[18] cum verbis paucis.

In omnibus vero diligenter est cauendum vt nullum menbrum prime diuisionis coincidat[19] cum alio menbro eiusdem subdiuisionis et eciam cum alio menbro secunde subdiuisionis (hoc est cum subdiuisione que debet fieri super secundam partem thematis), nec eciam cum aliquo menbro principalis diuisionis. Nam co\in/cidencia menbrorum repugnat nature diuisionis. Vnde semper laborandum est vt menbra subdiuidencia contineantur sub principali diuisione. Sic "animal" diuiditur in leonem, bouem, et capram. Si quis debet diuidere "animal" et dicat quod aliud est substancia animata, aliud inanimata, dupliciter peccat siue errat, quia primum est idem[20] cum eo quod debet diuidi,[21] et per consequens co\in/cidit cum eo; et secundum menbrum non continetur in[22] eo et ideo non se habet ad ipsum sicut pars ad suum totum. Et constat quod diuisum se debet habere ad

16. signatam] sanctificatam L.A; *see also next paragraph.*

17. modo] A; *om.* L.

18. fiant] stant (?) L.A.

19. coincidat] *both mss. write* concidat, *here and afterwards. But notice the two instances of interlinear insertion in the next sentences, in* L. *See further textual note* 65 *to* Vade.

20. idem] illud L.A.

21. diuidi] dici L.A.

22. in] *possibly* cu[m] L; cum A.

tions, not only in themselves but also in relation to the other parts of the thema. If that part contains something expressed by a noun, the subdivision can be made with adjectives, or genitive cases, or accusatives, or any other cases, as the subject requires. For example: If the thema contains the noun *Lord,* and it refers to God or to Christ, one can say, "God is to be feared, listened to, and loved," so that one can make keys and a rationale just as in the main division, namely: "He is to be feared as the most powerful, listened to as the most knowing, and loved as the most merciful." Or else: "Because of his power, knowledge, and mercy." For the other situations you can find many examples.

But if that part [of the thema] which has been divided was a verb form, then the [sub]division can be made by means of adverbs, gerunds and that [grammatical] case that has to be governed by it,[6] prepositions with their objects, or further modes as the subject matter requires. And the same must be observed in other situations. These subdivisions and their keys should always be made with few words.

In all this one must, however, beware diligently that no member of the first division coincides[7] with another member of its subdivision, nor with another member of the second subdivision (that is, the subdivision that should be made of the second part of the thema), nor with any member of the main division. To have coinciding members is against the nature of division. Hence one must always strive that the subdividing members are included in the main division. For example, "animal" is divided into lion, ox, and goat. Now, if someone has to divide "animal" and says that "some being is animate, another inanimate," he errs or is mistaken in two ways, because his first part ["animate being"] is the same as what he is dividing, and therefore coincides with it; his second part ["inanimate being"] is not included in it at all and therefore is

6. Tentative translation. I take *eum* in the text to refer to *gerundivum* (or *gerundium,* which may be intended). The meaning seems to be that a verb form in the thema may be divided by a gerund followed by (a noun) in the case required by the respective verb. An alternate meaning may be that such a division may be made with a gerundive plus noun or other word in whatever case is required; for instance: *Te salvum fecit > ostendendo per legem . . . , predicando per seipsum . . . , manifestando in martiribus . . . , humiliando se ad mortem* (Alcok).

7. "Coincides": has the same or a closely related meaning, such as "animal" and "animated being" in the following example.

diuidencia sicut totum ad suas partes, sicut eciam videmus manifeste in rebus corporalibus.

[IV]

Quantum autem ad menbrorum subdiuisionum confirmacionem per applicacionem[23] auctoritatum: primo debet repeti menbrum subdiuisionis cum verbo principalis thematis, et postea debet auctoritas cum cotacione libri seu capituli allegari. In qua auctoritate diligenter est aduertendum vt sit vocalis et realis. Tunc autem est vocalis quando in se habet verbum illud super quod fiebat subdiuisio, et tunc est realis quando clamat et probat illam sentenciam que in menbro subdiuisionis continetur. Si vero non inueniatur aliqua vna auctoritas que habeat istas duas condiciones, possunt due auctoritates adduci, quarum vna est vocalis et alia realis. Racio autem quare auctoritas adducenda [f. 178v] debet esse realis et vocalis est quia, nisi fuerit realis, non probat illud quod in subdiuisione assumitur, et nisi sit vocalis, non valet ad thema propositum magis quam aliud quodcumque proponendum. Iuxta hoc eciam diligenter est obseruandum vt in verbis quibus applicari debet auctoritas ad sentenciam subdiuisionis obseruetur ille modus loquendi qui magis congruit auctoritati, quia si auctoritas dicatur in prima persona, in verbis quibus applicari debet fiet mencio de prima persona, et eodem modo sciendum est de secunda et tercia. Si vero in menbro confirmando fiat mencio de vna persona et in auctoritate confirmante de pluribus personis, tunc in verbis conuertentibus debet dici: "Vnde de isto et sibi similibus potest dici illud quod scribitur tali loco." Si vero e contrario, vtpote si in verbo confirmante de vna persona, tunc in verbis conuertentibus debet dici: "Vnde de quolibet tali debet dici illud," etc. Et per simile iudicandum est de aliis modis lo-

23. applicacionem] ampliacionem L.A.; *see the beginning of the treatise and instances of* (auctoritas) applicari *throughout.*

not related to it as a part is related to its whole. It is clear that what is to be divided relates to its divisions as a whole to its parts, as we clearly see in corporeal objects.

[IV]

With respect to confirming the members of subdivisions by means of applying authorities: first we must repeat the member of the subdivision with the word of the main division, and then an authority must be quoted with citation of its book or chapter. One must diligently see to it that this authority agrees verbally and in its sense. It agrees verbally when it contains the same word that was subdivided; it agrees in sense when it expresses or proves the meaning that is contained in the member of the subdivision. Now, if no single authority can be found that fulfills these two conditions, one may quote two different authorities—one in verbal agreement, the other in sense. The reason why the authority to be adduced should agree in sense and verbally is this: unless it agrees in sense, it does not prove what is stated in the subdivision; and unless it agrees verbally, it is of no use for the proposed thema any more than anything else one could say. In this regard, one must diligently see to it that in the words to which the authority is to be applied for the meaning of the subdivision, that form of speech is used that agrees closely with the authority. If the authority is in the first person, in the words to which it is to be applied must be a reference to the first person, and the same with respect to the second and the third person. But if in the member that is to be confirmed a single person is mentioned, and the confirming authority uses several persons, then one must say in one's linking words, "Therefore of this and of others that are similar may be said what is written in such and such a place." But if the opposite is the case, namely, if [the passage to be confirmed contains several persons and] in the confirming quotation only one person is mentioned, then in one's linking words one should say: "Therefore, of each of these must be said," etc. And the same should apply to other speech forms[8] that

8. "Other speech forms" refers back to what was said in the first paragraph of part I, as does the preceding distinction between one and several persons.

quendi qui poterunt inueniri in qualibet auctoritate adducenda. Et in fine[24] collacionis debet dici verbum tale vel simile: "Propter hec et alia dicit," etc.

Et sic terminatur in generali ars faciendi collaciones propter artem iam dictam, que est communis tam collacioni quam sermoni.

[V]

Requiritur aliud speciale in sermonibus faciendum. Nam in quolibet menbro subdiuisionis possunt adduci diuerse auctoritates canonis uel sanctorum, et auctoritates canonis quandoque, si videtur expediri, possunt exponi ac diuidi artificialiter, acsi quedam auctoritas debeat[25] adduci pro principali themate. Sed iste modus procedendi est sumptuosus et difficilis, licet sit subtilis. Et prosequendo debent fieri inuenciones vel ad commendandum bonitatem vel ad detestacionem prauitatis. Item ad maiorem sermonis dilatacionem possunt duci exempla et narraciones de vitis sanctorum. Et diligenter notandum quod quandoque aliquid sensibile adducitur pro aliqua moralitate facienda, semper cauere debet predicator vt in exempli sui adaptacione habeat verba propria et examinata secundum exigenciam materie et exempli. Et in fine sermonis facienda est oracio secundum beatum Augustinum dicendo aliquid per modum oracionis, scilicet "quod nobis prestare dignetur," vel aliquid simile.

Iuxta predicta sciendum est quod in sermonibus precipue potest esse duplex diuisio thematis, et similiter duplex subdiuisio. Nam diuisio potest esse exterior vel interior, potest eciam thema sub- [f. 179] diuidi vel per diuisionem exteriorem vel interiorem.[26] Tunc autem thema diuiditur diuisione exteriori quando aliquod verbum in themate distinguitur secundum diuersas ipsius accep-

24. fine] ?; fto L.A. *The sentence remains puzzling, and perhaps collacionis is an error.*

25. debeat] A; debent L.

26. Nam ... interiorem] *suggested emendation required by the sentence sense.* Nam diuisio potest esse exteriorum, potest enim subdiuidi vel per diuisionem exteriorem vel interiorem L; nam potest esse exterior potest enim thema uel per diuisionem exteriorem uel interiorem A.

could be found in whatever authority is to be cited. And at the end of the collation something like the following must be said: "On account of this and other things it says," etc.

And thus ends in a general way the art of making collations by way of the technique that has been laid out, which is common to both collations and sermons.

[V]

In making sermons something special is required. For in any member of the subdivision several authorities from Scripture or the saints may be quoted, and the authorities from Scripture may sometimes, when it seems expedient, be explained and artfully divided, just as for the main thema some authority must be adduced.[9] This procedure, however, is lavish and difficult, even if it is subtle. And in the development one must find devices either to commend goodness or to reproach depravity. Also, in order to dilate the sermon further, one can bring in *exempla* and stories from the lives of the saints. And the preacher must be attentive that, whenever something concrete is cited for his moral teaching that is to be deduced from it, he must take heed that in applying his example he uses proper and carefully chosen words that his subject matter and his example require. And at the end of the sermon one must make a prayer, according to blessed Augustine, by saying something in prayer form, such as "which he may grant us," or something similar.

According to what has been said, we should know that sermons in particular may have a twofold division of the thema, and likewise a twofold subdivision. For a division can be exterior or interior, and a thema can be subdivided by an exterior or interior division. The thema is divided by an exterior division when a word in the thema is divided according to different meanings it has in Holy Scripture. For example, if one takes as one's thema the sentence *Truth has sprung out of the earth,*[10] one can say that, "*Earth* is, in Holy Scripture, sometimes

9. I understand the author to say that in a collation members of a subdivision *may* be confirmed with proof texts, just as *(acsi)* members of the division of the main thema *must* have some confirming proof text.

10. Ps 84:12 (85:11).

ciones in sacra scriptura. Verbi gracia: Si quis pro themate accipiat hoc verbum *Veritas de terra orta est,* potest dicere quod "*Terra* aliquando in sacra scriptura accipitur pro machina mundiali, aliquando pro vtero virginali, et aliquando pro Ecclesia militante, et aliquando pro Ecclesia triumphante. Sed in proposito accipitur *terra* pro vtero virginali de quo ortus est Filius Dei, qui in proposito *veritas* appellatur." Et ista diuisio exterior debet poni in principio sermonis ante diuisionem interiorem, et est pulcer modus introducendi thema. Interior diuisio thematis est quando tota sentencia in themate contenta per partes diuiditur et distinguitur per verba cognate et consimilis signacionis, sicut dictum est superius. Subdiuisio interior est quando omnia membra subdiuidencia continentur sub membro principali sine coincidencia[27] aliorum membrorum, sicut dictum est superius. Sed tunc est subdiuisio exterior quando propter maiorem edificacionis occasionem uel materie dilatacionem subdiuisio extenditur ad aliqua que non sunt contenta sub menbro principali. Et quamuis iste modus possit obseruari a predicatoribus ruralibus, tamen a scolaribus, qui debent ingenia sua exercere, nullatenus debet obseruari, etc.

27. coincidencia] concidencia L.A; *see above note* 19.

taken to mean the universe, sometimes the womb of the Virgin, sometimes the Church Militant, and sometimes the Church Triumphant. But in the stated thema *earth* is taken to mean the womb of the Virgin, from which the Son of God has sprung, who in the announced thema is called *Truth.*" This exterior division must, at the beginning of the sermon, be put before the interior division, and it is a beautiful way of introducing the thema. An interior division of the thema occurs when the entire meaning contained in the thema is divided into parts and differentiated by words of a cognate and similar meaning, as has been said above. An interior subdivision occurs when all members of the subdivision are contained in their principal member without coincidence of the other members, as was said earlier. But an exterior subdivision occurs when, for the sake of a greater degree of edification or of expanding the subject matter, the subdivision is extended to some matter that is not contained in the respective main member. Although this way may be practiced by country preachers, scholars, who should exercise their ingenuity, should in no way practice it, etc.

IV
VADE IN DOMUM

THE OPENING SENTENCE of *Vade,* quoting Matthew 9:6, introduces the image of a house, whose parts—foundation, walls, entrance door (with threshold, opening, key, and lock), windows, window panes, and roof—are then systematically applied to the standard six parts of a sermon. In its style and thought *Vade* is more sophisticated than its two companion pieces, as already shown in its consistent use of the house image for its structure. In addition, its author employs a refined technical vocabulary with such terms as *clavis, sufficientia,* and *pedis positio,*[1] which he discusses by defining them and explaining the definition's component parts. In many ways this treatise is closer to technical scholastic thinking than its companions; one can easily see the difference by comparing its explanation of the common requirement that the thema

1. Cf. the headnote to *Hic docet,* notes 3–5.

must make grammatical and lexical sense (in the fourth paragraph of part I, *Tercio principaliter*) with the corresponding parts in *Quamvis* and *Hic docet.* Like *Hic docet,* this work also comments on the difference between *sermo* and *collatio.*

SOURCES

The treatise has been preserved as follows:

Lincoln Cathedral Library, MS 234 (L), ff. 179v–182v.

London, British Library, MS Additional 24361 (A), ff.60–63. For more information on this and the above manuscript, see the headnote to *Quamvis.*

Wolfenbüttel, Herzog August Bibliothek, MS 4047 (82.8 Quodl.) (W).[2] Paper, end of the fifteenth century, containing one manuscript of twenty folios and nine incunables bound together. *Ars collacionandi siue sermocinandi,* "Vade in domum tuam," imperfect, ff. 1–16. Followed by excerpts from "Fulgentius," that is, moralized pictures, stories, canonical matter, and a *forma absolutionis.* In this version, the treatise is a compilation made up of most of the material of *Vade* but arranged in a different order, with parts from *Quamvis* and from other texts (perhaps including Thetford).

THE TEXT

Establishing a semicritical text for *Vade* presents an even greater challenge than it does for *Quamvis* and *Hic docet.* Here L and A contain many clear or putative errors, suggesting that their scribes, or perhaps rather the scribe of their exemplar, had greater difficulty understanding the more sophisticated text of *Vade* than that of the other two treatises, as can be seen in the textual notes.[3] On the other hand, in the respective passages—if they are present in W—W is clear and usually makes

2. Otto von Heinemann, *Die Augusteischen Handschriften,* in *Die Handschriften der Herzoglichen Bibliothek zu Wolfenbüttel,* Alte Reihe, Zweite Abteilung (Frankfurt a. M.: Klostermann, 1965–66), vol. 5, 251–52; and private communication from Dr. Bertram Lesser dated July 8, 2009.

3. Especially good examples occur at notes 41, 62, and 73.

good sense. It would have been chosen as the "best text" were it not that its entire composition seems to be secondary, for *Vade* is here clearly made of up of pieces from several different treatises, including the text as found in AL but here rearranged. I have therefore decided to continue to use L as my base text and have emended it from A and particularly W more frequently than was necessary in *Quamvis* and *Hic docet.*

VADE

TEXT

Lincoln Cathedral, MS 234
[F. 179]

UADE[1] IN DOMUM TUAM. Secundum Magistrum *Historiarum* in principio, sicut imperatoris maiestatis est tres in palacio mansiones possidere, idest auditorium in quo iura recte discernat, necnon et cenaculum in quo cibos grate distribuat, sed eciam thalamum in quo rite ipse requiescat, sic imperator noster Christus, qui vniuerse creature imperat, potencius[2] mundum pro auditorio, animam iusti habet pro thalamo, et sacram scripturam pro cenaculo optinet gloriose secundum illud Psalmi *In domo Dei ambulavimus cum consensu,* idest in sacram scripturam idipsum sencientes. Quia igitur in hac tanquam in domo quadam conuiuii varia virtute fercula seriose ministrantur, varia doctrine pocula [f. 179v] copiose propinantur (secundum Gregorium ix *Morum*), qui populum reficere intendis docendo Dei verbum, huius scripture sacre *vade in domum.* Et sic per hec verba sacra scriptura dupliciter descripta ad presens relucet, quia—

vt laborum[3] imperatrix, torporis extirpatrix, solercius operando, *Vade;*

1. *The text on f. 179 in L is nearly illegible and has here been edited with the help of A and W.*
2. potencius] L.A; patencius W.
3. laborum] L.A; laboris W. *The latter form would be required to establish the usual rhyme (with* torporis*); but see the repeated line in III.4,* p. 178.

VADE

TRANSLATION

GO INTO YOUR HOUSE.[1] According to the Master of the *Histories,* at the beginning, it is natural for the imperial majesty to have three chambers in his palace, namely, an audience hall, where he decides judicial cases; a dining hall, where he graciously distributes food; and also a bedroom, where he properly takes his rest.[2] In the same way, our emperor Christ, who rules over all creation, holds even more powerfully[3] in his glory the world as his audience hall, the soul of a just person as his bedroom, and Holy Scripture as his dining hall, according to the words of the Psalm, *In the house of God we walked with consent,*[4] that is, in Holy Scripture, by giving our consent. Since therefore in Scripture as in a banqueting house food is offered in successive dishes of varying strength [and] various cups of doctrine are offered to drink in plenty (according to Gregory in book 9 of his *Moral Commentary*),[5] you who intend to refresh the people by teaching the word of God, *go into the house* of this Holy Scripture. Hence, in these words Holy Scripture shines forth as for now described in two ways, namely:

as commanding work and uprooting torpor by working more diligently, *Go;*

1. Mt 9:6, etc.
2. Peter Comestor, *Historia scholastica* (PL 198:1053).
3. "Even more powerfully": W reads *patencius,* "more clearly."
4. Ps 54:15 (55:14).
5. Cf. Gregory, *Moralia in Job* 1.1.19 (PL 75:539).

vt quiescentis habitaculum, vt fugientis refugium, securius conseruando, *in domum.*

Labor torporem repellit longius, cum quiescenti ociose profectus[4] demandatur, *vade;*

territus[5] timorem euadit leuius, cum fugienti operose locus quietis datur, *in domum.*

Primum[6] actiuam, secundum[7] contemplatiuam vitam significat.[8]

Primam renuenti et ociose torpescenti precipitur[9] Prouerbiorum 6: *Vade ad formicam, o piger,* etc.

Secundam vero attingere et habere cupiditatem docet Psalmista sic Deum exorare: *Esto michi in Deum protectorem et in domum refugii vt saluum me facies,* Psalmo 30.[10]

Domus autem materialis artificialiter constructa fundamentum et murum, ostium[11] et fenestram, lumen[12] et tectum dinoscitur possidere. Que sex partes principales et in predicando vsuales mistice signant,[13] vt sic primum parti prime, secundum secunde, tercium tercie, quartum quarte, quintum quinte, et sextum sexte valeat applicari.

[I]

Sicut enim in domo materiali quoddam firmum[14] preiacitur fundamentum quod alia superedificanda, vt sunt[15] murus et tectum et luminaria,[16] valeat supportare, in sermone dumtaxat

4. profectus] W; prostratus L.A.

5. territus] L.A; interitus W. *This word should echo* labor *of the preceding line, but nothing fitting other than* terror *comes to mind. See also the repetition of these lines below in section III.4.*

6. Primum] W; prima L.A.

7. secundum] W; secunda L.A.

8. significat] W; preficiat L.A.

9. precipitur] W; precio L; precem(?) A.

10. Psalmo 30] *source of quotation;* pro tercio L.A; *om.* W.

11. ostium] W; *om.* L.A; *but see the development below in section III, also shared with* W.

12. lumen] limen L.A; luminis diffusionem siue lu' W.

13. signant] preficiant L.A, *perhaps intended as* prefigurant; W *lacks the sentence.*

14. firmum] *add* et L.A; *lacking in* W.

15. sunt] sicut L.A; *lacking in* W.

16. luminaria] A; liminaria L; *passage lacking in* W.

and as giving a dwelling to one who rests and shelter to one who is in flight by protecting him more securely, *into the house.*

Work drives torpor far away when he who lies in idleness is commanded to progress, *Go;*

and one who is terrified evades his fright easily when he, as he flees and works, is given a place of rest, *in the house.*

The former signifies the active life; the latter, the contemplative.

The person who rejects the former [i.e., the active life] and becomes indolent in idleness is bidden to *Go to the ant, o sluggard,* etc., Proverbs 6.[6] But in order to have the desire to reach and obtain the second, the Psalmist teaches to pray to God: *Be to me a God, a protector, and a house of refuge to save me,* Psalm 30.[7]

Now, a material house that is built according to the rules of building is known to have a foundation and a wall, a door and a window, a window pane and a roof. These also symbolize the six main parts that are usual in preaching, so that the first can be applied to the first part, the second to the second, the third to the third, the fourth to the fourth, the fifth to the fifth, and the sixth to the sixth.

[I]

For as in a material house first something firm is laid down as the foundation, which can then support other parts that are to be built on top of it, such as the wall and the roof and the window panes, so in a sermon, at least in a formal one, the thema is laid down first as its foundation, so that it may underlie and support the other parts that are later to be built on it, namely, the introduction, division, subdivision, and also the development. This foundation must be triangular, in that the thema that is to be chosen must have three properties, namely [1] strength, [2] appropriateness, and [3] completeness.

6. Prv 6:6.
7. Ps 30:3 (31:2).

formali pro fundamento thema[17] premittitur, ut aliis imposterum construendis, que sunt introduccio, diuisio, et subdiuisio, et eciam prosecucio, ipsum thema subsit et subiciatur. Hoc vero fundamentum et triangulare esse debet, tres proprietates continendo thematis assumendi vt sit [1] firmum, [2] congruum, et [3] perfectum.

[1] Vt autem huiusmodi fundamentum firmum reddatur, ex sacra scriptura sumi debet, dicente beato Gregorio 18 *Morum,* capitulo 28: "Qui ad vere predicacionis verba se parat, necesse habet vt a sacris paginis[18] originem sumat, vt omne quod dicit aut loquitur ad diuine auctoritatis fundamentum reuocet atque in eo fundamentum sue locucionis firmet."

[2] Secundo, hoc fundamentum debet esse congruum, et hoc quantum[19] ad ordinem in se, quantum ad terminum quo deriuatur,[20] et quantum ad terminum cui dirigitur. Primum requirit vt nomen cum verbo, casus cum persona, adiectiuum cum substantiuo rite[21] disponatur. Secundum requirit vt thema congruum habeat autorem a quo oritur. Propter quod dicunt aliqui quod dicta reproborum, cuiusmodi sunt ista: *Mitte te deorsum, Hec omnia tibi dabo si cadens adoraueris* [f. 180] *me, Quem teipsum facis,* et cetera consimilia, pro themate nullatenus assumi debent. Tercium eciam exigit quod thema conueniat auditorio cui predicatur. Quapropter volens predicare religiosis et assumat pro themate *Vos ex patre diabolo estis,* peccabit[22] in assumendo, eo quod thema debet esse conueniens persone et etati, sexui et statui, loco et tempori.

[3] Tercio[23] principaliter debet hoc fundamentum esse perfectum. Quod dupliciter ad presens intelligi potest. Aut quia perfeccio mouet intellectum ad aliquid penes veritatem uel falsitatem intelligendum, et sic requiritur quod thema sit oracio indicatiua

17. thema . . . perfectum] *a large tear in* L. *Missing text supplied from* A.

18. paginis] A; paginibus L; *passage lacking in* W.

19. quantum] *required by sense and parallelism;* consequenter L.A; *om.* W.

20. deriuatur] *suggested emendation required by meaning, for* diuiditur L.A; *om.* W.

21. rite] L; recte A; *passage lacking in* W.

22. peccabit] precauet L.A; *sentence lacking in* W.

23. Tercio] tercium L.A; *phrase lacking in* W.

[1] To make this foundation strong, it must be taken from Holy Scripture, as blessed Gregory says in book 18 of his *Moral Commentary,* chapter 28: "He who prepares himself for the words of true preaching must of necessity begin with Holy Scripture, so that everything he says or speaks about he refers to the foundation of divine authority and anchors in it the foundation of his own speech."[8]

[2] Second, this foundation must be appropriate, and this with respect to its own order, to its source, and to its intended purpose. The first requires that a noun agree properly with the verb, a grammatical case with the respective person, and an adjective with its substantive. The second requires that the thema have an appropriate author from whom it originates. Therefore, some say that the words of evil speakers, such as, *Cast yourself down,*[9] *All these I will give you if you fall down and adore me,*[10] or *Whom do you make yourself?*[11] and similar passages, must in no way be chosen for the thema. And the third requires that the thema is appropriate to the audience to whom it is preached. Hence, if one wants to preach to religious and takes as one's thema *You are of your father, the devil,*[12] one chooses very wrongly, because the thema must be appropriate to the persons [who hear it], their age, gender and status, place and time.

[3] Third, following the main numbering, this foundation must be complete. This for now can be understood in two ways. [a] Completeness moves the intellect to an understanding of something that is true or false, and this requires that the thema be a declarative sentence, either affirmative or negative. If it is affirmative, no negation must be

8. Gregory, *Moralia* 38.26 (PL 76:58).
9. Mt 4:6.
10. Mt 4:9.
11. Jn 8:53.
12. Jn 8:44.

affirmatiua uel negatiua—si affirmatiua, non debet addi negacio; si vero negatiua, non debet omitti[24] negatiua ne ipsius auctoritatis sentencia omittatur. Aliunde eciam potest thema esse perfectum, uel quia sua perfeccio mouet intellectum ad aliquid prosequendum, vt cum dicitur *Surge et ambula;* vel ad[25] aliquid fugiendum,[26] vt cum dicitur *Nolite diligere mundum;* vel ad aliquid optinendum, vt cum dicitur *Salua nos, perimus;* vel ad aliquid interrogandum, vt cum dicitur *Cuius est ymago hec?* Et consimiles quamuis quoad veritatem vel falsitatem inperfecte sint, habent tamen aliquid in se subintelligendum mediante quo perficitur intelleccio ad aliquid exequendum vel subintelligendum. Et ideo quelibet talis oracio, dummodo de canone Biblie fuerit assumpta, satis perfecta est et pro quolibet themate licite assumenda. Sunt tamen alie oraciones que tam in se quam de se imperfecte sunt, cuiusmodi sunt iste: *Loquente Iesu ad turbas, Sedente Iesu super montem Olilueti,*[27] *Ascendente Iesu in navicula.* Tales oraciones et consimiles nullatenus pro themate assumi debent, eo quod non moueant intellectum ad aliquid intelligendum.

Sic ipso fundamento firmius collocato, aliqualiter ad proposicionem congrue applicatur:

Hec est domus Domini, firma, et bene fundata est supra firmam petram. *Petra autem erat Christus,* in quo tota[28] scriptura tam vetus quam nouelle plenius continentur. *Aliud autem fundamentum preter illud quod iam positum est nemo potest ponere,* Corinthiorum 3.

[II]

Posito[29] sic fundamento, erigendus est murus, qui secunde parti sermonis satis competenter comparari potest, tum quia sicut in domo materiali post fundamentum immediate murus erigitur, sic in sermone saltem formali post thematis assumpcionem thematis introduccio immediate sequetur, tum eciam quia[30] secundum auctores grama-

24. uel negatiua . . . debet omitti] *suggested reconstruction as demanded by sense;* uel negatiua non debet addi negacio; si vero negatiua, debet omitti L.A, *lacking in* W.

25. vel ad] pro secundo L.A; vel W.

26. fugiendum] W; fun'tum L; funda'tum A.

27. super montem Olilueti] *thus source;* sub primo ol'i L.A; *sentence lacking in* W.

28. tota] totus L; *om.* A; *passage lacking in* W.

29. Posito] *add* Introduccio *marg.* L.

30. quia] *om.* L.A, *but required by the parallel syntactic structure;* W *lacks the passage.*

added; if negative, the negation must not be omitted lest the sense of the quoted authority be lost. [b] Second, the thema can be complete because in its completeness it moves the intellect either to follow something, as when it says, *Arise and walk;*[13] or to shun something, as when it says, *Do not love the world;*[14] or to obtain something, as when it says, *Save us, we are perishing;*[15] or to ask a question, as when it says, *Whose image is this?*[16] Though similar sentences may be incomplete with regard to truth or falseness, they still contain something to be understood by which their meaning is made complete in order to carry out or to understand something. And thus such a sentence, as long as it is taken from a biblical book, is sufficiently complete and may rightly be chosen as the thema. There are, however, other clauses that in and by themselves are incomplete, such as: *While Jesus was speaking to the crowds,*[17] *When Jesus was sitting on Mount Olivet,*[18] or *When Jesus entered into the boat.*[19] Such and similar clauses must in no way be chosen as the thema, because they do not lead the intellect to a full understanding.

When the foundation is thus firmly laid, it is in some way fittingly applied to one's purpose:

> This is the house of the Lord, strong and well founded on a firm rock. But *the rock was Christ,*[20] in whom all of Scripture, both old and new, is fully contained. *For no one can lay another foundation but that which is already laid,* Corinthians 3.[21]

[II]

After the foundation has thus been laid, a wall is to be raised, which may be quite fittingly compared to the second part of the sermon, both because just as in a material house a wall is raised right after the foundation, so in a sermon, at least a formal one, an introduction of the thema will follow immediately after the thema has been announced; and also because according to the grammarians the word *murus,* "wall," comes

13. Mt 9:5.
14. 1 Jn 2:15.
15. Mt 8:25.
16. Mt 22:20.
17. Mt 12:46.
18. Mt 24:3.
19. Mt 8:23.
20. 1 Cor 10:4.
21. 1 Cor 3:11.

ticales *murus* a muniendo dicitur, eo quod munit et roborat interius conseruanda. Et sicut murus munit et roborat, sic introduccio firmat et fortificat thema preassup- [f. 180v] tum. Iste murus quatuor ex lateribus resultans consistit, que sunt quatuor modi communiter vsitati in ipsius thematis introduccione, nam per auctoritatem, et racionem, per exemplum, et inducccionem solet ipsum thema vt pluries introduci.

[1] Quoad primum patet iam exemplum de themate iam assumpto et eius introduccione.

[2] Per racionem vero potest illud thema sic introduci:

Proprietas domus, condicio, et finis est vexatum quietare, timoratum gubernare,[31] et collocatum conseruare. Vt igitur[32] vexatus quieteris, timoratus gubérneris,[33] et collocatus conserueris, tibi ad presens dirigatur verbum cum sic dicitur: *Vade in domum tuam.*

[3] Per exemplum sic:

Sicut nauis in aqua saluat quos recipit ne maris fluctibus obruantur, sic domus in terra seruat quos operit ne tempestatibus exponantur. Varias ergo tempestates ceterasque timiditates vitare volenti proponitur remedium cum sic dicitur: *Vade in domum.*

Per exemplum thema tunc introducitur cum a simili[34] ad simile arguitur ad thema concludendum.

[4] Per inducccionem[35] potest illud thema breuiter introduci:

Sacre scripture carmina texentibus[36] domus trifaria intuenda relucet, videlicet—

domus carnis proprie[37] preciosa deformantis,
domus consciencie deformata reformantis,
et domus celestis ecclesie in patria triumphantis.

De prima Iob 4, de secunda Sapiencie 8, de tercia Psalmo 38 scribitur mani-

31. gubernare] W; gubernatum L.A.
32. Vt igitur] W; verbi gracia L.A.
33. guberneris] W; gubernari L.A.
34. a simili] W; simili L; simile A.
35. induccionem] W *and above;* introduccionem L.A.
36. Sacre scripture carmina texentibus] L.A; sacram scripturam inspicientibus W.
37. proprie] W; *propo'e* L.A.

from *munire,* "to protect," since it protects and gives strength to what is to be preserved inside. And just as a wall protects and gives strength, so the introduction strengthens and fortifies the chosen thema. This wall consists of four sides, which are the four ways commonly employed in this introduction of the thema. For the thema is most often introduced with an authority, with a reason, with an example, and with induction.

[1] With regard to the first an example has already been given in the just-stated thema and its introduction.[22]

[2] But the same thema can be introduced with a reason as follows:

The property of a house, its condition and purpose, is to provide rest for one who has labored, to guide the God-fearing person, and to protect a person who is placed in it. So, in order that you may find rest when you are tired, are guided as you fear God, and are protected when you are placed there, this word is spoken to you now which says, *Go into your house.*

[3] With an example [it can be introduced] as follows:

Just as on water a boat keeps those safe whom it takes in, that they do not perish in the waves of the sea, so on land a house keeps those it shelters that they are not exposed to tempests. Hence a person who desires to avoid tempests and other frightening things is given a remedy when it is said, *Go into* [*your*] *house.*

Thus a thema is introduced with an example when one argues from something similar to what occurs in the thema.

[4] With induction the same thema can be briefly introduced as follows:

To the writers of poems in Sacred Scripture, a house can mean three things:
the house of one's flesh, which deforms what is precious;
the house of conscience, which restores what has been deformed;
and the house of the Church in heaven, which triumphs in the fatherland.

Of the first it is manifestly written in Job 4,[23] of the second in Wisdom 8,[24] and of the third in Psalm 38.[25] *Go into the* first *house* and trample on it; *go into*

22. Reference to the initial paragraph, with the thema *Go into your house* and the authoritative quotation from "the Master of the *Histories.*"

23. Perhaps Jb 4:19.

24. Ws 8:16.

25. Perhaps Ps 25:8 (26:8).

feste. In primam *vade* ipsam calcando; in secundam *vade* ipsam mundando; et in terciam *vade* participando gaudiis beatorum,

vt sic inductiue de qualibet litera verificari potest thema preassumptum, cum sic dicitur *Vade in domum.* Quam inquam domum ut muris[38] roboremus consulit scriptura: *Vallemus muris et roboremus portas,* 2 Paralipomenon 14.

[III]

Sic posito fundamento muroque[39] erecto, ad ostium istius domus est vltra transeundum. Circa quod quatuor vt communiter concurrere dicuntur, videlicet limes,[40] apertura, clauis, et clausura.

Limes pedi est substratus;[41]
per aperturam fit pes illatus;
clauis aperit quod prius clauditur;
sed clausura firmat cum apponitur.
[1] Est ergo limes pedis posicio,
[2] apertura[42] thematis diusio,
[3] clauis menbrorum est declaracio,
[4] sed[43] clausura auctoritatis est confirmacio.

[1] Pedis posicio, secundum tradentes formam componendi sermonis et collacionis, est fundamentum a themate abstractum, conueniens fini, et substratum diuisioni. Dicitur primo "est fundamentum a themate abstractum," idest debet esse[44] tale quod [f. 181] actualiter[45] intelligitur in themate vel saltem congrue intelligi potest per ipsum thema vel aliquod verbum ipsius thematis preassumpti. Secundo debet esse[46] "conueniens fini," idest illis que[47] principaliter et finaliter dicentur in sermone vel collacione pro tunc probanda. Et tercio debet

38. muris] W; murus L.A.
39. fundamento muroque] fundamentoque L.A; *passage lacking in* W.
40. limes] *the word should be* limen, *but all three mss. read* limes (L *here* bonus), *here and in the following.*
41. substratus] W; subtractus L.A.
42. apertura] W; *om.* L.A.
43. sed] si L; et A; *om.* W.
44. substratum . . . debet esse] W; *om.* L.A.
45. actualiter] quod actualiter *(i.e.,* quod *repeated)* L.
46. Secundo debet esse] L.A; dicitur secundo W.
47. que] qui L.A; *phrase lacking in* W.

the second *house* and cleanse it; and *go into the* third *house* and share the joys of the blessed.

In this way one can from each literal quotation inductively verify the announced thema in the words *Go into the house.* And, as I say, in order for us to fortify this house, Scripture advises in 2 Chronicles 14: *Let us compass* [*these cities*] *with walls and fortify them with gates.*[26]

[III]

After the foundation has been laid and the wall raised in this fashion, one is to proceed further to the door of this house. This, as is commonly said, comprises four things together, namely the threshold, the opening, a key, and a lock. The threshold lies under the foot, through the opening one's foot is carried in, the key opens what had been closed, and the lock fastens when it is hung on the door. Thus, [in the sermon] [1] the threshold is the "placing of the foot"; [2] the opening the division of the thema, [3] the key the explanation of the parts, and [4] the lock the confirmation of an authority.

[1] The "placing of the foot," according to those who have handed on the form of composing a sermon and collation, is a base that has been drawn from the thema, it is fit for the preacher's purpose, and it underlies the division. First I say it is "a base that has been drawn from the thema," that is, it must be what is actually understood in the thema or at least what can be fittingly understood by the thema itself or by a word from the announced thema. Second, it must be "fit for the preacher's purpose," that is, for the things that will be said first and last in the sermon or collation and are to be proven. And third, it must "underlie the division," because the main division is to be built upon it.

26. 2 Chr 14:7.

esse[48] "substratum[49] diuisioni," quia super ipsum erigenda est diusio principalis.

[2] Thematis diuisio secundum eosdem est ipsius sentencie in themate incluse sub aliis verbis apericio siue explanacio. Et debent esse verba communia non extranea, plana non obscura, breuia non prolixa.

[3] Clauis appericio est diccionum quedam connexio[50] que diuisionis facte racionem apperit[51] et eiusdem diuisionis sufficienciam concludit. In principali enim diuisione, et maxime in sermone, reducenda sunt menbra ad aliquam sufficienciam sacre scripture vel alicuius alterius auctoris[52] autentici, vt si menbra sint quatuor, ad quatuor genera causarum vel ad quatuor virtutes cardinales vel ad aliquid consimile reduci debent. Si tria, ad tres[53] potencias anime vel ad tres personas in diuinis, vel ad tres virtutes[54] theologicas, et sic de aliis. Si duo, ad duplicem statum, scilicet vite actiue et contemplatiue, vel culpe et gracie et glorie, et sic de aliis reduci debent.

[4] Quarto requiritur clausura, que est auctoritatis confirmacio, vt facta[55] diuisio per auctoritates sacre scripture duplici conueniencia affirmetur, scilicet conueniencia literali siue vocali, et hoc quoad sensum,[56] et conueniencia sentenciali quoad intellectum, quia verbum diuisum et auctoritas adducta non solum in verbo aut litera sed eciam in sentencia conuenire[57] debent.

Exemplum omnium istorum patet in diuidendo thema preassumptum. Nam cum sic dicitur: "In hiis sacra scriptura dupliciter descripta ad presens relucet," ecce pedis posicio. Secundo, cum sic dicitur "vt laborum imperatrix et torporis extirpatrix,

48. Et tercio debet esse] L.A; dicitur tercio et W.
49. substratum] W; substractum L; subtractum A.
50. diccionum quedam connexio] W; ad duccionem quedam commixtio L.A.
51. apperit] apparenti L.A; aperiunt W.
52. auctoris] W.A; *apparently corrected to* doctoris(?) L.
53. tres] W; tria L.A.
54. virtutes] W; veritates L.A.
55. facta] W; fiat L.A.
56. sensum] L.A; *om.* W. *Scribal error for* sonum?
57. conuenire] W; queri (or conueri) L.A.

[2] The division of the thema, according to the same teachers, is the opening up or explanation with different words, of the meaning contained in the thema. And these words must be common not strange, plain not obscure, short not prolix.

[3] The opening of the key is some verbal connection that opens up the reason for the division that has been given and furnishes a rationale for the same division. For in the main division, and especially so in the sermon,[27] the parts are to be reduced to some rationale drawn from Holy Scripture or from another authentic author. Thus, if there are four parts, these must be reduced to the four kinds of causes, or to the four cardinal virtues, or to something similar. If there are three, to the three faculties of the soul, or to the three divine persons, or to the three theological virtues, and so on. If there are two, to the twofold state, that is, the active and contemplative life, or to that of guilt and grace and glory, and thus in other cases.

[4] And in the fourth place, a lock is necessary, which is an authoritative confirmation. Thus, the division that has been made must be confirmed with authorities from Holy Scripture that agree [with the division] in two ways, namely, literally or verbally (and thus in their sound[28]) and in their meaning (with respect to what they indicate). The divided words and the quoted authority must agree not only in their verbal or literal form but also in their meaning.

An example for all this can be found in dividing the previously given thema.[29] For where it says, "In these words Holy Scripture shines forth as for now described in two ways," this is the "placing of the foot." Second, where it says, "as commanding work and uprooting torpor,

27. "Especially so in the sermon": the author may be thinking of a difference between sermon and other forms of scholastic discourse (such as biblical commentary or quodlibet), or else between sermon and *collatio.*

28. All three witnesses use *conueniencia* for what elsewhere is called *concordancia.* This may be *verbalis* (using the same or a cognate word form) or *realis* (using a synonym) or both. See for example Basevorn, chaps. 7 and 22; Waleys, pp. 34–346; Fusignano, chap. VIII. The scribal *sensum* (cf. textual note 56) may be an error or else refer to the *sensible* word form in contrast to its *intelligible* meaning.

29. I.e., *Go into your house.*

Vade, et vt quiescentis habitaculum et fugientis refugium, etc.,[58] *in domum,*"[59] ecce thematis diuisio. Tercio, cum dicitur "labor torporem expellit, territus terrorem repellit,"[60] ecce clauium appericio.[61] Quarto, cum dicitur quod "primum actiuam, secundum contemplatiuam vitam designat," ecce ad sufficienciam menbrorum reduccio.[62] Et vltimo cum dicitur "*Vade ad formicam, o piger,* etc., *Esto michi in Deum protector et in domum refugii vt saluum,* etc.," ecce per auctoritates tam sentenciales quam vocales confirmacio. Qui non in diuidendo *intrat*[63] per hoc ostium sed *ascendit aliunde, ille fur est et latro,* Johannis 10.

[IV–V]

Ostio sic posito ponende sunt fenestre. Fenestra enim, vt dicit Brito, "dicitur [f. 181v] a *fos,* quod est lux, et *ministra,* quia ministrat lucem." Huiusmodi autem fenestre quandoque in tria, quandoque in quatuor lumina diuiduntur, prout necessitas exigit luminis diffundendi. Et signanter dico in tria vel quatuor, quia secundum Tullium in sua *Rethorica,* libro primo, si[64] subdiuisio in sermone sistat debita,[65] numerum quaternarium excedere non debet, nec[66] infra ternarium sumi non valet. Circa hanc partem sermonis est aliquid aduertendum, aliquid amplectendum, et aliquid fugiendum: [1] Sciencia diuidendi est aduertenda, [2] sufficiencia est amplectenda, [3] et co\i/ncidencia[67] est penitus fugienda.

[1] Quoad primum dicit Boicius libro primo *Diuisionum* quod omnis diuisio vel est generis in suas species, vel tocius vniversalis in sua singularia, vel vocis in suas signaciones, vel tocius in partes integrales, vel subiecti in accidencia, vel accidentis in sua subiec-

58. etc.] tunc L.A; securius conseruando, cum dicitur W.

59. domum] W; domo L.A.

60. labor . . . repellit] *but see the earlier version at the beginning of the treatise.*

61. appericio] A; apposicio L; *lacking in* W.

62. reduccio] W; redicio L.A.

63. intrat] dicat L.A; *sentence lacking in* W.

64. si] W; sicut L.A.

65. debita] W; de luce L.A.

66. nec] W; et ita L.A.

67. L (*or the exemplar of* L.A) *evidently found the form* concidencia *in his exemplar and corrected it by inserting \i/, though inconsistently. In classical rhetoric* concidentia *means something different.* W *writes* coincidencia *clearly and consistently.* See also textual note 19 to *Hic docet.*

Go; and as giving a dwelling to one who rests and shelter to one who is in flight, etc., *into the house,*" this is the division of the thema.[30] Third, where it says, "Work drives torpor away, and one who is terrified evades his fright," this is the opening of the keys. Fourth, where it says, "The former indicates the active life; the latter, the contemplative," this reduces the parts to a rationale. And lastly, where it says, "*Go to the ant, o sluggard,* etc., *Be to me a God, a protector, and a house of refuge to save me,* etc.," this is the confirmation with authorities that agree in both meaning and actual words.[31] [A preacher] who in his division does not *enter by this door but climbs up another way is a thief and a robber,* John 10.[32]

[IV–V]

When the door has been thus placed, the windows must be put in. As Brito says, a window, *fenestra,* "is so called from *fos,* meaning light, and *ministra,* because it administers light."[33] Such windows are sometimes divided into three panes, sometimes into four, just as the need for spreading the light requires. And I say "into three" or "four" meaningfully, because according to Cicero in book 1 of his *Rhetoric,* if there is a fitting subdivision of a speech, it must not exceed four nor have fewer than three members.[34] With respect to this part of the sermon, something is to be heeded, something to be included, and something to be avoided: [1] the art of making a division is to be heeded; [2] a rationale is to be included; and [3] coincidence is to be totally avoided.

[1] As to the first, Boethius says, in book 1 of his *On Division,* that all division is either of a genus into its species, or of a universal whole into its specific members, or of a word into its meanings, or of an integral

30. In exemplifying the division from the example given at the beginning of the treatise, L and A present an incomplete quotation; for the complete form see the text above. W is more concise and clearer: "Ut cum dicitur ulterius 'Primo describitur vt laboris imperatrix et torporis extirpatrix sollercius operando, cum dicitur *Vade;* secundo describitur vt quiescentis habitaculum et fugientis refugium securius conseruando, cum dicitur *In domum tuam,*' ecce diuisio in se.... Ut cum ulterius dicitur: 'Laboris torporem repellit longius cum quiescenti ociose profectus demandatur; interitus timorem leuius cum fugienti operose locus quietis datur,' ecce hic fit clauium apercio. Sed cum ulterius dicitur primum actiuam, secundum cotemplatiuam uitam significat, ecce hic fit ad sufficienciam reductio."

31. "Actual words": *go* and *house.*

32. Jn 10:1.

33. *Summa Britonis,* ed. Lloyd W. Daly and Bernadine A. Daly (Padua: Antenor, 1975), vol. 1, p. 261. *Fos* is the Greek word.

34. Cf. *Ad Herennium* 1.10.17.

ta. Vt in prefato themate poterit ostendi: Domus quedam est lignea, quedam lutea, quedam lapidea—ecce diuisio generis in suas species et tocius vniversalis in sua singularia. Vel sic: Quedam est domus materie corporalis, quedam pagine diuinalis, quedam anime internalis, et quedam glorie eternalis—ecce diuisio vocis in sua signata.[68] Vel sic: Domus resultat ex fundamento, muro, et tecto—ecce diuisio tocius in suas partes integrales. Consimiliter de aliis menbris exempla poni possunt que causa breuitatis ad presens omitto.

[2] Sufficiencia eciam est amplectenda a subdiuisione. Et voco prout sufficienciam numerum talem quo[69] maior in materia specificata nequeat reperiri. Exemplum ad hoc: Si quis de domo intenderet predicare et tantum de domo triplici tangere, insufficienter procederet, quia numerus ternarius non est maior numerus quo maior in hac materia nequeat reperiri, eo quod quartam domum reperire contigitur, vt superius est exemplatum.[70] Sed hic est notandum quod duplex est sufficiencia, scilicet nature et scripture. Prima sufficiencia est maximus numerus qui per naturam in materia specificata poterit reperiri. Secunda sufficiencia est certus numerus positus in sacra scriptura vel ab aliquo alio auctore autentico[71] in aliqua certa materia, ita quod ille sit maximus numerus ab illo auctore positus in tali materia, quamuis per viam nature maior numerus in eadem materia poterit reperiri.

[3] *Tercio est*[72] *co\i/ncidencia fugienda.*[73] [f. 182] *Et voco conciden-ciam quando in aliqua* multiplicacione vnum in alio includitur. Vel ad sciendum in genere quando est co\i/ncidencia et quando non, videndum est si partes sint opposite vel ita disparate[74] quod nulla sequatur

68. signata] *add* Quandoque in massa (A: ma'a) corporal', quandoque pagina diuinalis, quandoque anima internalis, et quandoque gloria eternalis domus mutuatur (A: uiricuatur) L.A. *I cannot make sense of this sentence, and it seems to add another example of* divisio vocis in sua signata. W *lacks the examples for the different kinds of division.*

69. quo] que L.A; W *expresses the idea differently.*

70. exemplatum] extra[c]tum L.A; *passage lacking in* W.

71. autentico] A.W; autentice L.

72. est] W; *add* de L.A.

73. fugienda] W; fun'da L; fundanda *corr. interlin. from* facienda, *crossed out* A.

74. disparate] desperate L.A.W.

whole into its constituent parts, or of a subject into its accidents, or of an accident into its subjects.[35] This could be shown with respect to the thema given above. One kind of house is of wood, another of mud, and another of stone—this is a division of a genus into its species as well as a division of a universal whole into its specific members. Or else: one kind of "house" is that of physical material, another that of Holy Scripture, another that of the soul within us, and another that of eternal glory—this is a division of a word into its different meanings.[36] Or else: a house is made up of foundation, wall, and roof—this is a division of an integral whole into its constituent parts. In the same way examples for the other parts [of the division] could be given, which I now pass over for the sake of brevity.

[2] Further, a rationale[37] for the subdivision must be included. And I call "rationale" that number than which no greater can be found in the matter under discussion. An example of this: If one were to preach about a house and were to speak only of three kinds of houses, the development would be insufficient, because three is not the greatest number than which no more could be found in this matter, as was exemplified above. But here we must notice that a rationale is of two kinds, namely natural and scriptural. The first is the greatest number that can be found naturally in the given subject matter. The second is a certain number mentioned in Holy Scripture or by some other authentic author with regard to a certain subject matter, so that that is the greatest number mentioned by that authority in such a matter, even if in nature a greater number in that matter could be found.

[3] Third, coincidence is to be avoided. I speak of "coincidence" when in a string of words one thing is included within another. To know in general when there is coincidence and when not, one must make sure that the parts are opposites or so different from each other

35. Boethius, *De divisione* (PL 64:875–892), especially at 877. *Vade* uses a slightly more rigorous scholastic pattern and terms.

36. "Different meanings" here include metaphors and figurative meaning.

37. "Rationale," *sufficientia:* a technical term in scholasticism for the explanation why a certain number of items, and why these particular items, are included in a group; for instance, why there are seven deadly sins, and why pride, anger, envy, etc. See Siegfried Wenzel, "The Seven Deadly Sins: Some Problems of Research," *Speculum* 43 (1968): 1–22, at 3–12.

ad aliam, et \si/ sic, tunc nulla est concidencia; si autem vna sequatur ad aliam, concidencia est.

In omnibus predictis currunt a pari sermo et collacio, nam collacio nichil aliud est quam forma sermonis. Imaginor enim in sermone duo, scilicet materiam et formam. Formam voco istum modum procedendi, materiam illud quod subest in modo dilatandi. Collacio abstrahitur a materia dilatandi in quanto minus[75] habet de dilatacione. Cum hoc quod habeat formam et perfeccionem propriam, melior est collacio, et hinc est quod communiter dicitur collacio quanto breuior, tanto melior. Verbi gracia: "Domus Domini illustretur: *Fenestram in ea facies,* Genesis 6."

Fenestris per luminaria sic distinctis, lux domum intrat et intrans diffunditur sparsim. Sicut diffusa multiplicatur[76] secundum ipsius loci debitam exigenciam, sic in sermone, distinccione[77] posita, intrare debent historie exemplaque sanctorum, dicta moralia, <originalia> doctorum autenticorum, multiplicari[78] debent, vt sic virtutes commendando et vicia repugnando intret lumen gracie in cordibus auditorum, quia *dulce lumen et delectabile est,* Ecclesiastici xi.

[VI]

Vltima pars domus est tectum, quod non est aliud quam quedam combinacio seu colleccio tegularum vel straminum siue aliorum cooperimentorum quibus ipsa domus finaliter perficitur. Sic in sermone et collacione fieri debet quedam conglutinacio et conchatenacio in eisdem predictorum, et sic opus preinceptum perfeccione consummetur. Tunc enim erit verum quod *perfectum est omne opus tabernaculi et tecti,* Exodi 30.

Sic ergo domui materiali sermo formalis merito comparatur, vt si—
fundamentum thematis assumptio,
murus assumpti sit introduccio,
ostium thematis sit diuisio,

75. minus] *suggested by sense;* vnus L.A; *passage lacking in* W.

76. sparsim . . . multiplicatur] W; sparsimque diffusa fuit multiplicanda L; A *is rather garbled.*

77. distinccione] W; duo L.A.

78. multiplicari] *evidently* et *has dropped out somewhere in the preceding line,* L.A; W *reads:* et doctorum.

that none goes with another. If this is the case, then there is no coincidence; but if one does go with another, then there is coincidence.

In everything that has been said, a sermon and a collation are parallel to each other, for a collation is nothing else but the [essential] form of a sermon. For I conceive that there are two things in a sermon, matter and form. "Form" I call a particular way of development, "matter" what underlies the development. A collation is reduced in the matter of the development, in that it has less of a development. Insofar as it has its own form and completeness, a collation is better, and hence it is commonly said that the shorter a collation, the better. For example: "The house of the Lord is to be illuminated: *You shall make a window in it,* Genesis 6."[38]

When the windows have thus been divided into panes, light enters into the house, and in entering it is spread about. As in its spreading it is increased according to what the particular place demands, so in a sermon, after a distinction has been introduced, there must be added multiple historical narratives, examples of the saints, moral sayings, and original quotations from authentic teachers, so that by commending virtues and reproving vices the light of grace may enter into the hearts of the audience, *for light is sweet and delightful,* Ecclesiasticus 11.[39]

[VI]

The last part of a house is its roof, which is nothing other than a combination or composition of tiles or of straw or of some other covering with which the house is finally completed. In the same way, in a sermon or collation there must be some gluing or chaining together of what has been said before, and in this way the work one has begun will be finished in perfection. For then it will be the case that *all the work of the tabernacle and the roof was finished,* Exodus 30.[40]

Thus, then, a formal sermon is rightly compared to a material house in that its foundation is the announcement of a thema, its wall is the introduction of what has been announced, its door is the division of the

38. Gn 6:16, referring to the ark. I assume the author here means that in a collation such linking words as "Hence it is said" or even more "This house is figuratively mentioned in" are omitted for greater brevity.

39. Not Sir but Eccl 11:7.

40. Ex 39 [!]:31.

fenestra subdiuisio siue distinctio,[79]
luminis diffusio sermonis dilatacio,
et ipsius domus tectum finalis conglutinacio.

Sic propalanti[80] ipsius Dei verbum merito dicatur thema preassumptum sacre scripture, *Vade in domum.*

Huius domus, scilicet sacre scripture, fundamentum, paries, et tectum, licet vario scemate a diuersis fabricentur, nexu tamen firmissimo inuicem connectuntur. Nam domus huius fundamentum prophete supponentes[81] normam nostre fidei primitus tradiderunt. Sacramentorum ministeria apostoli disponentes eius domus parietes[82] seriose construxerunt. [f. 182v] Sed dicta et facta Christi[83] predicantes huius domus[84] tectum perfecte consummauerunt. Ad huius eciam domus decorem et ornatum varios opifices ipsam decorantes summus ipse artifex ordinate[85] disponebat. Quorum quidem opificum Ambrosius et Hillarius, vt clarior domus fieret, fenestras apponentes[86] obscura scripturarum loca exponebant; Augustinus et Jeronimus contra hereticas prauitates turres construentes argumentis firmissimis hanc domum muniebant; magnus Gregorius et Johannes Crisostomus per varia scripture loca flores et ornatus pulcherrime sparserunt, aliter iuncturis et celaturis variis ipsam interius subtiliter ornauerunt. Et quamuis hec domus[87] sufficienter per predictos fuerit consummata, quamplures tamen postea doctores successerunt, vt Basilius et Eusebius, Johannes Damascenus, Cassiodorus, et Isidorus, Bernardus et Anselmus, alii quoque[88] quamplurimi quorum non est numerus, ad huius domus decorem atque fulcimentum. Sic igitur sacre scripture domo firmissime fundata, erecta parietibus, et tecto consummata, picturis, celaturis, et floribus exornata, necnon et turribus tutissime constipata, *perfecta est domus in omni opere suo,* 3 Regum capitulo 6.

In hanc perfectam[89] domum ille nos introducat qui sine fine vuiut et regnat. Amen.

79. subdiuisio siue distinctio] W; diuisio distruccio sit L.A.
80. propalanti] W; per preambulum L.A.
81. supponentes] suppo'tes L.A; supportantes W.
82. parietes] W; probitates L.A.
83. Christi] *add* o'a'item L.A; *om.* W. *Perhaps for* omni terre?
84. domus] annus L; *longer eyeskip* A; *om.* W.
85. ordinate] W; ordinare L.A.
86. apponentes] W; *add* et L.A.
87. domus] A; annus L; *clause lacking in* W.
88. quoque] W; *om.* L.A.
89. perfectam] perfecte L.A; *phrase lacking in* W.

thema, its window is the subdivision or distinction, its spreading of the light is the sermon's development, and the roof of this house is the final gluing together. In this way, to the one who preaches the word of God himself, the thema quoted above is rightly spoken: *Go into your house.*

Even if the foundation of this house, that is, [a quotation from] Holy Scripture, its wall, and its roof may be built up by different people in different forms, they are nevertheless tied together in a very firm bond. For the prophets laid the foundation of this house and handed on the norm of our faith. The apostles constructed the walls one by one[41] by setting forth the holy mysteries. And those who preached Christ's words and deeds finished the roof of this house in perfection. For the adornment and embellishment of this house its chief builder appointed workmen in good order. Among these, Ambrose and Hilary set in windows to lighten up the house by explaining dark passages in the Scriptures. Augustine and Jerome fortified this house against the perversions of heretics by building towers with very strong arguments. Gregory the Great and John Chrysostom spread flowers and most beautiful ornaments with the help of many different quotes from Scripture and otherwise decorated this house inside subtly at its joints and paneling. And while this house was thus sufficiently completed by those mentioned, still many other doctors followed them, such as Basil, Eusebius, John of Damascus, Cassiodorus, Isidore, Bernard, Anselm, and many others without number, to adorn and support it. Hence, after the house of Holy Scripture has been put on a strong foundation, built up by its walls, completed with its roof, adorned with pictures, paneling, and flowers, and securely fortified with towers, *the house is finished in all its works,* 3 Kings, chapter 6.[42]

May he lead us to this perfect house, he who lives and reigns without end. Amen.

41. "One by one": the translation "in earnest" is possible, but it is more likely that the author here thinks of the composition of the Apostles' Creed by the twelve apostles, of whom each was considered responsible for one statement in the creed.

42. 1 Kgs 6:38.

V
JEAN DE LA ROCHELLE

ROCHELLE, A FRENCH FRANCISCAN and Paris master (died 1245), closely associated with Alexander of Hales, wrote a number of important theological works.[1] A *Processus negociandi themata sermonum,* beginning "Cum plures sint modi negociandi circa themata" (Caplan 31 and Suppl 31), is ascribed to him in manuscript P. It presupposes its readers' knowledge of the parts of a scholastic sermon as they were expounded and discussed in many *artes praedicandi* including the preceding four works here edited. Instead of giving another systematic account of the scholastic sermon structure, Rochelle focuses on seven aspects of "negotiating"—that is, handling, or dealing with, or developing, a thema—analyzes them, and shows how to avoid errors or faults that might occur in their use. The seven parts cover the following:

I. The general way of developing a "root" and "branches" from the announced thema.

1. For a recent summary of his biography and secondary literature see L. Hödl, "J[ohannes] de Rupella," *Lexikon des Mittelalters,* vol. 5 (Munich/Zurich: Artemis-Verlag, 1991), col. 598. For his works see Jacques-Guy Bougerol, "Jean de La Rochelle, les oeuvres et les manuscrits," *Archivum Franciscanum Historicum* 87 (1994): 205–15.

II. Handling a thema that includes a second-person word form. This is the longest part of the treatises and considers several specific aspects: for instance, how to handle a thema that includes both second- and first- or third-person forms. In dealing with this, Rochelle even considers and distinguishes between various sequences (II.4.b), as when a second person is followed by a third or first (2-3), or the reverse (3-2), or split sequences (3-2-3 and 2-3-2).

III. Developing the thema by quoting a second authority that says the opposite, and dividing the latter.

IV. A notion is expressed in different words or things.

V. A word of the thema means different things (or notions). Parts IV and V deal with similes and metaphors.

VI. Developing the thema by quoting a second authority with the same meaning and dividing it; this is the opposite to part III.

VII. Developing an authority with three, or more or fewer (of the traditional four), senses that Scripture can have.

This is, therefore, a refined, highly technical, and critical reflection on aspects of constructing a sermon which in contrast to other treatises pays close attention to matters of grammar (II) and metonymy (IV–V).[2] Rochelle very helpfully defines his terms and constantly illustrates his points with examples. He also uses parts of the tree image—root, branches, and twigs—for the respective parts of the sermon, but again in a way that assumes that his readers are already familiar with them. For instance, in part I Rochelle discusses the "root," which is a bridge sentence between the announced thema and its division and corresponds to what *Vade* calls *pedis posicio.* He then adds that disjunctive conjunctions like *or* are to be avoided, but degrees of comparison of an adjective may be used. In a similar way, Rochelle deals with the protheme, with confirming authorities, and with various relations between these and the thema. The subjects he deals with are, therefore, quite detailed and concern seemingly minor matters, such as the gram-

2. By "metonymy" here is meant the allegorical meaning that can occur in the literal sense of biblical words. It is to be distinguished from allegorical meanings of things and persons mentioned in the Bible, that is, the three spiritual senses: "allegorical" or "typical," "moral" or "tropological," and "anagogical," as they are discussed in Fusignano, chap. IX.

matical person(s) contained in the chosen thema, authorities that contain a simile or metaphor, contrasting authorities, and the like.

SOURCES

The *Processus* has been preserved in the following manuscripts:

Lisbon, Biblioteca Nacional, Fundo Alcobaça, MS 130 (P).[3] Parchment, thirteenth century (the colophon to the preceding sermons, on (modern) f. 185v, gives "Era MCCLXXXVIII" as the date of completion, i.e., 1250 A.D.). iii (paper) + iv + 189 folios in one column, written by one hand (numbered consecutively 1–196 by a modern hand). Contains:

(1) A set of saints' sermons by Pelagius Parvus (Frei Paio de Coimbra), O.P. (died 1240), ff. 8–185v (modern foliation), preceded by an alphabetic index of sermon topics (ff. 6–7).
(2) Johannes de Rupella, O.F.M. (died 1245), *Processus negociandi themata sermonum,* ff. 186–191v. This is the only witness that identifies the author as "Magistri Johannis de Rupella ut credo fratris Ordinis Minorum" (f. 186).
(3) Additional themata and divisions, in schematic form, ff. 191v–195v.

London, British Library, MS Arundel 275 (R).[4] Parchment, fourteenth century, ninety-one folios. From the Carthusian house at Mainz. (1) through (5) written in a Gothic bookhand. Contents:

(1) *Sermons,* ff. 1–66, for Sundays and saints, in random order; at least one for St. Francis.
(2) Odo of Cheriton, *Parabolae,* ff. 66va–81vb. Listed in J. A. Herbert, *Catalogue of Romances in the Department of Manuscripts of the British Museum,* vol. 3 (London: British Museum, 1910), 46–49. The explicit ("Expliciunt parabole Magistri O. ad laudem ipsius qui est Alpha et O") is followed by two blank lines and, without title, by:

3. Thomas L. Amos, *The Fundo Alcobaça of the Biblioteca Nacional, Lisbon.* Volume I: *Manuscripts 1–150* (Collegeville, Minn.: Hill Monastic Manuscript Library, 1988), 14–15.

4. Cf. J. Forshall, *Catalogue of Manuscripts in the British Museum. New Series* (London: Trustees of the British Museum, 1834–40), part 1 (online: http://www.bl.uk/catalogues/manuscripts/HITS0001.ASP?VPath=html/37232.htm&Search=275&Highlight=F).

(3) Anon., *Ars predicandi,* "In predicacione debent esse vita, sapiencia vel sciencia, et eloquencia," ff. 81vb–83rb. Caplan 68 (unique). Followed at once without rubric or title by:
(4) Jean de la Rochelle, *Ars predicandi,* ff. 83rb–86rb. Ending with explicit after part III. Followed after two blank lines, with marginal rubric "Collaciones... qualiter fien[de]," by:
(5) Anon., *Exercitacio in collacionibus* (thus explicit), "Si quis vult exercitari in collacionibus," ff. 86rb–89vb. Caplan 169 (unique).
(6) Alphabetical list of Latin terms with German translation: "Abditum–verborgen... Spiracio passiua–lidenne geisting," f. 90ra–vb.
(7) A note "Terribilis est locus iste," ff. 90v–91.

Vatican, MS. Ottoboni latinus 396 (V).[5] Paper and parchment, early fifteenth century, in various hands, seventy-two folios. Contents:

(1) Philippus Riboci (Ribois), O.Carm., *Tractatus de sensibus sacre scripture,* ff. 2–13v.
(2) Jean de Châlons, O.Cist., *Ars brevis quedam ad faciendum sermones secundum formam sillogisticam,* "Hec est ars brevis et clara," ff. 14–29. Caplan 52.
(3) Franciscus Eiximenes, O.F.M., *Ars predicandi,* ff. 29v–44. Caplan 84. Edited by Marti de Barcelona (see note 5).
(4) Ramon Lull, *Ars abbreviata predicacionis,* "Cum hec sit maior ars," ff. 44v–50v.
(5) John of Wales, "In isto libello continentur quatuor capitula," ff. 51–59v. Caplan 62 and Caplan Suppl 62.
(6) Jean de la Rochelle, O.F.M., *Processus,* ff. 59v–61, without title or rubric, ending incomplete in part II, the text breaking off at the bottom of f. 61, with f. 61v left blank. Caplan 31.
(7) Ramon Lull, *Liber de ente simpliciter absoluto,* ff. 62–68v.
(8) Sermon for the Blessed Virgin, in Catalan, f. 69r–v.

THE TEXT

The work was edited by Gustavo Cantini, O.F.M., in "Processus negociandi themata sermonum di Giovanni della Rochelle, OFM," *Antonianum* 26 (1951): 247–70, on the basis of the Lisbon manuscript (P)

5. A description by A. Pelzer was given to and is quoted by Marti de Barcelona, O.M.Cap., "L'Ars Praedicandi de Francesc Eiximenes," *Homenatge a Antoni Rubiò i Lluch. Miscelània d'Estudios Literaris Històricis i Linguisticis* (Barcelona, 1936), 2:301–40, at 302.

collated against the Vatican codex (V), and perhaps with the help of a transcript made by a nineteenth-century Franciscan scholar. Cantini clearly had studied *artes praedicandi* and provided a reasonably accurate text, though a number of errors in P escaped his attention.[6] I have therefore re-edited the work from the three manuscripts.

Since R and V are incomplete, the base text has to be P. In the passages shared, none of the three is convincingly superior. Perusing the recorded variants for parts I–III will reveal that P itself is not free from scribal errors.[7] I therefore follow the methodology already used in the previous texts of analyzing variants and the text of P critically, and emending P wherever this seems justified by variants in the other witnesses and/or by the sense of the exposition. Fortunately, for part II, the longest and most difficult section of the treatise, R and partially V are available and offer much help to establish a sensible text. The textual notes record not only the readings of all manuscripts in cases of emendation (as before) but also substantive variants throughout this text.

P uses schemata quite extensively, and in order to give readers a taste of them I have, especially in section VII, reproduced the braces by following the head word with a double hyphen and then running in the aggregated members by a space. I have, further, added numerals and letters in square brackets here and there in order to facilitate the reader's understanding of the work's structure. In the translation I have similarly added some words or phrases in square brackets to make the exposition more transparent.

Another peculiarity of P is that its scribe was unusually careful and consistent in identifying biblical quotations by book or its author, chapter, and part of the chapter (a, b, etc.). But he did not always have all these at hand, and consequently left spaces for them with periods. Thus we find, for example, *Genesis xxii.c* and *Psalmus xvii.f* but only *Psalmus vii.*[space]. or *Sapiencie.*[space].[space]. or no source at all, as in *vnde.* [space].[space].*Volo.* I have not reproduced the blank spaces and have not supplied chapter numbers if they occur only in R or V.

6. A very clear example is P's reading of *pro themate* for an intended *pro prothemate,* required by the sense, at textual note 14; and the same for P's correct reading *pro prothemate* at the end of the same paragraph rendered by the editor as "Primo . . . sit pro themate" (Cantini, p. 258). See also the following reference.

7. See also the emended text at notes 71–72.

ROCHELLE

TEXT

Lisbon, Biblioteca Nacional, MS Alcobaça 130.
[*f. 186*]

INCIPIT PROCESSUS Magistri Johannis de Rupella, ut credo fratris Ordinis Minorum.

Cum plures sint modi negociandi circa themata, ut melius pateat qualiter uicia sint uitanda et qualiter circa singulos sit agendum, primum de primo hic notatur.

[I]

Primus modus est quando proposito themate assumitur una radix in hac forma:

[1] Ponatur pro themate *Sobrie et iuste et pie.* Eliciatur talis radix, scilicet "In[1] uerbis propositis describitur perfectio uiri iusti."

[2] De assumpta radice producantur immediate rami, qui de ipsa radice artifficialiter exeant et per sufficientiam. Verbi gracia, dicto quod "In uerbis propositis describitur perfectio uiri iusti," assumendum est ita:

Sed quia perfectio uiri iusti potest esse per ordinationem sui ad se, ad[2] proximum, et ad Deum, ideo tria dicuntur, scilicet ordinatio sui—

1. In] R.V; quia P.
2. ad] R.V; sui ad P.

ROCHELLE

TRANSLATION

HERE BEGINS THE TREATISE of Master John of Rochelle, as I believe a Friar Minor.

As there are many modes of handling themata, in order to clarify how faults should be avoided and how one is to deal with each mode, we will begin with the first.

[I]

The first mode occurs when from the announced thema a root is derived in the following form.

[1] Take as thema *Soberly and justly and piously.*[1] Let the following root be derived from this: "In the announced words the perfection of a just man is described."

[2] From this derived root must then immediately branches be produced, which grow from it by art[2] and with some rationale.[3] For example, once we have said that "in the announced words the perfection of a just man is described," we must continue as follows:

> But since the perfection of a just man can consist in his ordering himself with respect to himself, to his neighbor, and to God, three things are expressed [in our thema], namely his ordering himself—

1. Ti 2:12. In the view of *Vade* I.2–3 this would be an imperfect thema.
2. "Art": such logical procedures are definition, division, etc.
3. For "rationale" see the translation of *Vade,* note 36.

ad se, ibi *sobrie;*
ad proximum, ibi *iuste;*
ad Deum, ibi *et pie.*

Ecce qualiter tres rami producti sunt de proposita radice artificialiter et sufficienter: artificialiter quia ad uirum iustum pertinet esse[3] ordinatum; sufficienter quia non nisi predictis modis et ad ista tria potest ordinari. Caueatur autem ne in numeratione ramorum productorum huiusmodi, utpote *unus, duo, tres,* etc., connumerentur. Sed si uelit predicator ramos productos repetere, potest hoc facere ratione materie in hunc modum: "Ordinatio uiri iusti ad se notatur ibi *sobrie;* ad proximum ibi *iuste;* ad Deum ibi *pie,*" et sic de aliis quando erunt plures rami.

[3] Item caueatur ne in diuisione thematis huiusmodi disiuntiuis (scilicet aut, siue, uel, etc.) utatur; hoc enim pertinet ad lectores. Sed per[4] comparatiua nomina possunt partes repeti, sic: "Vtilis est ualde ordinatio prima, vtilior secunda, et utilissima tertia."

[4] Item, proposito themate, inducenda est alia[5] auctoritas prothegmatis, que uoce uel sensu conueniat cum themate. Voce, ut si assumpto themate predicto assumatur pro prothemate illud Sapientie *Sobrietatem et iustitiam,* etc.; sensu, ut si assumatur pro prothemate illud Michee *Indicabo tibi, o homo, quid sit bonum,* etc.

[5] Item caueatur ne ultra quam tertia concordantia inducatur. Voco autem "terciam concordanciam" quando auctoritas auctoritatem exponit. Ad quarum etiam euidentiam, plures utuntur tertiis concordanciis et quartis, auctoritatem per auctoritatem exponendo. Quod si cogat necessitas uti quarta concordancia aut

3. pertinet esse] R.V; pertinere est P.
4. per] P; *add* et uero et per R.V.
5. alia] R; illa P; aliqua V.

with respect to himself, in the word *soberly;*
with respect to his neighbor, in the word *justly;*
and with respect to God, in the words *and piously.*

Lo how three branches have been produced from the proposed root by art and with some rationale: by art, because a just man is characterized by being ordered; with some rationale, because one cannot order oneself except in the three ways mentioned and with respect to those three. In listing the branches that have been produced in this way, however, one should avoid using numbers, such as "one, two, three," and so forth. But if the preacher wants to mention the derived branches again, he may do so with reference to the subject matter in this way: "The ordering of a just man with respect to himself is indicated in the word *soberly,* with respect to his neighbor, in the word *justly,* and with respect to God, in the words *and piously.*" And likewise with others if there are more branches.

[3] Further, in the division of a thema of this kind the preacher must avoid using disjunctives, such as "but," "or," "else," and the like, for these are proper for lecturers.[4] But he may repeat the parts with the comparative forms of an adjective, such as: "The first ordering is useful, the second more useful, the third the most useful."

[4] Further, after the thema has been announced, another authority is to be introduced as the protheme, which should agree with the thema in its verbal form or meaning. In its verbal form: as when after announcing the given thema the words of Wisdom are taken as protheme: *Soberness and justice,* etc.;[5] in its meaning: as when the following words from Micah are taken as protheme: *I shall show you, man, what is good,* etc.[6]

[5] Further, the preacher must avoid introducing anything beyond a third concordant statement.[7] By "third concordant statement" I am speaking of explaining one authority by another. To wit, many preachers clearly use a third and even fourth concordant statement in their

4. Rochelle here distinguishes the style of preachers from that of lecturers on theology or philosophy.

5. Ws 8:7.

6. Mi 6:8.

7. By "concordant statement" the author means a sentence—not necessarily a biblical quotation—that repeats a word from the another (preceding) sentence. In the following examples this is *justice* and later *Eufrates.*

ultra, assumatur auctoritas que directe opponitur prime concordancie, et cum illa negociari poteris, inducendo semper in contrarium in[6] secundam et terciam concordanciam, que alias esset quinta et sexta. Verbi gratia, dico quod "In iusticia describitur ordinatio ad proximum"; statim diffinio iusticiam dicens: "Iusticia est uirtus reddens unicuique quod suum est"—ecce prima concordancia. Inde addo: "Propter hoc iusticia designatur per Eufraten, qui quam terram circumeat non habetur"—ecce secunda concordancia. Protinus adiungo: "Eufrates interpretatur frugifer, et figurat hoc uel illud"—ecce tercia concordancia, ultra quam non licet ibi directe inducere aliam. Sed si cogat necessitas diuertere inde ad mores, assumam[7] concordantiam ex opposito contra primam dicens: "At contra sunt quidam uiri iniusticie, qui de ordinatione ad proximum non curent, qui designantur per fluuium Farfar," etc.

[6] Circa istum modum notandum est[8] quod circa eundem ramum debent plures expositiones currere si contingat thema pluribus modis exponi. Verbi gracia, si in aliquo ramo contingat aliquem sanctum comendari aliqua uirtute, non oportet transire ad alium ramum donec moraliter dixeris quicquid moraliter intendis dicere circa eundem ramum. Item, moralitas induc- [f. 186v] ta circa eundem ramum debet esse eiusdem rnaterie de qua est comendatio uiri sancti, uel de uitio quod opponitur uirtuti de qua ille sanctus uel uir iustus comendatur. Si circa eundem ramum plures occurrunt ramusculi—hoc est, plures dictiones describentes principalem ramum—reducende sunt omnes ad aliquam sufficientiam qua euidenter appareat sufficienter descriptus principalis ramus. Nichil quod non sit ex

6. in] P; s. R; super V. 7. assumam] R.V; summam P.
8. est] R.V.; eciam P.

explaining one authority with another. Now, if there is need to use a fourth concordant statement or even more, you should take an authority that is directly opposed to the first concordant statement, and with that you will be able to develop your thema by continuing to introduce a statement that is opposed to the second and the third, which then would be the fifth and sixth overall. For example, I say that "justice means one's ordering oneself with respect to one's neighbor"; then I define "justice" at once by saying, "Justice is the virtue that gives to each his own"—this is the first concordant statement. Then I add: "Therefore, justice is symbolized by *Eufrates,* about which it[8] does not say what country it flows around,"[9]—the second concordant statement. I add further: "*Eufrates* means 'fruitful' and indicates this or that"—the third concordant statement. Beyond this one must not add another directly. But if it becomes necessary for me now to turn to human behavior, I may bring in a concordant statement that stands in opposition to the first and say: "But in contrast [to this definition] are some men of injustice, who do not care about their being ordered with respect to their neighbor; they are symbolized by the river Pharphar," etc.[10]

[6] Notice also with regard to this mode that, if the thema is to be explained in several ways, several explanations must be at hand for one and the same branch. For example, if in some branch a saint is to be commended for some virtue, one must not go on to another branch before one has said, in moral terms, what one intends to say in moral terms about this particular branch. Further, the moral matter that one introduces regarding this particular branch must be the same as the matter for which the saint is commended, or else it must be about the vice that is opposed to the virtue for which the saint or a just man is being commended. If several twigs spring from this branch—that is, several words that describe the main branch—these must all be reduced to some rationale in which the main branch will be seen to be described sufficiently. Nothing must be used in a sermon built according to this mode that does not belong to the properties of the branches either

8. I.e., Scripture.

9. Augustine, *De Genesi ad Manicheos* 2. *Eufrates* stands for justice.

10. Cf. 2 Kgs 5:12. For the negative symbolism of the river Pharphar see, for example, Bernard of Clairvaux, *Sententiae* 2.145.

proprietate ramorum significatione uocis, interpretatione nominis, uel aliqua alia facie in sermone secundum istum modum facto inducatur. "Faciem" in hoc loco uoco omnem circumstanciam conuenientem ex qua potest moraliter dici. Que hiis uersibus continentur:[9]

Res, persona, locus, factum, tempus, numerus, uox,
Hiis septem scripture sacre signa trahuntur.

Trahitur enim moralitas:

a re, ut quando *templum* materiale signat templum spirituale, idest, animam bene ordinatam;
a persona, ut *Dauid* signat uirum iustum;
a loco, ut *mons* in quo transfiguratus est Dominus signat eminentiam uite in qua uir sanctus transfiguratur per depositionem ueteris hominis et induitionem noui;
a facto, ut *Abraham immolauit arietem,* et signat quod quilibet debet immolare carnem suam cum uiciis et peccatis;
a tempore, ut *nox* peccatum, *dies* uero gratiam significat;
a numero, ut per septenarium septem uirtutes, uicia, dona, totum tempus designatur;
a uoce, ut nominis interpretatione.[10]

Nota quod circa istum modum parum aut nichil curat litteralis exposicio uel anagogica. Item nota quod circa istum modum non ualent themata in quibus sunt uerba secunde persone.

[II]

De secundo modo notanda sunt tria.

9. continentur] V; continetur P; notantur R.
10. interpretacione] R.V; interpositione P.

through its verbal meaning, or through the interpretation of a name,[11] or through some other aspect *(facies).* By "aspect" I here mean any pertinent circumstance[12] from which a moral quality may be drawn. These are contained in the following lines:

> Thing, person, place, deed, time, number, and word.
> From these seven the signs of Holy Scripture are derived.

For a moral meaning is derived:

> from a thing, as when the material *temple* designates the spiritual one, that is, the well-ordered soul;
> from a person, as when *David* indicates the just person;
> from a place, as when the *mountain* on which the Lord was transfigured signifies the height of a life in which a holy person is transfigured by putting off the old man and putting on the new;[13]
> from a deed, as when *Abraham offered a heifer,* and this signifies that everyone must offer up his flesh with its vices;[14]
> from time, as when *night* signifies sin, but *day,* grace;
> from a number, as when the number *seven* indicates the seven virtues, the seven vices, the seven gifts [of the Holy Spirit], or all time;
> from a word, as by the interpretation [*or* etymology] of a name.

Notice further that with regard to this mode the literal or anagogical interpretation [of Scripture] is of little or no use. And notice also that in this mode, themata that contain verb forms in the second person are of no use.

[II]

About the second mode three things must be noted.

11. "Interpretation of a name" refers to its putative (medieval) etymology.

12. The "circumstances" of an act form a major topic in classical and medieval rhetoric as well as in moral theology, especially in hearing confession; see for instance Higden's *Ars componendi sermones,* 45. They are usually listed in a hexameter: "Quis, quid, ubi, quibus auxiliis, cur, quomodo, quando." See Johannes Gründel, *Die Lehre von den Umständen der menschlichen Handlung,* Beiträge Bäumker 39.5 (Münster: Aschendorff, 1963).

13. Cf. Eph 4:22–24.

14. Gn 22:13.

[1]

Secundus modus non habet locum nisi in uerbis secundarum personarum, vel in uerbis[11] quibus sermo dirigitur ad secundas personas et de secundis. In uerbis secundarum personarum sed non de secundis, verbi gratia, in Apocalipsi *Hii qui amicti sunt stolis albis, qui sunt?* etc.—ecce, cum hic sermo dirigatur ad secundam personam, fit tamen mentio uel questio de tercia—; in uerbis secundarum personarum et de secundis, ut in Genesi *Det tibi Deus de rore celi,* etc. Fit autem directio sermonis ad secundam personam undecim de causis:
ratione—

questionis, vt in auctoritate predicta;
increpationis, vt in i Regum xxvi: *Quis es tu, qui inquietas regem?;*
irrisionis, Genesis iiii: *Videte ne forte sumat de ligno uite et uiuat in eternum;*
vocationis, Mathei iiii: *Venite post me, faciam uos fieri piscatores hominum*
exortationis, qui quidem modus maximum locum habet in omnibus epistulis Pauli et canonicis, ubi fit exortatio ad mores;
inperationis siue iussionis; Luce xvi: *Si uis ingredi ad uitam, serua mandata;*
postulationis siue deprecationis, Mathei ix: *Domine, si uis, potes me mundare;*
allegationis siue inductionis siue persuasionis, ut in I Regum xxvi: *Conclusit Deus hodie inimicum tuum in manus tuas;* Luce: *Dignus est ut hoc illi perficias, quia sinagogam hedificavit nobis;*
detestationis; Iohannis xi: *Tu discipulus eius sis;*[12]
enunciationis, et maxime uisionis prophecie; qui quidem modus maximum locum habet in omnibus auctoritatibus prophetarum que occurrunt per secundas personas;

11. secundarum … uerbis] R.V; *om.* P.
12. detestationis … sis] R.V; *om.* P.

[1]

The second mode concerns only second-person expressions, where an utterance is either directed to a second person or is about a second person. An example [of the first case] of a second-person expression, but one that is not about a second person, is the verse from Revelation: *These who are clothed in white robes, who are they?* etc.[15]—this utterance is directed to a second person, but it mentions or asks about third persons. An example of a second-person utterance that is also about a second person is Genesis: *May God give you the dew of heaven,* etc.[16] Now, an utterance may be directed to a second person in eleven ways, namely in the form of:

a question, as in the [first] quoted authority;
rebuke, as in 1 Kings 26: *Who are you who disturb the king?*[17]
derision, as in Genesis 4: *Behold, lest perhaps he take from the tree of life and live forever;*[18]
calling, as in Matthew 4: *Follow me and I will make you fishers of men;*[19]
exhortation: this mode occurs most frequently in the epistles of Paul and the canonical epistles, where these exhort to moral behavior;
command or behest, as in Luke 16: *If you would enter into life, keep the commandments;*[20]
prayer or request, as in Matthew 9: *Lord, if you wish, you can heal me;*[21]
allegation or presentation or persuasion, as in 1 Kings 26: *Today the Lord has shut your enemy into your hands;*[22] or Luke: *He is worthy that you should do this for him, because he has built us a synagogue;*[23]
loathing, as in John 6: *You be his disciple;*[24]
announcement, chiefly of a prophetic vision; this mode occurs most frequently in all the authoritative sayings of the prophets wherever they use second-person utterances;

15. Rv 7:13.
16. Gn 27:28.
17. 1 Sm 26:14.
18. Gn 3:22.
19. Mt 4:19.
20. Mt 19:17.
21. Mt 8:2.
22. 1 Sm 26:8
23. Lk 7:4–5.
24. Jn 9:28.

solicitationis[13] ad bonum, siue promotionis ad melius, vt *Surge qui dormis et exurge a mortuis et illuminabit te Christus.*

Cum ergo occurrerit aliqua auctoritas secunde persone, reducatur continuo ad aliquem predictorum istorum modorum [f. 187] in hunc modum: Ponatur pro themate illud *Iesu, fili Dauid, miserere mei.* Assumatur statim "Vox est auxilium petentis," et hoc habeatur pro radice, sicut in primo modo habebatur pro radice illud quod immediate extrahebatur de tota auctoritate.

[2]

Conuenit autem iste modus cum primo in quatuor:

Primo, quia inducenda est aliqua auctoritas pro prothemate[14] que sensu vel voce conveniat cum themate;[15] sed non oportet quod sit secunde persone sicut prima, sed sufficit quod sit principium novum inductum[16] uel quoad assignandam[17] insufficientiam praedicantis, siue ad excitandam deuotionem populi ad orationem, siue ad comendandam bonitatem Dei uelut predicanti gratiam docendi et populo audiendi conferentis. Omne enim prothema ductum primo et secundo modo debet aut simul hec tria amplecti, uel ad minus alterum istorum. Intelligas autem "amplecti" sensu uel uoce, sicut dictum est in primo modo. In tercio modo, quarto, quinto et sexto non oportet aliquod prothema adducere, cum ipse modus negociandi circa themata modorum predictorum sit ibi pro prothemate.

Secundo, quia non recipit ultra terciam concordantiam nisi eo modo quo dictum est supra in primo modo.

Tercio, quia non trahuntur moralitates secundum facies superius memoratas.

Quarto, quia si circa eundem ramum plures occurrerint ramusculi, hoc est, plures dictiones describentes principalem ramum, reducende sunt omnes ad aliquam sufficientiam que euidenter appareat, etc., sicut supra in primo.

13. solicitationis] V; sollicitudinis P.R; *cf. below II.4.d.*

14. pro prothemate] pro themate P.R.V.

15. que … themate] R.V; *om.* P *(eyeskip).*

16. inductum] R.V; indicatiuum P.

17. assignandam] P; allegandam R.V.

incitement to what is good, or moving to what is better, as in: *Rise, you who sleep, and arise from the dead, and Christ will enlighten you.*[25]

Therefore, when a second-person authority occurs, it should at once be turned into one of these listed modes in this way: if *Jesus, son of David, have pity on me* is announced as the thema, let the preacher at once say: "This is the voice of one who is praying for help." And let this then be as it were the root, just as in the first mode above what was immediately drawn from the entire [quoted] authority was taken as the root.

[2]

This mode agrees with the first in four respects:

First, because some authority is to be introduced as the protheme[26] that agrees with the thema in meaning or verbal form. However, it is not necessary that it be a second-person utterance as was the first [i.e., the thema], but it is enough that it be a new beginning introduced either to express the preacher's insufficiency, or to excite the audience's devotion for the [following] prayer,[27] or to commend God's goodness, who grants grace to the preacher for his preaching and to the people for their hearing. For every protheme that is formed in the first and second mode should contain either these three points together, or at least one of them. By "contain," understand either in its meaning or in its verbal form, as was said in the first mode.[28] In the third, fourth, fifth, and sixth modes it is not necessary to introduce a protheme, since the way of handling themata itself in the aforesaid modes takes the place of the protheme.

Second, because it receives nothing after the third concordant statement except in the way that was mentioned above, in the first mode.[29]

Third, because no moral meanings are derived according to the aspects *(facies)* that were listed above.[30]

Fourth, because if the given branch should have several twigs, that is, several words that describe the major branch, these must all be reduced to some rationale that seems evident, etc., as above in the first chapter.[31]

25. Eph 5:14.

26. See above at I.4.

27. According to other *artes*, the protheme is usually followed by a prayer recited by the preacher and his audience, often with an *Ave Maria*.

28. At I.1.

29. At I.5.

30. At I.6.

31. At I.2 and following.

[3]

Differunt hic et supra, quia supra[18] extrahendi erant ramusculi per artem et sufficientiam; hic autem per sufficientiam tantum, non per artem. Voco autem "extrahi ramusculum de ramo per artem" quando fit repetitio[19] ipsius rami, "sufficienter" quando aliqua facie ostenditur quod tot conueniant illi ramo et non plura. Verbi gratia, posito hoc themate *Iesu, fili Dauid, miserere mei,* et dicto "Vox est petentis auxilium," addo:

Petit a Iesu, petit pro se. Circa primum allegat tria: potentiam, scientiam, bonitatem.

Potentiam ibi: *Iesu;* interpretatur enim "saluator";

bonitatem ibi: *fili;* dicitur enim a *filos,* quod est amor;

sapientiam ibi: *Dauid;* de Dauid enim legitur ii Regum xxiii: *Sedens in cathedra sapientissimus inter tres.*

Ecce tres ramusculi sufficienter producti de principali ramo, quia ad hoc quod aliquis sufficienter efficiat uel aliquid operetur oportet quod possit, uelit, et sciat illud operari. Sed non exeunt artifficialiter, quia non fit repetitio principalis rami.

[4]

Habet autem modus iste suas regulas quibus innititur speciales, et sunt[20] numero undecim.[21]

[a] Quarum prima hec est: in omnibus expositionibus sacre scripture modus iste habet locum, maxime uero in anegogica et morali.

18. supra] R.V; sumpta P, *possibly corrected to* supra.
19. repetitio] R.V *(and see end of paragraph);* recuperatio P.
20. sunt] R.V; sub P.
21. undecim] xi P; x R; ix V.

[3]

There is, however, a difference between this mode and what was said earlier. Above [we said that] the twigs are to be drawn out by art and with some rationale, while here they are so drawn out only with some rationale, not by art. By "drawing out a twig from a branch by art" I mean repeating this branch; by "with some rationale," I mean showing with reference to some aspect *(facies)* that so many items belong to that branch and no more. For example, if I announce as thema *Jesus, son of David, have pity on me,*[32] and I have said "This is the voice of someone asking for help," I continue:

> He [i.e., Bartimaeus] asks Jesus, and he asks for himself. Concerning the former, he refers to three things: [Jesus'] power, goodness, and wisdom.
>
> His power when he says *Jesus,* whose name means "savior";
>
> his goodness when he says *son,* for *filius* derives from *philos,*[33] which means "love";
>
> and his wisdom when he says *David,* for of David we read at 2 Kings 23 that *he was sitting in the chair, the wisest among three.*[34]

Behold, three twigs that are drawn from the main branch with a rationale, because for someone to rationally act or do something, it is necessary that he is able, wills, and knows how to do so. But these twigs do not derive by art because there is no repetition of the main branch [i.e., *he asks Jesus*].

[4]

This mode has its own special rules on which it rests, and they are eleven in number.[35]

[a] The first is this: This mode occurs with all interpretations of Holy Scripture, but mostly with the anagogical and moral one.[36]

32. Mk 10:47.
33. *Philos:* the Greek word.
34. 2 Sm 23:8.
35. P and R contain only ten, V ends in the second.
36. Reference to the fourfold interpretation of Scripture; cf. Fusignano XI.

[b] Secunda, si in themate ocurrant due orationes quarum una respiciat secundam personam, altera[22] uero terciam, assumendum est ut predictum est in principio istius modi. Sed in negotiatione negociandum est circa primam partem secundum regulas positas in isto[23] modo, in secunda uero negociandum est circa regulas positas in primo[24] uel tercio uel quarto, et sic de aliis, secundum quod magis uiderit congruere. Verbi gratia, posito illo themate *Miserere mei, fili Dauid, quia fiilia mea male a demonio uexatur,* circa hoc totum *miserere mei,* etc., negociandum est secundum regulas hic assignatas et assignandas. In eo uero quod sequitur, *filia mea,* negociandum est secundum regulas aliorum[25] modorum que huic parti melius poterunt adaptari. Si uero e conuerso fieret—utpote si principium thematis esset prime uel tertie persone, finis uero secunde—non oporteret negociari secundum regulas quibus iste modus distinguitur ab aliis, nisi in productione ramusculorum a ramis, si occurrant. Verbi gratia, si secunde persone: tunc enim sufficit quod ramusculi de ramo exeant per sufficientiam, nec exigitur quod per artem. Verbi gratia, posito themate hoc Psalmi cix *Iurauit* [f. 187v] *Dominus et non penitebit eum: Tu es sacerdos in eternum secundum ordinem Melchisedec,* in ista particula *iurauit Dominus,* etc., procedendum est iuxta primum modum uel tercium uel[26] quartum, etc., et sic de aliis,[27] nec oportet quod reducatur ad regulas secundi modi nisi in productione ramusculorum de ramis, ut predictum est. Verbi gratia, posito hoc quod in diuisione thematis dictum est: “Sub hac particula *Tu es sacerdos,* etc., describitur officium sacerdotis,” et posset assumi ita:

22. altera] R.V; alia P.

23. isto (modo)] *apparently* P *found* i'o *in his exemplar, misunderstood it as "primo," and continuned with* uel ii'o . . . ; *or else an eyeskip occurred. Similar confusions appear in* R *and* V.

24. in secunda . . . in primo] V; uel secundo P *(see previous note); om.* R.

25. aliorum] R.V; aliquorum P.

26. uel] V *ends here.*

27. aliis] P; *om.* L.V *(garbled text). The sense of the sentence would require* alia (particula).

[b] Second: If two phrases or words appear in the thema of which one concerns the second person, the other the third,[37] it is to be taken as was said at the beginning of this mode [II.1]. But in handling it the preacher must deal with the first part according to the rules stated in this mode, with the second according to the rules given in the first, third, or fourth, and so on with the others, as seems to be most pertinent. For example, if the preacher has announced as his thema *Have pity on me, son of David, for my daughter is grievously troubled by a devil,*[38] he must deal with the complete clause *Have pity on me,* etc., according to the rules that have been and will be set forth here. But with what follows, *my daughter* [etc.], he must deal according to rules contained in other modes that can be more readily applied to this part. But in the opposite case—namely, when the beginning of the thema regards the first or third person, but its end the second—then he does not need to deal with it according to the rules that distinguish this mode from the others, except with regard to drawing out twigs from the branch, if there are any. For example, if [the second part is] in the second person, it is sufficient that the twigs arise from the branch with some rationale, nor do they need to do so by art. For instance, given a thema from Psalm 109: *The Lord has sworn and he will not repent: You are a priest forever according to the order of Melchizedek,*[39] with regard to the part *The Lord has sworn,* etc., one must proceed according to the first or third or fourth mode, and so on, and likewise with regard to the other [part], nor must it [i.e., the latter] be reduced to the rules of the second mode except in producing twigs from the branches, as has been said. For example, if in the division of the thema was said "In the part *You are a priest,* etc., the office of a priest is described," one could continue:

37. This paragraph discusses how to handle authorities that contain sequences (of grammatical persons) 2-3; 3-2; 3-2-3; and 2-3-2.

38. Mt 15:22.

39. Ps 109:4 (110:4).

Dicit autem tria de sacerdote—
ipsam dignitatem sacerdotalem, ibi *Tu es sacerdos;*
perpetuitatem, ibi *in eternum;*
formam uel modum, ibi *secundum ordinem Melchisedec.*

Idem[28] dico si uerba secunde persone ueniant in medio auctoritatis, ita dumtaxat ut in principio uel fine auctoritatis sint uerba tertie persone, ut patet in hoc uersu Psalmi cix.a: *Dixit Dominus domino meo, sede a dextris meis,* in qua quidem auctoritate uerba media pertinent ad secundam personam, prima et ultima ad terciam; vnde in principio dicitur *Dominus,* in ultimo *inimicos.* Si uero in principio et fine auctoritatis sint uerba secunde persone, ut hic Psalmo cvii.a: *Exurge, gloria mea, exurge, psalterium et citara, exurgam diluculo. Confitebor tibi,* etc., negociandum est secundum regulas istius modi per totum, excepto quod intermedium potest reduci ad primum modum conuenienter,[29] et tunc inuenienda est in illa particula una radix que extrahatur artificialiter et sufficienter. Quique rami siue ramusculi sic educti ex parte ante debent conuenire cum sua radice, ex parte post cum ramo principali immediate subsequente.

[c] Tercia regula est quod de proposito themate non sunt extrahendi rami de radice; non enim ponitur radix sed aliquid quasi[30] pro radice; nec proprie uocantur rami sed partes exeuntes ab illo toto. Que quidem partes exire habent non artifficialiter nec sufficienter, sed sufficit quod per aliquem numerum. Verbi gratia, posito themate *Fili Dauid, miserere mei, quia filia mea male a demonio uexatur* et dicto[31] "Vox est petentis auxilium siue allegantis pro filia," statim assumatur:

28. Idem] R; ideo P.
29. conuenienter] P; congrventer R.
30. quasi] P; aliud R.
31. et dicto] R; *om.* P.

He [i.e., the Psalmist] declares three things about a priest:
his priestly dignity, when he says *You are a priest;*
its perpetuity, when he says *forever;*
and its form or manner, when he says *according to the order of Melchizedek.*

I say the same if second-person words appear in the middle of an authority, while at its beginning or its end stand words in the third person. This is the case in the verse of Psalm 109: *The Lord has said to my lord, Sit on my right* [*until I make your enemies your footstool*].[40] In this authority the words in the middle are in the second person [i.e., *Sit on my right*], while the first and last ones are in the third person: in the beginning *The Lord,* and in the end *enemies.* But if at the beginning and at the end of an authority stand second-person words, as in Psalm 117: *Arise, my glory, arise, psaltery and harp, I will arise early in the morning. I will praise you,* etc.,[41] then one must handle the quotation according to the rules of this [second] mode in its entirety, except that the middle part can be conveniently reduced to the first mode, and then one must find in that part a root that may be drawn out by art and with some rationale. Any branches or twigs thus drawn from the preceding part must agree with their root; those that are drawn from the subsequent part must agree with the main branch that immediately follows.

[c] Third: No branches of the announced thema are to be drawn out of a root, because there is no root but rather something that takes the place of the root; nor are those parts properly called "branches" but rather "parts that derive from the whole" [authority]. By their nature such parts arise neither by art nor with some rationale; it is enough if they arise with the help of some numeral. For example, if the preacher has announced as thema *Son of David, have pity on me, for my daughter is grievously vexed by a demon*[42] and said: "This is the voice of one praying for or mentioning her daughter," he should at once continue:

40. Ps 109:1 (110:1).
41. Ps 107:3 (108:1–2).
42. Mt 15:22.

Tria sunt que reddunt petitionem istius domine exaudibilem—

persona a qua petit;
modus petendi;
res pro qua petit.

Persona a qua petit, ibi *Fili Dauid;* modus petendi, ibi *miserere mei*—qui enim uult sibi misereri, miseriam ostendit; res pro qua petit siue fit peticio, ibi *filia mea,* etc.

Licet autem partes huiusmodi per quandam enumerationem exeant, non tamen in repetitione earum dicam "prima," "secunda," "tercia." Immo ab huiusmodi et ab[32] "aut" et "uel" abstineatur penitus, sicut dictum est in primo modo. Repetantur autem partes sicut patet in themate immediate supra posito.[33]

[d] Quarta regula: Ad ornatum istius modi facit vt, si thema habeat plures partes, quot rationes assignantur circa primam, totidem circa quamlibet aliarum sequentium assignentur. Verbi gratia, posito pro themate illud Ezechielis xxviii: *Tu signaculum similitudinis plenum sapientia et decore,* et dicto "Vox est comendantium beatum Bernardum[34] uel quemlibet[35] sanctum," et assumpto "Quatuor sunt in quibus commendatur beatus Bernardus,[36] scilicet in *signaculo, similitudine, sapientia,* et *decore,*" si dicatur quod "Triplici de causa dicitur beatus Bernardus[37] Dei *signaculum,*" totidem cause assignande sunt quare dicatur *similitudo,* et totidem quare dicatur *sapientia,* et totidem quare dicatur *decor.*

Notandum circa hoc quod si tres[38] predicte rationes assumantur de proprietatibus *signaculi,* omnes alie assumende sunt de proprietatibus sequentium partium; et si prime[39] ab effectibus, et alie similiter[40] ab effectibus. Idem dico de omni alia facie a quacumque rationes prime partis extrahantur.

32. ab] P; *add* hiis coniunctionibus R.
33. posito] R; posita P.
34. Bernardum] P; Franciscum R.
35. quemlibet] P; alium R.
36. beatus Bernardus] P; *om.* R.
37. beatus Bernardus] P; *longer om.* R.
38. si tres predicte] sic res predicte P; sic predicte tres R.
39. prime] R; proprie P.
40. alia similiter] P; secunde R.

There are three things that render the petition of this woman worthy to be heard:

the person who is asked,
her way of asking,
and the thing for which she is asking.

The person who is asked, in *Son of David;* her way of asking, in *have pity on me*—for he who has pity on someone shows pity; and the thing for which she is asking or makes her petition, in *My daughter,* etc.

But even if the parts in this way arise through some enumeration [i.e., "three things"], in repeating them I should not say "the first," "the second," "the third." Such a procedure, as well as using a word like "but" and "or," must be completely avoided, as was said in our first mode. Let the parts be [simply] repeated as is shown in the thema given immediately above.

[d] Fourth, to embellish this mode: If the thema has several parts, the same number of reasons that are given for the first part must also be given for each of the following parts. For example, let the thema be Ezekiel 28: *You were the seal of resemblance, full of wisdom and beauty*[43] and say "This is the voice of people who commend blessed Bernard or any saint," and then continue: "There are four things in which blessed Bernard is commended, namely in *seal, resemblance, wisdom,* and *beauty.*" Now, if the preacher then says that blessed Bernard is called God's *seal* for three reasons, he must adduce the same number of reasons why he is called *resemblance,* and the same number why *wisdom,* and the same number why *beauty.*

With regard to this it should be noted that if these three reasons are taken from the *properties* of a seal, all the others must similarly be taken from the *properties* of the following parts; and if the first are taken from the *effects* of a seal, then the others must be similarly taken from its *effects.* The same, I say, applies to any other aspect *(facies)* from which such reasons are drawn.

43. Ez 28:12.

Instantiam autem [f. 188] non[41] habet ista regula in uno, utpote quando occurrit proprium nomen. Tunc enim oportet negociari circa interpretationem nominis proprii, quod non potest fieri circa alias partes non habentes proprium nomen. Quando autem ita occurrit proprium nomen, si de re nominis uel que significantur per illud nomen possunt haberi rationes congruentes[42] rationibus aliarum partium, bene quidem. Verbi gratia, posito themate hoc Genesis: *Non uocaberis ultra Iacob, sed Israel erit nomen tuum,* et dicto "Vox est sollicitantis ad melius," et assumpto:

> Duo sunt que describuntur:[43]
> status actiuorum, ibi *non uocaberis ultra Iacob,* a quo reuocat;
> et status contemplatiuorum ad quem sollicitat,[44] ibi *sed Israel erit nomen tuum,*

statim potes procedere in hunc modum:

> *Iacob* signat statum actiuorum propter tria. Sicut enim actiui habent pugnare contra tres hostes—scilicet mundum, carnem, et diabolum— ita Iacob pugnauit contra tres hostes:
> primo contra fratrem suum Esau, per quem intelligitur caro;
> secundo contra Laban, qui interpretatur dealbatio, per quem mundus intelligitur;
> tertio contra angelum, per quem intelligitur diabolus.

Hoc dicto, statim dicendum est:

> *Israel* significat statum contemplatiuorum propter tria, quia Israel (sicut ipse dicit Genesis) uidit *Deum facie ad faciem,* vidit terram promissionis,[45] vidit et intrauit Egiptum, ad significandum quod contemplatiuus debet tria contemplari: Deum ad fruendum, bona patrie ad diligendum, peccatum proximorum ad compaciendum,[46] quia ut dicit Gregorius, "Vnusquisque talem misericordiam a Deo est accepturus qualem ipse proximo suo dederit."

Si autem in prima parte processissem per expositionem siue interpretationem nominis dicens: "*Iacob* interpretatur luctator," deberem in

41. non] *om.* R.P; *required by sense.*
42. congruentes] R; congruentibus P.
43. describuntur] R; describit P.
44. et status . . . sollicitat] R; *om.* P.
45. promissionis] *add* Genesis P, *perhaps due to the word having been misplaced in a schema.*
46. peccatum proximorum ad compaciendum] P; peccata preteritorum ad dolendum et compaciendum R.

There is one exception to this rule, namely, when there is a proper noun. For then it is necessary to deal with the interpretation of the name, which cannot be done in the other parts if they do not [also] contain a name. But when a proper noun thus occurs that reasons can be derived from the object thus named or from what that name signifies, and these reasons are the same as for the other parts, then it is all right. For example, if the thema is the verse in Genesis *You will not be called Jacob any longer but your name will be Israel,*[44] and you say, "This is the voice of one calling to something better," and next:

Here are two things described:
the state of active people, in *You will not be called Jacob any longer,* from which he calls back;
and the state of contemplatives to which he calls, in *Your name will be Israel,*

then you can at once proceed in this fashion:

Jacob indicates the state of active people for three reasons. For just as active people naturally fight against three enemies—that is, the world, the flesh, and the devil—so Jacob fought against three enemies:
first against his brother Esau, by whom we understand the flesh;
second against Laban, whose name means "white-washing," whereby we understand the world;
third against the angel, by whom we understand the devil.

And when this much has been said, one is to continue at once:

Israel indicates the state of contemplatives for three reasons. For Israel (as he himself says in Genesis) saw *God face to face,*[45] saw the Promised Land, and saw and entered into Egypt. This signifies that a contemplative must contemplate three things: God to enjoy, the goods of his homeland to love, and his neighbors' sin to have compassion—for as Gregory says, "Everyone will receive that mercy from God which he himself has shown to his neighbor."[46]

Now, if I had, in the first part, proceeded by an explanation or interpretation of the name and said, "*Jacob* means 'wrestler,'" then I should in the second part proceed in like fashion and say, "*Israel* means 'a man seeing God.'"

44. Gn 35:10.
45. Gn 32:30.
46. Cf. Defensor, *Scintillarium* 5.8 (CCSL 117, p. 23), attributed to Augustine.

secunda parte similiter procedere dicens: "*Israel* interpretatur uir uidens Deum."

Notandum etiam circa idem quia quotquot interpretationes accipiuntur de uno proprio nomine, tot accipiende sunt de alio, si plura sint ibi propria nomina circa eundem ramum uel ramusculum. Si uero circa diuersos ramos principales, tunc non est necessarium; si autem fiat, non est inconueniens. Si autem de re nominis non possunt haberi alique rationes et oportet negociari circa interpretationem nominis, tunc a diuersis partibus thematis assumantur diuerse rationes, ita quod quelibet pars habeat differentes rationes, id est, rationes sumptas a diuersis faciebus. Ita tamen quod semper sit conuenientia in numero, ita quod, si in prima parte assignentur tres rationes, totidem in quolibet[47] assignentur, et etiam ab ipso nomine assumantur totidem interpretationes, si habeantur materie congruentes.

[e] Quinta regula est quod omnes partes posite in sermone secundum istum modum reducende sunt ad—

[i] diuersos status,[48]
[ii] conditionem,
[iii] professionem,
[iv] perfectionem,
[v] ordinationem.

Ad cuius euidentiam notandum quod est multiplex status,[49] conditio, professio, perfectio, ordinatio.[50]

[i] Status:

vie-patrie, uiuentium-fruentium, uiatoris-comprehensoris.

Incole-peregrini, currentium-tendentium ad brauium.

Pugnantium-triumphantium, flentium-gaudentium, debilium-firmorum.

Spei-rei, fidei-intellectus, laboris-quietis.

Meriti-premii, Marthe-Marie. [f. 188v]

47. quolibet] P; qualibet parte R.
48. ad diuersos status] *written twice* P.
49. status] *written twice* P.
50. *In* P, *the following list uses multiple schemata, not reproduced here.*

With regard to the same matter one should also notice that, in case there are several proper nouns connected with the same branch or twig, the same number of interpretations[47] that are given for one name must be given for the other as well. This is not necessary when it occurs with regard to *different* main branches; but if it is done, it is not unfitting. However, if no reasons can be found regarding what a name stands for, and one has to apply an interpretation of the name, then different reasons must be taken from different parts of the thema, so that each part has different reasons, that is, reasons taken from different aspects *(facies)*. But this must be done in such a way that there is always agreement in number, so that, if in the first part three reasons are given, the same number must be given in every other part, and likewise for the name itself the same number of interpretations must be given, if suitable material is available.

[e] Fifth: All parts placed in a sermon according to this mode must be reduced to different

[i] status
[ii] conditions
[iii] professions
[iv] degrees of perfection
[v] sequences

One must therefore be aware that there is a multiplicity of status, conditions, professions, degrees of perfection, and sequences.

[i] [Regarding the] status [one can differentiate between]: this life and our true home, those living here and those who enjoy blessedness, the wayfarer and him who has arrived, the inhabitant and the pilgrim, those who just run and those who aim for the prize, the fighting and the triumphant, those who weep and those who rejoice, the weak and the strong, hope and possession, faith and understanding, labor and rest, merit and reward, Martha and Mary, those who sow and those who reap, seed and fruit, and similar pairs.

47. Medieval texts frequently offer more than one "etymology" of a name. See for example the three different "etymologies" given for *Israel* in Fusignano X. Other examples occur with some regularity in the *Legenda aurea*.

Seminantium-metentium, siue seminis-fructus, et hiis similia.

Status bonorum-malorum, spine-lolii, vt in canone, sanorum-egrorum.

Filii ire-filii gratie, miserorum-felicium, lucis-tenebrarum, mortis[51]-uite.

Vetus Adam-nouus Adam, vetus homo-nouus homo.

Filii seculi-lucis, filii Dei-diaboli.

Habens caracterem agni-bestie, et sic de hiis similibus.

Ad hunc statum possunt reduci: ignorantes-scientes.

Vel possunt habere proprium statum sic:

peregre proficiencium-errancium,

vigilantium-dormientium, occulorum-pedum, cecorum-uidentium.

Rei opace-diaphane siue transparentis.[52]

Noctis-diei, vespere-mane, solis-lune.

Domus fenestre clausa-aperta, speculi-feni.

Incipientium-progredientium-pervenientium, qui quandoque dicuntur inchoantes-proficientes-consumati.

Status—

Ciues Ierusalem-Babilonie, heredes-servi.

Filii ancille-libere, filii Agar-Sare.

Filii carnis-spiritus, sarmentum-uitis.

Quandoque intrantes-euntes-exeuntes, quandoque in statu preceptorum-consiliorum-supererogantium.[53]

Extirpantes uicia-seminantes uirtutes-colligentes fructus.

Status legalis, qui quandoque dicuntur legales—

Lege nature-scripture-gratie; quandoque lex umbre-figure ueritatis. [f. 189]

Lex Ade-Moysi-Christi.

Ad hoc potest reduci status Ecclesie, vt dicatur matrimonium iniciatum-ratum-consumatum;

vel itinerancium prefiguratum-prenunciatum-adimpletum.

51. mortis] R; meroris P.

52. transparentis] transponentis P.

53. supererogantium] interrogantium P; R *lacks the sentence.*

The status [can also be differentiated between] the good and the evil, thorns and grapes as said in Scripture,[48] the healthy and the sick, the sons of wrath and those of grace, the miserable and the blessed, light and darkness, death and life, the old Adam and the new, the old man and the new, the children of this world and the children of light, the children of God and the children of the devil, being like a lamb or like a beast, and so on.

To the same differentiation can be reduced the ignorant vs. those who know; or to those who progress in their pilgrimage vs. those who wander astray, the vigilant vs. those who sleep, eyes vs. feet, the blind vs. the seeing, something opaque vs. something diaphanous or transparent, night vs. day, evening vs. morning, sun vs. moon, an open window vs. a closed one, mirror vs. ?,[49] beginners vs. those in progress and those who have arrived.

[And further] the status of: citizens of Jerusalem vs. citizens of Babylon, heirs vs. servants, sons of the slave woman vs. those of the free woman, sons of Hagar vs. those of Sarah, children of the flesh vs. those of the spirit, brushwood vs. vine. Sometimes they can be divided into those who enter, who go on, who exit; or those who live according to the commandments vs. those who follow the [evangelical] counsels, and those who go even further; those who weed out their vices vs. those who plant virtues and those who gather the fruits.

Also the legal status can be differentiated, according to the law of nature, of scripture, and of grace; sometimes the law of darkness, of prefiguration, and of truth; the law of Adam, Moses, and Christ. Likewise, states in the Church, as marriage can be differentiated into proposed, entered, and consummated; or the status of a journey, as differentiated between planned, undertaken, and completed.[50]

48. Rochelle may be thinking of Mt 7:17 (gathering grapes from thorn bushes) or Lk 6:44 (figs from thorn bushes).

49. I cannot make sense of the (clearly written) *feni,* in opposition to *speculi.* Is Rochelle thinking of something like *phenomeni*? or, less likely, of *fenum,* "hay," set in opposition to *spicula,* "a small ear of grain, etc."? or more far-fetched, of *speculum* as the title of a book vs. *fen,* a chapter (as in Avicenna)?

50. Tentative translation.

[ii] Condicio:

Clericorum-laicorum, religiosorum-secularium.

Prelatorum-subditorum, doctorum-discipulorum, actiuorum-contemplatiuorum.

Matrimonium-predicatorum, virginum; coniugatorum-uiduarum-virginum; patriarcharum-prophetarum-apostolorum-euangelistarum.

[iii] Professio complectitur conditionem et statum.

[iv] Perfectio:

In se-in comparatione; que quandoque potest dici perfectio in intellectu-in affectu.

In cognitiva-affectiva; in fide-moribus.

In scientia-vita; interior-exterior; in animo-corpore.

Perfectio in uirtutibus theologicis, idest: infusis-theoricis, id est acquisitis.

Item perfectio quoad Deum-proximum-se; in significatiua-affectiua-operatiua.

Quandoque in memoria-intellectu-voluntate; quandoque corde-ore-opere.

Perfectio in fide-spe-caritate; in bono innato-infuso-in acquisito.

Secundum ierarchiam supercelestem-celestem-humanam; secundum rationalem-irascibilem-concupiscibilem;

secundum precepta-consilia-supererogationes.[54]

Perfectio quoad proximum superiorem-parem-inferiorem.

[v] Ordinatio quoad incipientes-progredientes-peruenientes; quandoque secundum bonum-honestum-utile.

Quandoque secundumn uerum-bonum-arduum,

et breuiter ad hunc modum possunt reduci omnes differentie date de statu [f. 189v] et conditione.

Item, breuiter per omnes easdem differentias per quas currit perfectio, currit ordinatio.

[f] Sexta regula: Si plura propria nomina occurrunt in eodem thema et non possunt haberi tot interpretationes de uno quot de alio, pro-

54. supererogationes] R; interrogationes P.

[ii] Conditions [can similarly be distinguished]: cleric and lay, religious and secular, prelates and subjects, teachers and disciples, active and contemplative, matrimony and preachers, virgins; married people, widows, and virgins; patriarchs, prophets, apostles, and evangelists.

[iii] Professions include both conditions and status.

[iv] Perfection: in itself and in comparison with something else, which sometimes may be said to be perfection in intellect vs. affect; in the cognitive vs. the affective power; in faith and in works; in knowledge and in living; interior vs. exterior; in the soul and in the body. Perfection with respect to the theological virtues: infused vs. acquired. Similarly perfection with respect to God, to one's neighbor, and to oneself; or in understanding, desire, and deed. Or in one's memory, intellect, and will; or in heart, mouth, and deed. Perfection [further] in faith, hope, and love; with regard to the innate, infused, or acquired good. [Further, degrees of perfection] with regard to hierarchies: above-heavens, heavenly, and human; with regard to the rational, irascible, and concupiscible [faculties of the soul]; with regard to the commandments, the counsels, and works beyond; and with respect to one's neighbor: a superior, an equal, or an inferior.

[v] In a sequence: those who begin, progress, and have arrived; or the good, the honorable, the useful; or else what is true, good, and difficult. In brief, all the differences that have been given with respect to status and condition can be reduced to this last mode. And similarly, a sequence occurs likewise in all the differences that occur in degrees of perfection.

[f] Sixth: If there are several proper nouns in one and the same thema and one cannot find the same number of etymologies for one as for another, one should proceed according to different aspects *(facies)* in

cedatur secundum diuersas facies in eisdem. Verbi gratia, negocietur circa unum nomen per interpretationes nominis, circa aliud per proprietates sumptas de re nominis uel secundum aliam aliquam faciem.

[g] Septima regula: Si in aliquo themate dirigitur sermo ad secundam personam ratione questionis, non oportet quod alique trahantur partes ab eo quod ponitur quasi pro radice; sed magis[55] congruit ut se extendat ad inquisitionem similium questionum que in sacra scriptura reperiuntur et sue congruunt[56] materie. Verbi gratia, si ponatur pro themate Canticorum *Que est ista que ascendit quasi aurora?* et dicto "Vox est querentium et admirantium beatitudinem beate Marie," statim assumere poteris:

Tres inuenimus questiones factas de beata Maria secundum eius triplicem statum: natiuitatis, conceptionis filii sui, et assumptionis. Ideo:

quandoque queritur Canticorum: *Que est ista que progreditur;*

quandoque Canticorum: *Que est ista que ascendit de deserto sicut uirgula fumi;*

quandoque Canticorum: *Que est ista que ascendit de deserto deliciis affluens;*

et ita negocietur circa questiones illas.

[h] Octava regula est: Dictiones consignificatiue in quacumque parte thematis inueniantur[57] possunt reduci ad quamcumque partem uolueris principalem, et possunt ramusculi sufficienter deduci ab illa.

[i] Nona regula est: In quacumque parte thematis inuenitur nomen quod supponitur[58] principali uerbo, ab eodem inchoandum est primo in negociacione.[59]

[j] Decima[60] regula est: Si fiat conuersio ad secundam personam ratione detestationis uel exhortationis et huiusmodi, et dicto eo quod iam[61] ponitur quasi pro radice, non oportet aliquas partes ex

55. magis] *interlinear addition, illegible* P.
56. congruunt] R; congruit P.
57. Dictiones . . . inueniantur] P; quando dictiones in quacumque parte thematis inueniuntur R.
58. supponitur] R; supponat P.
59. negociacione] R; negociacionem P.
60. Decima] P; decima et ultima R.
61. iam] *an abbreviated word hardly legible, possibly* tunc? P; *om.* R.

them. For example, one may deal with one name by way of its etymology, and with another by way of the properties belonging to the object named or according to any other aspect.

[g] Seventh: If a thema contains an expression directed to a second person in the form of a question, it is not necessary to draw any parts from what is, as it were, put as the root, but it is more fitting for the preacher to look for similar questions in Scripture that agree with his subject matter. For example, if you take as thema the verse from Canticles *Who is she that rises like the dawn?*[51] and you have said "This is the voice of those who ask about and admire the beauty of blessed Mary," you can at once continue:

> We find three questions concerning blessed Mary, according to her threefold status: her nativity, the conception of her son, and her assumption. Therefore—
>
> at one point the question is asked, in Canticles, *Who is she that comes forth?*[52]
>
> at another point, in Canticles, *Who is she that rises from the desert like a pillar of smoke?*[53]
>
> and at yet another point, in Canticles, *Who is she that rises from the desert flowing with delights?*[54]

and then you can deal with those questions.

[h] Eighth: Synonymous words, in whatever part of the thema they may be found, can be reduced to any main part of the thema that you wish, and then twigs can be drawn from it with some rationale.

[i] Ninth: In whatever part of the thema one finds a noun that relates to the main verb as its subject, one must begin from it first in one's development.

[j] Tenth: If there is an address of a second person in the form of loathing or exhortation and such, once one has said something that is then placed as the root, then it is not necessary to derive parts from it, but it suffices to take the entire unit at once and say: "This is to be commended" or "to be detested" or "This is commended or detested in

51. Sg 6:9.
52. Sg 6:9.
53. Sg 3:6.
54. Sg 8:5.

ea producere, sed sufficit totum illud assumere in communi et dicere: "Hoc est commendabile" uel "detestabile" siue "Hoc[62] commendatur uel detestatur in sacra Scriptura propter tres uel quatuor rationes," quas uolueris assignare. Conuertas enim te ad materias,[63] ad effectus, et ad alias facies, et ex hiis poteris assumere quot uolueris rationes.

[III]

Tercius modus est per antithesim, idest per oppositionem,[64] uidelicet, quando aliqua auctoritas proponitur, et deinde contrarium eidem assumitur, et post per diuisionem assumpte[65] habetur per contrarium diuisio proposite.[66] Verbi gratia, posito pro themate illud Ysaie i: *Quiescite agere peruerse, discite benefacere,* iste est processus istius modi: Primitus fit processus de malo quam de bono, posito themate:

In Ieremia legitur de peccatoribus: *Sapientes sunt ut faciant mala, bene autem facere nescierunt.* Sicut due sunt partes iusticie, scilicet declinare a malo, facere bonum, sic due sunt partes iniusticie. Vnde propheta in propositis uerbis duo mala peccatoribus inproperat, scilicet facere malum, declinare a bono, que sunt due partes iniusticie siue iniuste. Ab isto autem duplici modo reuocat Dominus peccatores hic per prophetam Ysaiam dicens: *Quiescite agere,* etc. *Peruerse* enim agit qui ordinem faciendorum agendo peruertit. Vnde notandum quod triplex ordo debet esse in homine. Debet enim esse ordinatus quoad se, proximum, Deum. Agit ergo peruerse qui se deordinat ad ista tria. Ex inordinatione[67] sui ad se potest homo agere peruerse [f. 190] tripliciter—

> cogitando; Ecclesiastici ii: *Ve duplici corde;*
> loquendo, scilicet de Deo blasphemando, vnde talis debet lapidari;
> operando.[68]

Ex inordinatione sui ad proximum tripliciter—

> corde; Psalmus: *Locuntur pacem cum proximo suo;*

62. siue Hoc] R; si P.
63. materias] P; materiam R.
64. oppositionem] appositionem P; *phrase om.* R.
65. assumpte] P; auctoritatis assumpte R.
66. proposite] P; auctoritatis proposite R.
67. inordinatione] R; ordinatione P.
68. operando] *add* Psalmus Operantur iniquitatem in viis eius ambulant R.

Holy Scripture for three or four reasons," which you may want to give. You should turn to its subject matter, to its effects, and other aspects, and from these you can assume however many reasons you wish.

[III]

The third mode uses antithesis or opposition; that is to say: an authority is quoted and then its opposite is taken up, and after that, by dividing what has thus been taken up, one gets through antithesis [back] to the division of the announced authority. For example, let us take as thema the words of Isaiah 1: *Cease to act perversely, learn to do well.*[55] The development in this mode is then as follows: First one expands on the evil part rather than the good one. Thus, after announcing the thema [one says]:

In Jeremiah we read about sinners: *They are wise to do evil, but they do not know how to do good.*[56] Just as there are two parts to being just, namely, turning away from evil and doing good, so there are two parts to being unjust. Therefore in the quoted words the prophet reproaches sinners for two evils, namely, doing evil and turning away from good, which are the two parts of being unjust. From this twofold way the Lord here calls sinners back through the prophet Isaiah when he says: *Cease to do,* etc. For a person acts *perversely* when in his actions he perverts [i.e., turns around] the right order of what is to be done. Hence we must note that there should be a threefold order in a person. He must be ordered with respect to himself, to his neighbor, and to God. Therefore a person acts perversely when he is disordered in regard to these three. By disordering himself with respect to himself a man may act perversely in three ways:

in his thought; Ecclesiasticus 2: *Woe to them who are of a double heart;*[57]
in his words, by blaspheming God, for which he ought to be stoned;[58]
and in his deeds.

By disordering himself with respect to his neighbor, in three ways:

in his heart; the Psalm verse *They speak peace with their neighbor,* [*but there are evils in their hearts*];[59]

55. Is 1:16–17.
56. Jer 4:22.
57. Sir 2:14.
58. Cf. Lv 24:14 and following.
59. Ps 27:3 (28:3).

uerbo; Psalmus: *Uerbum iniquum constituerunt aduersum* [*me*];

opere; Psalmus: *In uia hac quam ambulabam* [*absconderunt laqueum mihi*]; Ysaias x: *Vnusquisque proximo suo auxiliatur et fratri suo dicit: Confortare;* Michee: *Concupierunt agros.*

Contra tales Dominus in Matheo: *Ommia quecumque uultis ut faciant uobis homines,* etc.

Ex inordinatione sui ad Deum potest agere peruerse tripliciter—

cogitando; vnde de hiis Psalmus: *Cogitaverunt et locuti sunt nequitiam;*

loquendo; Psalmus: *Iniquitatem in excelso locuti;*

operando; Psalmus cvii.a: *Posuerunt aduersum me,* etc.;

Peruerse cogitando—loquendo—operando contra nos ipsos—proximum—Deum. Recte ergo dicitur: *Quiescite agere peruerse.*[69]

Sed quoniam non sufficit declinare a malo nisi faciat bonum, ideo sequitur: *discite benefacere.* Ad eadem ordinatur homo benefaciendo ad que ordinatur male agendo. Quando ergo discemus benefacere? Ordinando nos ad nos ipsos—ad proximum—ad Deum. In huiusmodi autem ordinatione docet nos Deus per prophetam Micheam vi: *Indicabo tibi, o homo,* etc.

[IV]

Quartus modus est quando res aliqua significatur in diuersis. Habetur iste modus in auctoritatibus parabolam continentibus. Verbi gratia, posito pro themate illud Psalmi ci: *Similis factus sum pellicano solitudinis:*

Inuenitur de beato Thoma in legenda sua quod fuit ordinatus quoad—

se per mundiciam castitatis; vnde, sicut legitur ibi, portabat cilicium ne caro superbiret;

Deum per deuotionem contemplationis, vnde quando persecutores inuaserunt eum, et ipse peragebat uespertinam sinaxim;

69. peruerse] R *adds:* cogitando, loquendo, et operando. Explicit ars predicandi, *and text ends.*

in his words; the Psalm verse *They established an unjust word against me;*[60]

and in his deeds; the Psalm verse *In this way where I walked they have hidden a snare for me;*[61] Isaiah 10: *Everyone shall help his neighbor and say, Be of good courage;*[62] Micah: *They have coveted fields.*[63]

Against these the Lord says in Matthew: *Whatever you would that people should do to you,* etc.[64]

And by disordering himself with respect to God he can also act unjustly in three ways:

in his thoughts; whence the Psalm says of them: *They have thought and spoken wickedness;*[65]

in his words; the Psalm: *They have spoken iniquity on high;*[66]

and in his deeds; Psalm 107: *They repaid me,* etc. [*evil for good*].[67]

Thus we act perversely in our thoughts, words, and deeds, against ourselves, our neighbor, and God. Therefore it is rightly said, *Cease to act perversely.*

But since it is not enough to turn away from evil without doing good, the quoted verse continues: *Learn to do good.* In doing good a man is ordered with respect to the same things as he is in doing evil. So, when shall we learn to do good? By ordering ourselves with respect to ourselves, to our neighbor, and to God. With regard to this ordering of ourselves, God teaches us through the prophet Micah 6: *I will show you, o man,* etc.[68]

[IV]

The fourth mode occurs when something is indicated by different [words or images]. This mode is found in authorities that contain a parable.[69] For example, let the thema be Psalm 101: *I have become like a pelican of the wilderness.*[70]

In his legend we find that blessed Thomas[71] was well ordered with respect to—

himself by chastity; therefore, as we read there, he wore a hair shirt so that his flesh would not grow proud;

God by devout contemplation; therefore, when his killers rushed in on him, he himself was saying vespers;

60. Ps 40:9 (41:8).
61. Ps 141:4 (142:3).
62. Is 41:6.
63. Mi 2:2.
64. Mt 7:12.
65. Ps 72:8 (73:8).
66. Ps 72:8 (73:9).
67. Ps 108:5 (109:5).
68. Mi 6:8.
69. Here and elsewhere Rochelle uses *parabola* in the sense of similitude or metaphor.
70. Ps 101:7 (102:6).
71. Evidently St. Thomas (Becket) of Canterbury.

proximum per opera pietatis, vnde sicut ibi legitur, pro grege suo mortuus est, iuxta illud *Bonus pastor animam suam,* etc.

Propter hoc beatus Thomas potest comparari—

turturi, qui est castissmus inter alias uolucres. Vnde uox angelorum comendancium eius castitatem potest esse in Canticis: *Vox turturis,* idest, comendatio castitatis beati Thome, *audita est in terra nostra uiuentium;*

thuri, cuius fumus eleuatur in celum. Vnde Dominus uolens ipsum erigere et gratia implere, dicit de ipso et consimilibus: *Vadam ad montem mirre et ad collem turis,* idest, ad beatum Thomam, cuius desiderium eleuatur in celum;

pellicano, sicut in auctoritate premissa, quia sicut pellicanus se exponit pro filiis, sic iste fecit pro suis. Vnde conuenienter potest dicere illud Psalmi ci: *Similis factus sum pellicano.*

[V]

Quintus modus est quarto contrarius, quando res una significat plura. Et habet modus iste locum in auctoritatibus parabolam continentibus. Verbi gratia, posito pro themate illud Genesis ix.d: *Archum meum ponam in nubibus et erit signum federis inter me et inter terram,* iste est modus procedendi in quinto modo sic:

Archus in sacra scriptura significat—

Ad litteram [f. 190v], instrumentum quo iacitur sagitta; vnde Genesis xxii.c legitur de Agar: *Abiit seditque e regione,* etc.

Sacram scripturam; vnde Psalmus vii: *Archum suum tetendit et parauit illum.*

Tetendit ostendendo comminationes, *parauit illum* per sanctos expositores. In isto archu corda est Nouum Testamentum flectens duriciam Ueteris. Habet enim arcus similitudinem cum sacra scriptura, quoniam sicut archus tentus minas et timorem incutit hostibus, ita Dominus per sacras scripturas peccatoribus.

Constanciam sanctorum, vnde Psalmus xvii.f: *Posuisti ut archum ereum brachia mea.*

and his neighbor by works of compassion; therefore, as we read there, he died for his flock, according to the verse *The good shepherd* [*gives*] *his life*, etc.[72]

For this reason Thomas may be compared—

to the turtledove, who is the most chaste of all birds. Therefore, it may be the voice of angels who praise his chastity in Canticles: *The voice of the turtle-dove*—that is, the praise of blessed Thomas's chastity—*is heard in our land;*[73]

to frankincense, whose smoke rises to heaven. Therefore, when God wanted to raise him and fill him with grace, he said of him and others like him: *I will go to the mountain of myrrh and to the hill of frankincense,*[74] that is, to blessed Thomas, whose desire was focused on heaven;

and to the pelican, as in the quoted authority, because just as a pelican offers himself for his young, so did he for his own. Wherefore we may fittingly say Psalm 101: *I have become like a pelican.*

[V]

The fifth mode is contrary to the fourth, [namely] when one and the same object signifies several different things. This mode can be found in authorities that contain parables. For example, if as thema Genesis 9 is chosen: *I will set my bow in the clouds of heaven, and it will be a sign of the covenant between me and the earth,*[75] the way of proceeding in the fifth mode then is as follows:

In Holy Scripture "bow" means:

Literally the instrument by which an arrow is shot; whence we read in Genesis 22 of Hagar that she *went away and sat* [*as far from him as a bow can shoot*].[76]

Holy Scripture, as in Psalm 7: *He has bent his bow and made it ready.*[77] He has *bent* it by showing his threats, he has *made it ready* by means of the holy exegetes. In this bow the string is the New Testament, which bends the hardness of the Old. For the bow is like Holy Scripture: just as a bent bow threatens and frightens the enemies, so does the Lord threaten and frighten sinners by means of Holy Scripture.

The constancy of the saints, as in Psalm 17: *You have made my arms like a bow of gold.*[78]

72. Jn 10:11.
73. Sg 2:12.
74. Sg 4:6.
75. Gn 9:13.
76. Gn 21:16.
77. Ps 7:13 (7:12).
78. Ps 17:35 (18:34).

Fortitudinem malorum, vnde I Regum ii: *Archus fortium superatus est.*

Futurum iudicium; vnde Psalmus lix.b: *Dedisti metuentibus te significationem,* idest signum crucis, *ut fugiant a facie arcus.* idest ab impugnatione futuri iudicii. Iste archus quasi extensus iam minatur sed nondum ferit, quia iudicium nos terret sed nondum infertur.

Potest etiam significare quemlibet sanctum post peccatum, uel post impugnationem Ecclesie ad unitatem fidei gratia Dei conuersum; et specialiter beatum Paulum, ut in uerbo proposito. Vnde de beato Paulo posset dici illud Ecclesiastici xliii.b: *Vide archum et benedic qui fecit illum; ualde speciosus est in splendore suo.* Est enim beatus Paulus speciosus dupliciter, per—

carnis castitate; vnde: *Volo omnes homines* [*esse sicut meipsum*];

boni exempli ostensionem; vnde: *Comendemus*[70] *nosmetipsos.*

Ad istam speciositatem nos inuitat ubi dicit: *ab omni specie mala abstinete uos.* Sed quia triplex fuit status eius, scilicet—

peccati ante conuersionem,
gratie post conuersionem,
apostolatus post conuersionem,

secundum hoc bene conuenit ei illud quod dicitur *Archum meum ponam in nubibus celi. Nubes* enim prelati, sacerdotes, et rectores Ecclesie dicuntur, quia sicut nubes inter celum et terram medie sunt, sic ipsi inter Deum et homines; clari et pulcri, sicut Psalmus dicit xvii: *Pre fulgore in conspectu eius nubes,* scilicet rectores ualde fulgidi mediatores debent esse; vnde Apocalipsis viii.s: *Vidi aquilam uolantem inter celum et terram clamantem: Ve, ve, ve habitantibus terram* retributionis, et secundum hoc conuenit ei quod sequitur: *et erit signum federis inter me et inter terram.* Hec tria que beato Paulo conueniunt in propositis uerbis describuntur. Potuit ergo dicere Dominus: *Archum meum,* idest beatum Paulum, *ponam in nubibus,* idest inter me et homines. Uel aliter, *in nubibus,* idest inter apostolos, qui significantur per nubes; vnde Ysaiae lx.b: *Qui sunt isti qui ut nubes uolant?*

70. comendemus] P; commendamus *source.*

The strength of evil men, as in 1 Kings 2: *The bow of the mighty is overcome.*[79]

The future judgment, as in Psalm 59: *You have given those who fear you a warning,* that is, the sign of the cross, *that they may flee from before the bow,*[80] that is, from the assault of the future judgment. This bow, as it is so to speak bent, threatens us now but does not yet strike, for the judgment frightens but is not yet brought upon us.

It can further mean any saintly person who, after sinning or after assaulting the Church, has been brought back by God's grace to the unity of faith. And in particular it may refer to blessed Paul, as in the announced thema. Whence of blessed Paul might be said Ecclesiasticus 43.b: *Look upon the bow and bless him who made it; it is very beautiful in its brightness.*[81] For blessed Paul is beautiful in two ways:

through the chastity of his flesh; whence: *I would that all [men were just like myself]*;[82]

through providing a good example; whence: *We commend ourselves.*[83] To this beauty he invites us when he says: *Refrain from every kind of evil.*[84]

Now Paul was in three states, namely—

that of sin before his conversion;
that of grace after his conversion;
and that of being an apostle after his conversion.

In accordance with this, the words *I will set my bow in the clouds of heaven* apply well to him. *Clouds* indicate prelates, priests, and rectors of the Church, for just as clouds are intermediary between heaven and earth, so are those intermediaries between God and men, bright and beautiful, as Psalm 17 says: *At the brightness before him the clouds [passed],*[85] that is, rectors should be very bright mediators; whence Revelation 8: *I saw an eagle flying between heaven and earth and crying, Woe, woe, woe to the inhabitants of the earth* (of retribution).[86] And for that reason, what follows [in the thema] also applies to him: *And it/he will be a sign of the covenant between me and the earth.* These three things that apply to blessed Paul are [thus] described in the quoted words [of the thema]. Therefore the Lord could say: *I will set my bow,* that is, blessed

79. 1 Sm 2:4.
80. Ps 59:6 (60:4).
81. Sir 43:12. *Arcus* here seems to refer to the rainbow, a meaning not considered in the present context.
82. 1 Cor 7:7.
83. 2 Cor 5:12.
84. 1 Thes 5:22.
85. Ps 17:13 (18:12).
86. Rv 8:13. "Of retribution" may be misplaced and rather modify "eagle."

[VI]

Sextus modus est quando ad expositionem et diuisionem auctoritatis proposite reducitur expositio et diuisio auctoritatis assumpte; et est iste modus quasi tercio oppositus. Tercius enim currit per antithesim, sextus uero currit per thesim, quando scilicet due auctoritates ponuntur sibi ipsis concorditer ad inuicem respondentes. Verbi gratia, ponatur pro themate:[71] *Ueniens ueniet et non tardabit; iustus meus ex fide uiuit.*

Veni, Domine, et noli tardare; relaxa facinora plebi tue.[72] In Ysaia, ubi famulatum sanctorum patrum innotescit apud Deum, tria allegantur, scilicet aduentus, acceleratio, causa aduentus.

Aduentus Christi, ibi: *veni, Domine;*
acceleratio, ibi: *noli tardare;*
causa, ibi: *relaxa facinora plebi tue.*

Sed quia, ut dicitur in Psalmo, *prope est Dominus omnibus inuocantibus eum in ueritate,* exaudiens est Deus Pater preces eorum, respondens [f. 191] eis tria promittit eis: aduentum, accelerationem, utilitatem.

Aduentum Christi ibi: *veniet;*
accelerationem ibi: *non tardabit;*
utilitatem ibi: *iustus meus ex fide uiuit.*

[VII]

Septimus modus est quando aliqua auctoritas inducitur simul triplici expositione exponenda, uel pluribus uel paucioribus. In quo quidem firmiter est tenendum ut quot membra in prima expositione proponuntur, tot in ceteris habeantur. Hic est modus procedendi in isto modo sic:

71. ponatur pro themate] *om.* P; *required by context.*
72. Veni . . . tue] *om.* P; *required by the following development.*

Paul, *in the clouds,* that is, between me and humans. Or in another way: *In the clouds,* that is, among the apostles, who are symbolized by clouds, as in Isaiah 60: *Who are those who fly like clouds?*[87]

[VI]

The sixth mode occurs when an explanation and division of a [second] assumed authority is used to explain and divide the authority chosen [as the thema]. This mode is, as it were, the opposite of the third mode, for the third mode employs contrast, this sixth mode uses identity, namely, when two authorities are quoted that correspond to each other precisely in their meaning. For example, let the thema be: *In his coming he shall come and not delay; the just man lives by faith.*[88]

Come, Lord, and do not delay; loosen the bonds of your people. When in Isaiah[89] the obedient service of the holy fathers before God is shown, three things are announced, namely his coming, its speed, and its cause.

The coming of Christ, in *Come, Lord;*
its speed, in *Do not delay;*
and its cause, in *Loosen the bonds of your people.*

But since, as is said in a Psalm, *The Lord is near to all who invoke him in truth,*[90] God the Father hears their prayers, and in answering them he promises them three things: His coming, its speed, and its usefulness

The coming of Christ, in *He shall come;*
its speed, in *He will not delay;*
and its usefulness, in *The just man lives by faith.*

[VII]

The seventh mode occurs when an authority is introduced that is to be explained at one and the same time by a threefold exposition, or by more or fewer [expositions].[91] In doing this it must be strictly observed that the same number of members is to be developed in all expositions as there are in the first. The way of development according to this mode, then, is this:

87. Is 60:8.

88. Hb 2:3–4.

89. The quoted text is not from Isaiah but from the Mass for the Fourth Sunday in Advent (Sarum Use).

90. Ps 144:18 (145:18).

91. As the illustration shows, by "exposition" the author here refers to the four senses of Scripture.

Regum: *Misit rex Salomon et tulit Iram de Tiro, filium mulieris uidue de tribu Neptali patre Tirio, plenum sapientia et intelligentia et doctrina ad faciendum omne opus.* Hec uerba ubi proposita possunt exponi tripliciter—

[a] hystorialiter siue literaliter,
[b] allegorice de aliquo sancto,
[c] moraliter ad edifficationem nostram.

[a] Secundum literalem expositionem sollicitant nos ad quatuor requirenda—

Quis fuit iste *Salomon,*
Iram,
vnde vocatus fuit,
ad quid.

[b] Verba ista secundum quod exponuntur de beato N. reddunt ipsum comendabilem in quatuor, scilicet in sua—

[i] mirabili uocatione. In qua occurrunt tria secundum personas: persone—

vocantis,[73] *Salomon,*
vocati, *Iram,*
terminus a quo uocatus fuit, *Tyrus.*

Fuit ergo in sua uocatione comendabilis tripliciter allegorice: ratione—

vocantis, quia *Salomon rex,* idest Christus, qui est pax nostra, rex regum, uocauit eum;

vocati, quia *Iram,* qui interpretatur uigilans plasmationi, idest uanitati sui, mundi, ut contempneret;

termini a quo uocatus fuit, quia *a Tyro,* qui interpretatur angustia, quia beatus N. uiderat se errasse, tempus amisisse, Deum offendisse. Ideo erat in quadam indicibili angustia positus.

Vocavit ergo rex Salomon Iram, beatum N, se et mundum studiosissime contempnentem, de omissis eiulantem. Quere concordantias in legenda.

[ii] Felici inchoatione, in qua habuit perfectionem in ra-

73. vocantis] *om.* P, *but see the next division, and clearly required by meaning and parallel structure.*

In the Book of Kings: *King Solomon sent and brought Hiram from Tyre, the son of a widow of the tribe of Nephthali, whose father was a Tyrian, full of wisdom and intelligence and skill to do all works.*[92] The quoted words can be expounded in three ways:

[a] as history or literally,
[b] allegorically in reference to some saint,
[c] and morally for our edification.

[a] In their literal exposition they urge us to ask four questions—

who was that *Solomon,*
[who was] *Hiram,*
from where was he called,
and to what [was he called].

[b] When these words are applied to blessed N., they show him to be commendable in four things, namely in—

[i] the admirable way he was called, in which three personal names occur, namely, the person—

who called, *Solomon,*
who was called, *Hiram,*
and where he was called from, *Tyre.*

In his being called he was thus commendable allegorically in three ways: because of—

who called: because *king Solomon,* that is, Christ, who is our peace, the king of kings, called him;

who was called: because *Hiram*—whose name means "watchful about his nature," that is, about being vain about himself and the world—[was called] so that he might despise these;

and where he was called from: because *from Tyre,* whose name means "anxiety," for blessed N. had realized that he had gone wrong, had wasted time, and had offended God. Therefore he found himself in some unspeakable anxiety.

Thus, King Solomon called Hiram, that is blessed N., who most eagerly despised himself and the world and bewailed what he had omitted. Look for fitting quotations in his legend.

[ii] His happy beginning, where he attained perfection in the rational,

92. 1 Kgs 7:13–14.

tionali, irascibili, concupiscibili, secundum fidem, spem, caritatem. Et propter hoc dicitur—

filius mulieris uidue; idest natus per fidem;[74] Augustinus: "Mulier uidua mater Ecclesia";

Tyrus, idest factus per spem;

Neptalicus, idest latus per caritatem.

[iii] Feliciori[75] progressione, in qua habuit ordinationem [f. 191v] ad—

se,
Deum,
proximum;

et propter hoc dicitur—

sapientia,
intelligentia,
doctrina,

que est contra—

luxuriam,
motus in Deum,
motus in proximum.

[iv] Felicissima consumatione, quia fuit *ad faciendum omne opus,* et merito, cum egregie esset perfectus et perfecte ordinatus, sicut ostensum est supra. Uel erat ad omne opus. *Omne* enim signum est uniuersale et requirit tria appellata, quod miro modo congruit beato N., quia fundauit triplicem ordinem—

penitentium,
pauperum dominarum,
contemplatiuorum,

in quibus est perfectio uite et doctrine.

Et vocauit Dominus Deus exercituum in die illa ad fletum, et ad planctum, ad calvitium, et ad cingulum sacci, et ecce gaudium et letitia.[76] Vocat—

ad caluicium contra concupiscentiam occulorum,
ad sacci cingulum contra concupiscentiam carnis,
ad lamentum contra superbiam uite.

74. idest natus per fidem] *om.* P. *A phrase like this is required by the structural parallelism of the subdivision.*

75. Feliciori] *as demanded by the schema;* felici P.

76. Et vocauit . . . letitia] *om.* P, *but clearly required by the following sentences. This*

irascible, and concupiscible parts of his soul, according to faith, hope, and love. And for that reason he is called—

the son of a widow; that is, born by faith; Augustine says: "The widow is the Church";

of Tyre, that is, made by hope;

of Nephthali, that is, taken by love.

[iii] His happier progress, where he had become well ordered with respect to himself, to God, and to his neighbor. And for that our quote speaks of *wisdom, intelligence,* and *skill,* which are opposed to lechery, to going against God, and to hostility to one's neighbor.

[iv] His most happy fulfillment, because he was [prepared] *to do all works;* and rightly so, since he was eminently perfect and perfectly ordered, as has been shown above. Or else, he was [ready to do] all works, for *all* signifies universality, which requires three items.[93] This applies marvelously to blessed N., because he founded three orders—one of penitents, another of poor women, and the third of contemplatives, in which is the perfection of life and of skill.

And the Lord, the God of hosts, in that day called to weeping and to mourning, to baldness, and to girding with sackcloth; and behold, joy and gladness.[94] He calls—

to baldness against the lust of the eyes,

to girding with sackcloth against the lust of the flesh,

and *to mourning* against the pride of life.[95]

93. Cf. Joannes Balbus, *Catholicon,* under *Omnis:* "Ut dicunt quidam, *omnis* in singulari numero ad minus requirit tria appellatiua."

94. Is 22:12–13.

95. For "lust of the eyes," etc., see 1 Jn 2:16.

Vocat—

ad citharam letitie propter mali presentis ablationem,

ad stolam glorie propter boni eterni adeptionem,

ad coronam uictorie propter hostis antiqui superationem.

[c] Verba ista moraliter exposita inuitant nos ad quatuor requirenda ex parte regis: ad—

humilitatem, quia[77] cum esset tantus illum uocare uoluit, iuxta illud *quam magnus* etc.;[78]

discretionem, quia uocavit, non—

luxuriosum,

ebriosum,

ociosum,

sed *plenum*—

sapientia,

scientia,

doctrina.

Item ad perfectionem duplicem, scilicet rationis—

interiorem, que respicit inuestigatiuam, iudicatiuam;[79]

exteriorem, que respicit interpretatiuam, ut simus pleni—

sapientia,

intelligentia,

doctrina,

ut sic meremur uocari a Domino.

Amen.

Explicit processus.

---

biblical quotation and its exposition to superationem *may seem to interrupt the development from* [*b*] *to* [*c*]. *But its division on* vocat *ties in with the earlier development of* vocatio *in* [*b.i*] *and may represent an afterthought jotted down here, either by Rochelle or a scribe; or else Rochelle took* tulit *in the original quotation from* 1 *Kgs* 7:13–14 (Misit rex Salomon et tulit...) *to mean "vocavit." P clearly reads "tu." (i.e., tulit).*

77. quia] qui P.

78. quam magnus etc.] P, *perhaps Sir* 25:13: Quam magnus qui invenit sapientiam et scientiam, sed non est super timentem Deum.

79. iudicatiuam] indicatiuam P.

He calls—

to the harp of *gladness* because present evil has been taken away;

to the stole of glory because eternal good has been embraced;

and to the crown of glory because the ancient foe has been overcome.[96]

[c] When interpreted morally, these words invite us to four things to be sought on the part of the king, to—

humility, because even though he [i.e., God?] is so great, he wished to call him [i.e., blessed N.?], according to the words *How great* [*is he who finds wisdom and knowledge; but there is none above him who fears the Lord*];[97]

discretion, because he called, not a person who is lecherous, a drunkard, or an idler, but one who is *full of wisdom, knowledge, and skill;*

and a twofold perfection of our reason, namely an interior one, which is concerned with investigation and judgment,

and an exterior one, which is concerned with interpretation; so that we may be *full of wisdom, intelligence, and skill,* and thus merit to be called by the Lord.

Amen.

Here ends the treatise.

96. Rochelle may be thinking of Sir 6:32: *You shall put on* [*wisdom*] *as a robe of glory, and you shall set her upon you as a crown of glory.*

97. Sir 25:13.

APPENDIXES & INDEXES

A

REFLECTIONS ON *ARTES PRAEDICANDI*

The edited texts draw attention to several major features of medieval sermon making as it was taught in the *artes praedicandi.* First is their insistence on, their preoccupation with, the biblical text. All five works—and indeed every *ars praedicandi*—declare that the scholastic sermon is to be built on a short text, and that this text is to be chosen from Scripture. This is precisely what thousands of medieval sermons in fact do. Such insistence would imply that a text that otherwise looks like a sermon but is not built on a *biblical* phrase should not be considered a "sermon." Hence discourses that contain a thema, divide it, and then develop its parts, but use as their thema a text from Aristotle[1] or Gratian,[2] should not be considered to be sermons but sermon-like discourses or speech acts, such as the *introitus* or introductory addresses to university courses, *principia,* or graduation speeches.[3] Modern scholars—and I must include myself—are not always conscious of this dis-

1. See for example the speech edited and discussed in Wenzel, "A Sermon in Praise of Philosophy," *Traditio* 50 (1995): 249–59, and further bibliography there.

2. Some examples are given by F. Donald Logan, "The Cambridge Canon Law Faculty: Sermons and Addresses," in *Medieval Ecclesiastical Studies in Honour of Dorothy M. Owen,* eds. M. J. Franklin and Christopher Harper-Bill (Woodbridge: Boydell Press, 1995), 151–64, at 160–64. An extreme case is Petrarch's *collatio* which he delivered on being crowned poet laureate. It is structured like a scholastic sermon but based on a verse from Virgil's *Georgics;* see *Scritti inediti di Francesco Petrarca,* ed. Attilio Hortis (Trieste: Lloyd Austro-Ungarico, 1874), 311–28.

3. But notice that the reverse is also the case: academic or other speech acts that are by their nature not sermons may be based on a biblical verse. Thus, many *introitus* to lecture courses on the Bible, on Peter Lombard's *Sentences,* or on philosophy, law, or the arts, do in fact have a biblical thema. For examples see Wenzel, "Academic Sermons at Oxford in the Early Fifteenth Century," *Speculum* 70 (1995): 305–29; or the end-of-semester speech by Frisby translated in Wenzel, *Preaching in the Age of Chaucer: Selected Sermons in Translation* (Washington, D.C.: The Catholic University of America Press, 2008), 298–35.

tinction between sermon and academic speech, but it should be observed.[4]

But preoccupation with the biblical text goes beyond choosing it as the basis of a sermon and properly dividing it. The parts of the division must be confirmed, that is, a reason must be given for what the preacher declares about the part he is dealing with, and that reason must be supported with a biblical quotation that contains the same or a cognate word, or at least the same notion. For instance, in dealing with the thema *The youth shall dwell with the virgin,* the preacher may deal with the key terms *youth, dwell,* and *virgin.* About *youth* he may declare that it is the nature of a young person to be beautiful and a source of joy. Applying this thought, for instance, to preaching at Christmas, the preacher can then say that we rejoice in the beautiful face of the Christ Child, which causes us joy. This thought is confirmed with the Psalm verse *I will go to the altar of God, who gives joy to my youth.* In other words, the logical development of the biblical thema which the preacher builds will always have to be supported with biblical proof texts. For that, sermon makers had to have such reference aids as collections of distinctions or biblical concordances close at hand.

The urge to prove, to confirm any statement with a biblical authority leads to a second main feature of the sermon structure taught by these works, their strictly logical construction and coherence. The entire discourse, the subject matter a preacher wants to speak about, is to be grounded on a scriptural verse or phrase as its "foundation" or "root," from which everything else develops, as it were, organically. The image of root, trunk, branches, and twigs used by some authors is more than a simple literary device; it signals the intimate and organic connectedness of the sermon parts. This organic connectedness appears not only between thema and general development but shows up in minor and even the most minute connections, such as between thema and protheme, or between thema, division, subdivision, and supporting authorities. What results gives the impression of being a verbal construct of essentially biblical material, erected in accordance with logical rules and such verbal devices as word repetition (the "verbal concordance") and, especially in the divisions, parallelism and end rhyme. To show how this is to be achieved seems to

4. It must be said, though, that medieval writers themselves occasionally referred to such speeches as *sermo.* See for example, "Incipit quidam sermo in philosophia editus Bononie...," with the thema "Philosophia est divinarum humanarumque rerum cognitio cum studio bene vivendi," Gianfranco Fioravanti, "*Sermones* in lode della filosofia e della logica a Bologna nella prima metà del XIV secolo," in *L'insegnamento della logica a Bologna nel XIV secolo,* eds. Dino Buzzetti, Maurizio Ferriani, and Andrea Tabarroni, Studi e memorie per la storia dell'Università di Bologna, new series, vol. 8 (Bologna: Istituto per la storia dell'Università di Bologna, 1992), 165–85, at 177. In medieval Latin *sermo,* of course, meant "speech" in general, while the stricter technical term for what we call sermon would have been *praedicatio.*

be the main, even exclusive, concern of the authors of *artes praedicandi* when they speak of sermon structure (those authors of what I have called "comprehensive" *artes* do of course speak of other things as well). To modern readers such constructs may well appear artificial and lifeless, but it might help us to think of them as the structural skeletons on which individual preachers would put, according to their ability and the perceived needs, the flesh of condemning vices, commending virtues, praising a saint, and even commenting on social ills. That they in fact did so is obvious to anyone who has taken the time to read a number of the many thousands of extant medieval sermons.

To this structural concern should be added a third major feature, their repeated approval of and demand for elegance and beauty. Frequently some advice is given *ad decorem sermonis,* to beautify the sermon. Similarly, the adjective *pulcher,* in one form or another, occurs with some regularity. In *Quamvis,* for instance, it is applied to one kind of introduction (the *manuduccio*), the division, an introductory *sententia,* the development *(processus),* examples, and logical deductions. Similarly, Fusignano several times labels one way of dealing with a part of the sermon as *modus pulcer* or *pulcrior.* In this connection it should be stressed that the adjective *curiosus* and its noun *curiositas* here clearly do not signal a negative quality, such as being "curious" or "far-fetched," but rather something positive like being "executed with care" or simply "elegant." For medieval preachers and their manuals of instruction, the rhetorical beauty of human discourse, or more simply *eloquentia,* was a quality not to be neglected.[5]

One means to enhance the beauty of a sermon is to develop its parts with a variety of rhetorical devices, including *exempla* or pious stories.[6] As a number of modern students have pointed out, in late-medieval preaching the desire to entertain with "quaint" stories and jokes tended to overshadow the preacher's earnest commitment to teaching faith and morals. Their criticism was anticipated, long before, by Dante, FitzRalph, Wyclif, Gascoigne, and many others—sufficient to testify that in the practice of actual preachers the use of such devices had gained dominance and was noted with disapproval. It is well to point out that in contemporary manuals for sermon making, shorter as well as longer ones, it was at best given very minor attention.[7]

5. The key text for this notion, as for so much else in medieval preaching theory, is Augustine's *De doctrina Christiana,* book 4.

6. Fusignano XV.

7. For further remarks on the use of the Bible in medieval preaching as well as modern assessments of late-medieval sermon rhetoric, see my contribution to the *New Cambridge History of the Bible,* vol. 2, eds. Richard Marsden and E. Ann Matter (Cambridge: Cambridge University Press, 2012), 680–92.

B

THE LIFE AND TRANSMISSION OF LATE-MEDIEVAL *ARTES PRAEDICANDI*

The text of *Quamvis,* its appearance in various forms and manuscripts, and beyond this the manuscripts used for the texts here edited, furnish a limited yet significant amount of data that yield some insights into the "life" of *artes praedicandi* during the later Middle Ages.

As noted in the introduction, *Quamvis* has been preserved in four manuscripts (L, A, O, and U). It also exists in an abbreviated form (G) and in addition furnishes the substance of a compilation beginning with its opening words and enriching it with material from other *artes praedicandi* (C; see the section on sources in the headnote to chapter II). The author of C, after copying the opening sentence that announces the three parts of sermon making to be discussed in the treatise, evidently felt the need for a definition of "sermon," found it in a short work perhaps written by John of Wales, which he copied in its entirety, and then returned to the text of *Quamvis,* to copy it to its end. Such compilatory work can be found in other *artes praedicandi* as well. A fine large-scale example is Ranulph Higden's *Ars componendi sermones,* which, as Higden himself tells us without specifying titles and authors, combines material from several works of the same kind, including (as will be shown in appendix C) *Quamvis.* Another good example is the version of one of the companion pieces of *Quamvis,* i.e., *Vade,* in the Wolfenbüttel manuscript (W). In this version, the text of *Vade* appears rearranged and enriched with extracts from *Quamvis,* Higden or his sources, and others.

But these borrowings, rearrangements, abbreviations, and compilations of *Quamvis* do not exhaust what can be said about the work's "life" and influence. We can add to them a case which reveals more clearly the hand of its author, who is here even named. This is the treatise entitled *De modo sermocinandi,* beginning "Fecunda gratia Salvatoris," written by the Austin friar Geoffrey Schale and preserved in manuscript G. *Fecunda* is a short *ars praedicandi,* shorter than *Quamvis* (approximately 3,630 against 4,360 words), which deals succinctly with all the main features of a scholastic sermon: thema; antethema or protheme leading to a prayer; introduction; division or distinction, here called the *fundamentum* of the sermon; development (*prosecucio,* of which four kinds are selected and discussed); and conclusion. The parts are briefly discussed, with a minimum of illustration; but in the section on development, Schale provides a lengthy example of developing the three parts of a divided thema, each part using a different kind of development: scriptural authorities and quotations from the doctors, *figura,* and authorities with their explanations. The fourth kind, *per introducciones,* he then continues, was already illustrated in an earlier paragraph and is not much used by modern preachers. Now, the illustrative thema that is here divided and developed at such length is *Habitabit iuvenis cum virgine,* a verse that can serve as the "give-away" or "rhetorical DNA" of *Quamvis* (see also appendix C). Schale uses further material from *Quamvis* throughout his work, such as the lexical meaning of the three key terms of the illustrative thema ("*Habitare* est morari per spacium..."), their confirmation with biblical authorities ("Primo delectamur ex Dei venientis ad nos morosa requie..."), the three kinds of *virginitas,* and others. His borrowings also include four modes of introducing the thema, the first of which—by authorities from Scripture—he illustrates with, again, material taken from *Quamvis* ("In Lege precepit Dominus" in the latter, and ending with *Habitabit*). In fact, having done so, Schale continues: "And the same can be done in the other four [!] ways at the preacher's pleasure." And he adds: "On these see above, at the beginning of the third preceding folio."[1] The reference is exact, and the referred passage occurs in the same manuscript (G) on f. 105—in a version of *Quamvis.*

However, Schale's four ways are slightly different from those in *Quamvis,* and in general we have here a case of borrowing material and working with it independently, similar to that of Ranulph Higden (to be discussed in appendix C). For while in the three developed parts Schale uses further material from *Quamvis,* he expands it to much greater length. Yet all three parts uniformly end with the repeated citation of the thema, *Habitabit iuuenis cum virgine.* Schale's work, then, seems to be not simply an abbreviation or rewrite but an original treatise

1. "Et sic potest fieri de aliis quatuor modis ad placitum predicantis, de quibus vide supra in folio tercio proximo precedente in principio," f. 107v. Notice the discrepancy between Schale's announcing four modes and then, in the quoted sentence, implying that there are five. *Quamvis,* indeed, has five ways of introducing the thema.

that borrows material from *Quamvis.* Its originality in comparison with *Quamvis* is shown, for instance, in Schale's applying the term *distinctio* to the four senses of Scripture, or in his paying greater attention to the antethema that ends with the prayer and to different (illustrated) forms of the closing formula.

In addition to this literary vitality of a single treatise, the study of *Quamvis* reveals a second feature of late-medieval *artes praedicandi.* In the five manuscripts in which the treatise has been preserved—in whatever form—it is always accompanied by one or more different treatises of the same kind. Besides the two companion pieces *Hic docet* and *Vade,* these are works by Fusignano, Thomas Waleys, Geoffrey Schale, Simon Alcok, the anonymous "Circa artem faciendi sermonem," and the equally anonymous "Ad habendum materiam" (see the manuscript descriptions under "Sources" in the headnote to chapter II). What here appears in a nutshell can be asserted as a general observation: that in their manuscripts medieval *artes praedicandi* like to travel in groups of two or more, whether they were copied by the same scribe or collected and bound into one volume. This is true, not only of shorter works like *Quamvis* but also of longer ones, such as the treatises by Thomas Waleys and Fusignano. Even the comprehensive *artes* by Ranulph Higden or Eiximenes are found in manuscripts together with other arts of preaching. Nor is such fellowship limited to works of the late Middle Ages but can be equally found in earlier ones. For example, a very popular treatise on eight modes of dilation, the *Ars dilatandi sermones* by Richard of Thetford, who wrote ca. 1245, appears in one manuscript with what may be considered the earliest work on the art of preaching, *De arte praedicatoria* by Alanus of Lille, who died in 1203.[2]

One may be tempted to think that such grouping shows attempts to create anthologies, that is, books that collect into one volume a number of works by the same author or of the same genre.[3] Several manuscripts could easily qualify as anthologies of *artes praedicandi.* A good example is V, described in the headnote to chapter V, which contains five *artes* in sequence. Another case, from England, is manuscript G, with four *artes* appearing in a row. However, examination of these two and of similar codices reveals that the *artes* they contain are

2. In Oxford, Bodleian Library, MS Bodley 848, a (late) thirteenth-century English manuscript from the Benedictine abbey of Reading. See Falconer Madan, H. H. E. Craster, and N. DenholmYoung, *A Summary Catalogue of Western Manucripts in the Bodleian Library at Oxford…,* 7 vols. (Oxford: Clarendon Press, 1895–1953), Nr. 2601, vol. 2, 446–47; and N. R. Ker, *Medieval Libraries of Great Britain. A List of Surviving Books,* 2nd ed. (London: Royal Historical Society, 1964), 157.

3. Cf. Siegfried Wenzel, "Sermon Collections and Their Taxonomy," in Stephen G. Nichols and Siegfried Wenzel, eds., *The Whole Book: Cultural Perspectives on the Medieval Miscellany* (Ann Arbor: The University of Michigan Press, 1996), 7–21, at 19–20.

nearly always accompanied by different materials for use in preaching, such as distinctions (as in M), articles on theological and moral topics including vices and virtues (L, U, G, O, B), exempla collections (G, U, R), lists of the properties of things (G), sermons (L, U, G, O, B, P, R, V), biblical material (memory verses in A, commentary on the Decalogue in O, exposition of the four senses in V; lists of the books of the Bible, concordances of the gospels, explanations of biblical names elsewhere), etc. Even longer works can be found in the company of *artes praedicandi,* such as the *Dieta salutis* (L), *Speculum sacerdotis* (L), *Secreta secretorum* (U), Innocent III's *De miseria condicionis humanae* (U), Bernard's *Meditationes* (U), *De venenis* (O), Defensor's *Scintillarium,* the *Elucidarium,* Grosseteste's *Templum Dei,* the *Qui bene presunt* by William of Wetheringsett, and much else—all materials that would be useful to a preacher at his desk and in the pulpit and are quoted again and again in extant sermons.[4] If one wanted to call such codices "anthologies," it would be more appropriate to call them anthologies not of arts of preaching but rather of material for preachers.

4. For more details on the works mentioned see Wenzel, "The Appearance of *Artes praedicandi* in Medieval Manuscripts," forthcoming. Of special interest in this respect may be the presence of matters that more properly belong to rhetoric (L) or philosophy (U)—traces of the (undergraduate) schoolroom?

C

QUAMVIS AND RANULPH HIGDEN

Comparison of *Quamvis* and Higden's *Ars componendi sermones* reveals a hitherto unacknowledged source of the latter and establishes that *Quamvis* itself must have been composed before 1340. That the two works are somehow related is suggested at once by the fact that both use the biblical passage *Habitabit iuvenis cum virgine* in their illustrations. Although a particular biblical text may occur again and again in a variety of *artes praedicandi,* it is also the case that individual authors tried to exemplify their teaching with their own examples, using new and different proof texts. *Habitabit* is a *rara avis:* in the *artes* known to me, it occurs only in Higden, *Quamvis, Fecunda,* and the mixed text of *Vade in domum* in manuscript W. None of the other *artes* I know—major as well as minor—use this verse. It may therefore be considered a give-away, a family trait, a piece of rhetorical DNA. The relations between *Quamvis* on one hand and *Fecunda* and *Vade in domum* on the other are discussed in appendix B. What, then, is the relation between *Quamvis* and Higden?

The relationship can be best demonstrated from the section on how to introduce the thema. The key passages there shared by the two works are as follows:

QUAMVIS, I	HIGDEN, CHAPTER XIV
Habito ergo competenti themate, introducatur vel per aliquam propriam manuduccionem, vel per simile in natura, vel per aliquam sacram scripturam, vel per auctoritates sanctorum vel philosophorum.	Immo resumpto themate potest introduccio fieri multis modis, utpote per scripturam, per argumentum, per exemplarem manuduccionem, per simile in natura, per vulgare dictum.

These are then exemplified with the respective sections in *Quamvis* (here placed in the order in which they appear in Higden:

QUAMVIS	HIGDEN
	[a] per scripturam [p. 35]
	[a.1] *Nupcie factae sunt*... explained according to the four senses of Scripture; then Higden adds a second example, for the feast of the Annunciation:
	Item in Annunciacione dominica, thema sit *Habitabit iuvenis cum virgine.*
[c] Per sacram autem scripturam introducitur thema sic: In Lege precepit Dominus quod summus sacerdos non acciperet viduam repudiatam aut meretricem sed virginem de stirpe sua. Modo autem Filius Dei est summus sacerdos. Quod patet quia ei dictum est: *Tu es sacerdos in eternum secundum ordinem Melchisedech.* Debet igitur Filius Dei sibi matrimonio virginem copulare incorruptam.	Poterit introduci per scripturam sacram Biblie: Preceptum erat in lege quod summus sacerdos non acciperet sibi in coniugem nec repudiatam nec meretricem, set solummodo virginem de stirpe sua. Set Filio Dei dictum est: *Tu es sacerdos in eternum, etc.* [p. 36] Debuit ergo habere virginem.
Et licet hoc mistice verificetur de Christo et Ecclesia, vnde dicit Apostolus: *Despondi enim vos vni viro virginem castam exhibere Christo,*	Et quamvis hoc mistice verificetur de Christo et Ecclesia, secundum illud Apostoli Ad Corinthios: *Despondi vos uni viro virginem castam,* etc.
hoc tamen ad literam verificatum fuit de Christo Filio Dei et Virgine gloriosa, cum qua tanquam cum matre, tanquam cum sponsa et sorore, hodierna die incepit habitare, sicut preuidit Ysaias dicens: *Habitabit iuuenis cum virgine.*	hoc tamen ad litteram fuit verificatum de Christo et Virgine gloriosa, cum qua tamquam cum matre, tamquam cum sponsa et sorore, cepit hodie habitare, sicut previdit Ysayas dicens: *Habitabit iuvenis cum virgine.*
[d] Per scripturam sanctorum introducitur sic thema sicut predictum: Nichil ita discordes reconciliat vel amoris fedus confirmat sicut vinculum matrimoniale. Vnde cum nostra natura diuinam ininimiciam quam incurrerat non poterat tollerare (quia penam mortis pro ista quilibet incurrebat),	**[a.2]** Item introducitur illud thema per scripturam sanctorum sic: Nichil apud nos ita discordes consiliat sicud vinculum matrimoniale. Set quia nostra natura non potuit tollerare divinam offensam quam per peccatum incurrit,
necesse habuit de aliqua virgine speciosa sibi prouidere, cuius matrimonio hec inimicicia posset tolli et nos secure ad eum tanquam ad generum nostrum (quia ad sponsum sororis nostre), ymmo pocius	necesse fuit aliquam sponsam virginem Christo provideri cuius matrimonio offensa illa tolleretur; et nos ad Christum tamquam ad generum nostrum fiducialius accedere possemus, immo ad

QUAMVIS	HIGDEN
ad hominem de nostro genere (quia ad filium sororis nostre) possemus accedere. Vnde Augustinus 4 *Confessionum* dicit: "Descendit huc ipsa vita et tulit mortem nostram, et occidit eam, et de habundancia vite sue intonuis clamans vt [f. 172] redeamus hinc ad eum, idest in illud secretum vnde processit ad nos, idest in ipsum purum virginalem vterum, vbi ei nupsit humana creatura, caro mortalis, ne semper esset mortalis. Et inde tanquam sponsus processit de talamo suo."	hominem de genere nostro tamquam ad filium sororis nostre, unde dicit Augustinus, 4 *Confessio-num:* "Descendit huc illa vitaque tollens mortem occidit ipsam, intonuitque clamans ut redeamus hinc ad eum in illud secretum, unde venit ad nos—hoc est virginalem uterum ubi nupcit ei natura nostra, caro mortalis, ne semper foret mortalis."
Ista sponsalia preuidit Ysaias dicens: *Habitabit iuuenis cum virgine.*	Ipsa sponsalia previdit Ysayas cum dixit: *Habitabit iuvenis cum virgine.*
[e] Auctoritate philosophica vel poetica introducitur thema sic: Dicit Seneca in quadam epistula ad Lucillum: "Miraris homines ad Deum ire, Deus ad homines, ymmo quod melius est, in homines venit." Certum est quod in nullum hominem magis quam in hominem cuius se filium vocat, dicens: Filius hominis venit querere et saluum facere quod perierat, etc. Ipse enim solus vere est filius hominis, quia solius matris, non alterius hominis, quia non habet hominem patrem eius sicut ceteri homines, eo quod ipse de sola intemerata virgine generatus est, sicut preuidit Ysaias propheta dicens: *Ecce virgo concipiet et pariet filium.* De hac virgine intelligitur illud poeticum: "Virgo decora nimis, Dauid de semine regis." Et de ipsa et prole sua illi versus poetici possunt intelligi: "Iam redit et virgo, redeunt Saturnia regna, Nam noua progenies celo dimit titur alto." Et hoc quia isto die noua progenies dimittitur in vterum virginalem, vt impleatur Ysaie prophete vaticinium dicens: *Habitabit iuuenis cum virgine.*	[a.3] Item introducitur idem thema per scripturam philosophicam seu poeticam, sicut dicit Seneca in quadam [p. 37] epistola ad Lucilium: "Miraris homines ad deum venire aut deum ad homines? Immo quod magis est in homines venit." Set si in homines venit, in nullum magis quam in illam cuius se filium vocat qui dicit: *Venit filius hominis querere et salvare quod perierat.* Ipse vero solus est filius hominis quia filius solius matris; non enim dicitur filius hominum quia non habuit hominem patrem sicut ceteri hominum habent; quemadmodum previdit Ysayas dicens: *Ecce virgo concipiet.* De qua virgine posset intelligi illud poeticum: "Virgo decora nimis David de semine regis et de eius prole." Recitat Augustinus in quadam omelia de Adventu quosdam versus virgilianos: "Iam reddit et virgo, redeunt saturnia regna; iam nova progenies celo dimittitur alto." Nam isto die mittebatur pro genius celi in uterum virginis et iam impleatur illud Ysaye: *Habitabit,* etc.
	[b] per argumentum,
[a] Si accipiatur hoc thema *Habitabit iuuenis cum virgine,* posset introduci tali manuduccione: Si inter duo regna esset iugis guerra et	[c] Item introducitur thema per exemplarem manuduccionem sic: sit thema ut prius, *Habitabit iuvenis cum virgine,* et dicatur sic: Quando inter duo regna est ingens [*var.* iugis!]

QUAMVIS	HIGDEN
periculosa contencio, non posset meliori modo et firmiori concordia stabiliri quam, si vnus rex haberet filium iuuenem et decentem et alius filiam virginem pudore et decore pollentem qui possent matrimonii vinculo copulari,	guerra et periculosa, non possit firmiori modo concordia stabilire quam si filius unius regis filiam alterius desponsaret;
mergerentur. Sed postquam primum peccatum continua fuit guerra inter regem terrenum et celestem, et continua pugna, que sedari nullo pacto potuit donec filius regis celestis eam sibi coniungeret federe sempiterno. Ista coniunccio fuit hodie celebrata, sed diu ante preconizata per prophetam dicentem *Habitabit enim iuuenis cum virgine.*	set modo est ita quod post peccatum primum ingens guerra fuit inter regnum celeste et terrenum, que sedari non potuit donec filius celestis filiam terrenam sibi coniungeret federe maritali. Hec coniunccio fuit hodie celebrata, set diu ante per prophetam enunciata [p. 39] quando dixerat *Habitabit,* etc.
	[d] per simile in natura,
[b] Sed per simile in natura introducitur sic: Animalia fortissima et ferocissima, cuiusmodi sunt elephas et vnicornis, hoc modo feritatem dimittere dicuntur: Elephas ad cantum virginis et ad [f. 171v] ostensionem vberum eius que lambet suauiter mitescit. Vnicornis cum sit eciam animal ferocissimum et nullo modo vel arte posset eius ferocitas edomari, tandem adducta virgine in eius gremio mansuescit.	**[d.1]** Item introducitur thema per similem in natura, sic: Animalia fortissima elephas et unicornus sic capiuntur quod scilicet elephas in cantum virginis mitescitet, unicornus in gremio virginis mansuescit.
Sic Filius Dei fortissimus, ostensis illis vberibus Virginis de quibus scriptum est: *Beatus venter qui te portauit et vbera que suxisti,* vbera illa lambens et suggens, prius tamen adductus per cantum Virginis que cecinit *Magnificat anima mea Dominum,* etc., mitis effectus est.	Sic Filius Dei fortissimus ostensis virginis uberibus, de quibus dicitur in Luca: *Beatus venter qui te portavit et ubera que succisti,* emollitus per cantum virginis; quando cecinit *Ecce ancilla Domini,* mitis effectus est.
In huius eciam gremio ille vnicornis fortissimus Dei, qui angelum et hominem sibi resistentem, idest sapienciam appetentem que sibi apropriatur, cornu vindicte interemit, mansuetissimus est effectus quando *edificauit sicut vnicornis sanctificium suum in terra quam fundauit in secula,* scilicet in gremio virginis, implens illud vaticinium Ysaie dicentis: *Habitabit iuuenis cum virgine.*	Similiter et iste unicornus ferocissimus Dei Filius, qui hominem et angelum sibi resistentem ac supra quam debuit appetentem prostravit, mitis effectus est quando edificavit, sicut unicornus, sacrificium suum in gremio virginis implens illud Ysaye *Habitabit,* etc.
	[d.2] in arte
	[d.3] in historia
	[e] Item fit introduccio per vulgare proverbium sic: Sit thema *Habitabit iuvenis cum virgine*…

This comparison thus shows that (1) both works initially list five ways of introducing the thema, though they are not entirely the same, for Higden includes "argumentation" and "proverbs," which do not appear in *Quamvis.* However, (2) all five ways listed and exemplified in *Quamvis* also occur in Higden, fairly much in verbal agreement, but in a different order: *Quamvis* c-d-e-a-b. (3) The five ways and illustrations of *Quamvis* are built into a different structure in Higden, where some appear as subgroups:

Quamvis c = Higden a.1, second example
d = a.2
e = a.3
a = c
b = d.1.

(4) In *Quamvis,* each of the five ways is illustrated with an example that leads to the same biblical verse, *Habitabit.* In contrast, Higden illustrates his ways with examples that lead to different biblical verses; *Habitabit* is only one of them.

It would appear, then, that in contrast to the unified illustrations of the five ways in *Quamvis,* Higden has collected material from different sources, including *Quamvis.* This work of collecting or compiling resulted in the awkward fact, for instance, that in his section a.1 he introduced the four senses of Scripture, which are then taken up again and explained at greater length in his chapter XIX, as the eighth mode of amplifying the thema (p. 65). Moreover, Higden himself declared in his preface: "I gathered together excerpts from various authors,"[1] and evidently *Quamvis*—or its source—was one of them.[2]

Higden's borrowing from *Quamvis* extends into other parts of his *Ars componendi sermones.* Thus, the example of a faulty division of *Habitabit* and the correct way ("Hic tria notantur...*requiescet* etc.," above, p. 116) appears in Higden's chapter XV (pp. 43–44), and Higden's continued illustration of the correct way to divide this thema ("Similiter condicio iuvenis....Potest ergo thema sic dividi...*que Dei sunt,* etc.," pp. 44–45) similarly parallels sections in *Quamvis* (above, p. 116). Further borrowings occur in Higden's chapter XVII, on the two modes of dilating the sermon, including the three forms of *virginitas* (pp. 54–55), the three good qualities of a virgin (p. 56), and more. Higden also uses the rare

1. Edition p. 5, translation p. 34. For the other sources of Higden's section on the introduction, see edition, pp. 76–77.

2. The relation between *Quamvis* and Higden here demonstrated is, therefore, the reverse of that claimed by Jennings: "Higden's brief, but intriguing, discussion of sermon forms caught the attention of Thomas Penketh," translation, p. 77, n. 90; see also her edition, p. xl. For Penketh's supposed authorship of *Quamvis,* see the headnote to chap. II.

term *impactio* (p. 55; cf. *Quamvis,* p. 122) as well as the discussion of such complicated sermon structures as *sermo piramidalis, linearis,* and *circularis* (which he calls *circularitas,* p. 57, in a much shorter discussion). None of these technical terms (except *circularitas* and *circulatio*) appear in the *artes* I have studied.

D

MODERN EDITIONS AND TRANSLATIONS OF *ARTES PRAEDICANDI*

In general, the section *"Ars praedicandi"* in James J. Murphy, *Rhetoric in the Middle Ages: A History of Rhetorical Theory from Saint Augustine to the Renaissance* (Berkeley and Los Angeles: University of California Press, 1974), 269–355, contains many helpful and often detailed summaries, as does Dorothea Roth, *Die mittelalterliche Predigttheorie und das "Manuale Curatorum" des Johann Ulrich Surgant,* Basler Beiträge zur Geschichtswissenschaft, 158 (Basel: Helbing und Lichtenhahn, 1956).

Alan of Lille, *De arte praedicatoria* (not listed by Caplan): PL 210:111–198. Translation: Alan of Lille, *The Art of Preaching,* trans. Gillian R. Evans (Kalamazoo: Western Michigan University Press, 1981).

Alcok, Simon, *Tractatus de modo dividendi thema pro materia sermonis dilatandi* (Caplan 8): Mary F. Boynton, "Simon Alcok on Expanding the Sermon," *Harvard Theological Review* 34 (1941): 201–16.

Alexander of Ashby, *De artificioso modo predicandi* (Caplan 67 and Suppl): Alexander Essebiensis, *Opera theologica,* eds. Franco Morenzoni and Thomas H. Bestul, 2 vols., Corpus Christianorum Continuatio Medievalis 138 (Turnhout: Brepols, 2004), 1:21–33, sermons on 33–71, and an abbreviated version of *De artificioso* on 73–104. An earlier edition in Morenzoni, "Aux origines des *Artes praedicandi:* Le *De artificioso modo predicandi* d'Alexandre d'Ashby," *Studi Medievali,* third series, anno 32, fasc. 2 (1991): 887–935.

Alfonso d'Alprão, *Ars praedicandi, conferendi, collationandi, arengandi, secundum multiplicem modum,* or *Tractatus et ars de modo praedicandi* (Caplan 44, 72, and Suppl 72): Albert G. Hauf, "El 'Ars praedicandi' de

Fr. Alfonso d'Alprão, OFM. Aportacion al Estudio de la Teoria de la Predicacion en la Peninsula Iberica," *Archivum Franciscanum Historicum* 72 (1979): 233–329.

Anon., "Ad habendam materiam" (Caplan Suppl 1): Servus of Sint Anthonis Gieben, "Preaching in the Thirteenth Century. A Note on Ms. Gonville and Caius 439," *Collectanea Franciscana* 32 (1962): 310–24.

———, "Dic nobis" (not listed by Caplan): Siegfried Wenzel, "A Dominican (?) Ars Praedicandi in Sermon Form," *Archivum Fratrum Praedicatorum* 78 (2008): 51–78.

———, *Forma praedicandi,* "Predicacio est thematis assumpcio" (Caplan 121): Woodburn O. Ross, "A Brief Forma Praedicandi," *Modern Philology* 34 (1937): 337–44.

———, "Si vis sermonem ex arte conficere" (Caplan 170): Gillian R. Evans and David L. d'Avray, "Unusual 'Ars Praedicandi,'" *Medium Aevum* 49 (1980): 26–31.

Borgsleben, Christian, *Ars predicandi,* "Cum in his temporibus" (Caplan Suppl 155a): S. G. Buchwald, "Die 'Ars Praedicandi' des Erfurter Franziskaners Christian Borgsleben," *Franziskanische Studien* 8 (1921): 67–74.

Francesc Eiximenes, *Modus sermocinandi,* or *Ars predicandi populo* (Caplan 84 and 73, and Suppl): Marti de Barcelona, OMCap., "L'Ars Praedicandi de Francesc Eiximenes," *Homenatge a Antoni Rubio i Lluch. Miscelania d'Estudios Literaris Historicis i Linguisticis* (Barcelona, 1936) 2:301–40.

Geraldus de Piscario, *Ars faciendi sermones* (Caplan 140): Ferdinand M. Delorme, OFM, "L'*Ars faciendi sermones* de Geraud du Pescher," *Antonianum* 19 (1944): 169–98.

Guibert de Nogent, *Liber quo ordine sermo fieri debeat,* PL 156:11–21. Translation by Joseph M. Miller, "Guibert de Nogent's *Liber quo ordine sermo fieri debeat:* A Translation of the Earliest Modern Speech Textbook," *Today's Speech* 17 (1969): 45–56.

Guibert de Tournai, *Rudimentum doctrinae.* Partial edition in Servus Gieben, "Rudimentum doctrinae di Gilberto di Tournai, con l'edizione del suo Registrum o tavola della materia," in *Bonaventuriana: Miscellanea in Onore de J.G. Bougerol,* 2 vols. (Rome: Edizioni Antonianum, 1988), 2:621–80.

Henry of Hesse, *Tractatus solemnis de arte et vero modo predicandi* (Caplan 14 and others; cf. Charland 43–44): Harry Caplan, "'Henry of Hesse' on the Art of Preaching," *PMLA* 48 (1933): 340–61; repr. in Harry Caplan, *Of Eloquence: Studies in Ancient and Mediaeval Rhetoric,* eds. Anne King and

Helen North (Ithaca, N.Y.: Cornell University Press, 1970), 135–59. Edition and translation.

Humbert of Romans, *De eruditione religiosorum praedicatorum* (not listed by Caplan): Approaches the form of a "comprehensive" *ars praedicandi* but without a systematic discussion of sermon technique. Edited by Josephus Catalanus (Rome: Typis Antonii de Rubeis, 1739). Scattered remarks on sermon structure occur in book I, which has been translated as *Treatise on Preaching* by the Dominican students of the Province of St. Joseph and edited by Walter M. Conlon, OP (Westminster, Md.: The Newman Press, 1951).

Jean de la Rochelle, *Processus negociandi themata sermonum* (Caplan 31): Gustavo Cantini, OFM, "*Processus negociandi themata sermonum* di Giovanni della Rochelle, OFM," *Antonianum* 26 (1951): 254–70.

Martin de Cordoba, *Ars praedicandi* (Caplan 192): Fernando Rubio, "*Ars praedicandi* de Fray Martin de Cordoba," *La Ciudad de Dios* 172 (1959): 327–48.

Nicholas d'Oresme, *Ars sermocinandi* (not listed by Caplan): Franco Morenzoni, "À propos d'une *Ars praedicandi* attribuée à Nicole Oresme," *Archivum Franciscanum Historicum* 99 (2006): 251–81.

Pseudo-Aquinas, *Tractatulus solemnis de arte et vero modo predicandi* (Caplan 217): Translation only: Harry Caplan, "A Late Mediaeval Tractate on Preaching," *Studies in Rhetoric and Public Speaking in Honor of James A. Winans,* ed. A. M. Drummond (New York: The Century Company, 1925), 61–90; repr. Harry Caplan, *Of Eloquence: Studies in Ancient and Mediaeval Rhetoric,* ed. Anne King and Helen North (Ithaca, N.Y.: Cornell University Press, 1970), 40–79.

Pseudo-Bonaventure, *Ars concionandi,* "Omnis tractatio scripturarum" (Caplan 114): *Opera sancti Bonaventurae,* ed. Patres Collegii S. Bonaventurae (Quaracchi: Collegium S. Bonaventurae, 1882–1902), vol. 9, pp. 8–21. This text combines three *artes.* The third is the treatise by Richard of Thetford (see below). Translation by Harry C. Hazel, "Bonaventure, *Ars Concionandi,*" Ph.D. dissertation, Washington State University, 1972.

Ranulph Higden, *Ars componendi sermones* (Caplan 156): Margaret Jennings, *The Ars Componendi Sermones of Ranulph Higden O.S.B.* (Leiden: E. J. Brill, 1991). Translation by Margaret Jennings and Sally A. Wilson, Dallas Medieval Texts and Translations 2 (Dudley, Mass.: Peeters, 2003).

Richard of Thetford, *Ars dilatandi sermones* (Caplan 154): part 3 of Pseudo-Bonaventure, *Ars concionandi,* inc. "Quoniam aemulatores," see above.

Also edited with translation by George J. Engelhardt, "Richard of Thetford: *A Treatise on the Eight Modes of Dilatation*," *Allegorica* 3 (1978): 77–160.

Robert of Basevorn, *Forma praedicandi* (Caplan 116): Th.M. Charland, *Artes Praedicandi: Contribution à l'histoire de la rhétorique au moyen âge* (Paris: De Vrin, 1936), 233–323. Translation by Leopold Krul, OSB, in *Three Medieval Rhetorical Arts*, ed. James J. Murphy (Berkeley and Los Angeles: University of California Press, 1971), 109–215; repr. in Medieval and Renaissance Texts and Studies, vol. 228 = MRTS Reprint Series 5 (Tempe, Ariz., 2001).

Thomas of Chobham, *Summa de arte praedicandi* (not listed by Caplan): Franco Morenzoni, Thomas de Chobham, *Summa de arte praedicandi*, Corpus Christianorum Continuatio Mediaevalis 82 (Turnhout, 1987).

Thomas of Todi (or a Truderto), *Ars sermocinandi ac etiam collationes faciendi* (Caplan 16 and Suppl): June Babcock, "*Ars sermocinandi ac etiam collationes faciendi* of Thomas of Todi, MS. Paris, Bibl. Nat. 15965," M.A. thesis, Cornell University, 1941.

Thomas Waleys, *De theoria sive arte praedicandi* (Caplan 32): Th.M. Charland, *Artes Praedicandi: Contribution à l'histoire de la rhétorique au moyen âge* (Paris, 1936), 328–403. Translation by Dorothy E. Grosser, "*De modo componendi sermones,*" M.A. thesis, Cornell University, 1949.

William of Auvergne, "Verbum Dei propter Christum" (Caplan 179 and Suppl): A. de Poorter, "Un Manuel de prédication médiévale, le Ms. 97 de Bruges," *Revue Néo-Scolastique de Philosophie* 25 (1923): 192–205. The attribution has been questioned; see Franco Morenzoni, "À propos d'une *ars praedicandi* attribuée à Nicole Oresme," *Archivum Franciscanum Historicum* 99 (2006): 251–81, at 252.

INDEX OF BIBLICAL QUOTATIONS

Page numbers refer to both text and notes.

GENERAL INDEX

Page numbers refer to both text and notes.

The Art of Preaching: Five Medieval Texts and Translations was designed in Minion and typeset by Kachergis Book Design of Pittsboro, North Carolina. It was printed on 55-pound Natures Natural Recycled and bound by Sheridan Books of Ann Arbor, Michigan.